Writing Pathways: Performance Assessments and Learning Progressions, Grades 6–8

Lucy Calkins with Audra Kirshbaum Robb
and Colleagues from the Teachers College
Reading and Writing Project

Photography by Peter Cunningham

HEINEMANN ◆ PORTSMOUTH, NH

Thanks especially to Tom Corcoran and to his colleagues from the Center on Continuous Instructional Improvement at Teachers College, Columbia University. Their work with us has been funded by a grant from the William and Flora Hewlett Foundation. We're grateful to the foundation for the guidance we've received in learning progressions and performance assessments in relation to school reform.

We would also like to thank the following teachers, who went above and beyond in helping us collect, sort, and obtain permissions for the amazing student work included here: Katherine Messer, Lindsay Powell, Howard Banner, Caroline Ebrahim, Julie Heller, Aileen Florio, Sonja Cherry-Paul, and Stacey Fell.

DEDICATED TO TEACHERS™

firsthand
An imprint of Heinemann
361 Hanover Street
Portsmouth, NH 03801–3912
www.heinemann.com

Offices and agents throughout the world

Cataloging-in-Publication data is on file with the Library of Congress.

ISBN-13: 978-0-325-05953-2

Production: Elizabeth Valway, David Stirling, and Abigail Heim
Cover and interior designs: Jenny Jensen Greenleaf
Series includes photographs by Peter Cunningham and Nadine Baldasare
Composition: Publishers' Design and Production Services, Inc.
Manufacturing: Steve Bernier

Printed in the United States of America on acid-free paper
18 17 16 15 14   PAH   1 2 3 4 5

Contents

*All the assessment tools are also provided on the CD-ROM, including some
additional materials for grades 3–5 and 9.*

Letter to Teachers

EXPECTATIONS HAVE NEVER BEEN HIGHER for young writers—nor for you, as a teacher of writing. By making these expectations clear, understandable, and kid-friendly and by giving you the tools you need to empower students to "own" the expectations, this book (in combination with the K–8 *Units of Study in Opinion/Argument, Information, and Narrative Writing*) can go a long way toward enabling you and your students to meet those soaring expectations. But a word to the wise: this book will be exponentially more potent if your school system not only puts *Writing Pathways* and the accompanying *Units of Study* into your hands, but if the system also helps you and your colleagues have time to study student work in the company of one another. My colleagues and I have been dazzled by the results when teachers are given opportunities to clarify their shared goals for writers, to norm expectations across a grade level, and to become at home providing students with the feedback they need. It's not this book alone that can provide you with the direction and skills that are so crucial, but this book in combination with opportunities for conversation with colleagues.

The first version of *Writing Pathways* was written to undergird *Units of Study in Opinion, Information, and Narrative Writing, K–5*. Those tools have exceeded my wildest expectations and proved to be far more invaluable to teachers and students than I had dreamt possible. Teachers have told us that because *Writing Pathways* provides crystal clear trajectories of writing development, the book has allowed their students to work with zeal toward self-improvement. They have told us that *Writing Pathways* helps them realize that there is extraordinary power in rubrics, checklists, and benchmark texts that fit tongue and groove into a curriculum aligned to them. Assessment and instruction can be extraordinarily potent when they support each other. The response to *Writing Pathways, K–5* has been so intense and so positive that I couldn't resist improving the entire project, and so this 6–8 *Writing Pathways*

not only supports higher grade levels, but it also represents a revision of the initial book.

You will find that the expectations built into the rubrics, tools, and benchmark texts contained in this book ask a lot of students—and of you. To the best of our ability, we've tried to align everything in *Writing Pathways, 6–8* to the expectations of the Common Core State Standards (CCSS)—and yes, those expectations are high. The expectations in the checklists and rubrics you will find here reflect the ambitiousness of the Common Core (and by that, I refer not only to the ambitiousness of the actual standards but also of the exemplar texts in Appendix C of the CCSS, because those texts offer an interpretation of the standards).

For teachers, parents, and students in schools that have not taught writing in the past, the CCSS expectations (and those in this book) can feel like pie in the sky. I've seen teachers guffaw incredulously at samples of student writing in the Common Core. It is not surprising that people in any school system that has treated writing as a frill, as an extra-credit option, will feel that the standards contained in the Common Core and in this book are inaccessible. After all, consider what students' math skills would be like if only a handful of teachers taught math and if the math instruction that did happen was invented off the cuff by each teacher alone, with no effort to establish a coherent cross-grade curriculum.

But when writing is truly regarded as a basic (remember the old emphasis on "reading, 'riting, and 'rithmetic"?) and when teachers are given the help they need to teach writing well, the standards are suddenly more accessible. The K–8 series, *Units of Study in Opinion/Argument, Information, and Narrative Writing*, gives students the opportunity to proceed along a through-line of skills and strategies to reach the ambitious demands called for by the CCSS (and reflected in the checklists, rubrics, and student samples throughout this book).

Although the new expectations are substantial, they are also plausible in instances when teachers across an entire school engage in the teaching of writing. An eighth-grade teacher might well panic after reading the expectations for her grade—but she is apt to be consoled when she looks between the expectations for eighth grade and those detailed for seventh. This teacher will realize that, actually, if students entered her eighth grade meeting the seventh-grade standards, then sure, the expectations for eighth grade would be within reach. The problem, of course, is the *if*.

A study of the standards—say, those detailed in the provided chart—shows a few things. First, the expectations of any one grade level can look unreasonable when seen in isolation, but always, when those expectations are seen in relation to the preceding grade's expectations, the step-up seems absolutely doable.

Let's look, for example, at the difference between the seventh- and eighth-grade standards in the Common Core for informative/explanatory writing. As we compare and contrast expectations across the two grades, let's underline the expectations that are new in grade 8.

CCSS Informative/Explanatory Writing Standards highlighting the differences between the standards for seventh- and eighth-graders

Grade 7 Students	Grade 8 Students
Write informative/explanatory texts to examine a topic and convey ideas, concepts, and information through the selection, organization, and analysis of relevant content.	Write informative/explanatory texts to examine a topic and convey ideas, concepts, and information through the selection, organization, and analysis of relevant content.
Introduce a topic clearly, previewing what is to follow; organize ideas, concepts, and information, using strategies such as definition, classification, comparison/contrast, and cause/effect; include formatting (e.g., headings), graphics (e.g., charts, tables), and multimedia when useful to aiding comprehension.	Introduce a topic clearly, previewing what is to follow; organize ideas, concepts, and information into broader categories; include formatting (e.g., headings), graphics (e.g., charts, tables), and multimedia when useful to aiding comprehension.
Develop the topic with relevant facts, definitions, concrete details, quotations, or other information and examples.	Develop the topic with relevant well-chosen facts, definitions, concrete details, quotations, or other information and examples.
Use appropriate transitions to create cohesion and clarify the relationships among ideas and concepts.	Use appropriate and varied transitions to create cohesion and clarify the relationships among ideas and concepts.
Use precise language and domain-specific vocabulary to inform about or explain the topic.	Use precise language and domain-specific vocabulary to inform about or explain the topic.
Establish and maintain a formal style.	Establish and maintain a formal style.
Provide a concluding statement or section that follows from and supports the information or explanation presented.	Provide a concluding statement or section that follows from and supports the information or explanation presented.

Although a study of the standards is important, it is also important to note that bulleted standards are only one part of the actual standards; the following exemplar of student writing reveals far more about the standards than these lists alone. The geographical report is included in Appendix C to the Common Core State Standards is an example of eighth-grade standards for informative/explanatory writing. It was completed as homework for an eighth-grade English class, and even at a glance reminds us that the expectations are nothing to sneeze at. Let's look at even just an excerpt of the full report (an annotated analysis of this writing sample can be found on page 43 of Appendix C, http://www.corestandards.org/assets/Appendix_C.pdf, Google search term "Common Core Standards Appendix C"):

An excerpt from "A Geographical Report," Seventh-Grade Informative/Explanatory Student Sample, Common Core State Standards, Appendix C

Vernal pools have a large assortment of rare and exotic flora and fauna (plants and animals). Five of them are on the federal list of endangered

Teachers can't teach writing in a vacuum, unable to assume any prior instruction at all. This piece of writing is proof. The ambitious new expectations of the Common Core must lead to a schoolwide, cross-grade commitment to teach writing. Writers grow like oak trees, in the fullness of time, and for any teacher to bring her students to the ambitious levels of the CCSS, those students need the opportunity to grow over time.

But the good news is that you need not feel empty-handed when you ask, "How can we approach current Common Core expectations in writing?" The treasure chest of assessment tools, experiences, theories, and techniques that we offer in this book will bring the results of three decades of work to you.

—Lucy Calkins

species, and one more is a candidate for listing. The plants and animals in vernal pools are unusual because they have only developed recently compared to other changes in evolution. As scientists study the pools more intently they are finding more and more unknown species. There are temporary pools in other places around the world, but California's vernal pools are different because of their long drought phase, which causes the plants and animals to adapt to the climate. They go into a dormant phase. For example, fairy shrimp lay eggs before the drought which hatch when it gets moist enough to be active. Some plants, in a short period of time, develop seeds; others appear to die out, but quickly spout again from the rain. Many of these species cannot survive outside vernal pools, and some are "endemic" (species found only in a very restricted geographical area).

Chapter 1

An Assessment Toolkit

IT FEELS AUDACIOUS to be writing a book about assessment at this time, when the world has gone so data-crazy that many teachers flinch at just the mention of assessment. But the truth is that we cannot let assessment be regarded as part of The Dark Side. There is good reason for the emphasis on assessment. For example, John Hattie, author of *Visible Learning* (2008), reviewed studies of more than twenty million learners to understand the factors that maximize achievement—and found that it is important for a learner to have crystal clear, ambitious goals, to be given feedback that highlights progress the learner has made toward these goals, and finally, to know of next steps that are within reach. The checklists, rubrics, and benchmark texts within this resource, in conjunction with the sequence of writing units laid out in *Units of Study in Argument, Information, and Narrative Writing*, allow you to provide students with that sort of potent assistance so that your students aren't just writing, writing, writing, but are instead working with deliberateness toward specific goals.

The tools contained within this resource provide your students with clear pathways forward, helping them answer not only the question "How am I doing?" but also the more important question "How can I improve?" By providing them with checklists, rubrics, and texts that illustrate a pathway forward in argument, information, and narrative writing, you help your students develop a sense of efficacy, of "I can do this, if I work hard." With these tools, students can become evidence-based close readers of their own writing. While learning to write, then, they can also learn that when a person applies strategies, works hard, and doesn't give up, that person's work gets visibly better.

But the checklists are not only designed to lift the level of *students' writing*; they are also designed to lift the level of *your teaching*. There is widespread agreement among researchers that the one factor that matters more than anything else in student achievement is the quality of your teaching. This explains the ever-increasing focus on teacher evaluation. Whether your school system has adopted teacher evaluation frameworks from Charlotte Danielson, Robert Marzano, Kim Marshall, or others, chances are good that your school leaders are more and more intent on evaluating your teaching and, more specifically, on evaluating the extent to which your instruction is assessment-based. When observers watch your teaching, they want to know what your goals are, how you use data about your students to determine those goals, and how you will assess students' progress toward the goals. Again, that focus on goal-driven instruction comes from research on the factors that accelerate achievement. It has become especially urgent, then, that you get the help you need to keep your finger on the pulse of your students' learning.

Writing provides you with a perfect forum for becoming a more assessment-based teacher, because the results of instruction in writing are both visible and, when instruction is solid, dramatic. Writing is one of the few subjects in which you can make a covenant with your students, promising them that if they use what you teach and work hard, their work will become dramatically better within just a few weeks. If your instruction doesn't result in visible changes in your students' writing, something is wrong. By staying attuned to your students' progress, you will be able to adjust your teaching, extending whatever you are doing that *is* yielding results and altering that which is *not*. If you are keeping an eye on your students' progress, this means you can try something as a teacher—perhaps creating small tutorial centers where students who are strong at a skill help those who are less strong—and then *presto!* You watch to see if the strategy results in improved writing. If this yields progress, you have the evidence to support using that teaching strategy more often. By giving you a way to track your students' progress, then, this resource gives you a way to track and facilitate your own progress. Your attentiveness to results provides you with a feedback loop and with a self-correcting system.

Of course, you can learn not only when your own teaching yields results, but also when a colleague's teaching yields results. *Units of Study in Argument, Information, and Narrative Writing, Grades 6–8* has been written with the hope that colleagues across your grade level and your school need not teach alone. Whereas once upon a time it was possible for you to close the classroom door and teach in isolation, expectations are high enough now that it is hard to imagine any teacher thinking it wise to attempt to teach without support from colleagues. This system helps you be part of a collaborative system of continuous improvement.

Michael Fullan, one of the foremost authorities on change, points out that the problem in education is not resistance to change but the presence of too many changes, uncoordinated with existing systems and with one another, implemented in superficial or ad hoc ways. The field of education is often characterized by a constant frenzy of efforts to grasp at yet one more magic solve-all—and this is premised on the hope that somewhere, there is a program to buy, to install, that will provide the magic solution. But the truth is that if there is a magic solution, it is an engagement in a persistent cycle of teaching, observing the results of teaching and then responding thoughtfully to what one sees. What's called for is that you, as a teacher, as well as your colleagues and your students, study student work and develop and adapt curriculum in light of what the evidence shows. In the end, the greatest contribution these tools make is that they help both you and your students self-assess, collaborate with other learners, learn from feedback, and work collectively toward challenging, clear goals. And in the end, if there is a magic formula in education, a secret to success, it is this process of continuous improvement.

There is a growing body of research suggesting that the use of performance assessments embedded within curriculum improves instruction and supports students' building higher-order, complex skills (Goldschmidt et al., Educational Assessment, 2007 (12): 239–66; Pellegrio, Chudowsky, and Glaser, Knowing What Students Know, 2001; Wood et al., "Refocusing Accountability: Using Local Performance Assessments to Enhance Teaching and Learning for Higher Order Skills," 2007, available at www.fairtest.org/refocusing-accountability; Google search term "Fairtest refocusing accountability").

A SET OF TOOLS

It is important to keep in mind that this book is one piece of a larger system, *Units of Study in Argument, Information, and Narrative Writing*, meant to work in concert with the other pieces. That said, this particular book is chock-full of resources and writing assessment tools that can be used across a district, school, or classroom. These tools can enable you to grasp where your students are in their writing development and to figure out what help they need to take next steps. The system of teaching and learning that is embedded in the series makes progress in writing concrete and attainable and allows students to share ownership of this progress. The tools within just *Writing Pathways*—each of which has been piloted in thousands of classrooms and is aligned to the CCSS—include:

- **Three learning progressions.** These learning progressions (one in argument, one in information, and one in narrative writing) are based upon thirty years of research-based practice in writing development and are aligned to the Common Core State Standards. These are written to communicate expectations to students and to those of you who teach students, so they are written in straight, clear language. These progressions not only help you track students' progress across the three kinds of writing, locating a student's current level of work and the next steps the student should take, but they also help you see the cross-currents between the three types of writing, so that you can help a student realize that lessons learned in narrative writing can transfer to information writing, and so forth.

- **Student-friendly checklists.** These checklists allow students to assess their own writing, set goals for themselves, and with your help, work to make palpable progress toward those

Learning Progression for Argument Writing

	Grade 6	Grade 7	Grade 8	Grade 9
	STRUCTURE			
	The writer explained the topic/text and staked...	The writer laid out a well-supported argument...	The writer laid out an argument about a topic/...	The writer presented an argument about... offering...

Learning Progression for Argument Writing

	Grade 3	Grade 4	Grade 5
	STRUCTURE		
Overall	The writer told readers his opinion and ideas on a text or a topic and helped them understand his reasons.	The writer made a claim about a topic or a text and tried to support her reasons.	The writer made a claim or thesis on a topic or text, supported it with reasons, and provided a variety of evidence for each reason.
Lead	The writer wrote a beginning in which she not only set readers up to expect that this would be a piece of opinion writing, but also tried to hook them into caring about her opinion.	The writer wrote a few sentences to hook his readers, perhaps by asking a question, explaining why the topic mattered, telling a surprising fact, or giving background information. The writer stated his claim.	The writer wrote an introduction that led to a claim or thesis and got his readers to care about his opinion. The writer got his readers to care by not only including a cool fact or jazzy question, but also by telling readers what was significant in or around the topic. The writer worked to find the precise words to state his claim; he let readers know the reasons he would develop later.
Transitions	The writer connected his ideas and reasons with his examples using words such as *for example* and *because*. He connected one reason or example using words such as *also* and *another*.	The writer used words and phrases to glue parts of her piece together. She used phrases such as *for example, another example, one time,* and *for instance* to show when she wanted to shift from saying reasons to giving evidence and *in addition to, also,* and *another* to show when she wanted to make a new point.	The writer used transition words and phrases to connect evidence back to her reasons using phrases such as *this shows that...* The writer helped readers follow her thinking with phrases such as *another reason* and *the most important reason.* She used phrases such as *consequently* and *because of* to show what happened. The writer used words such as *specifically* and *in particular* to be more precise.
Ending	The writer worked on an ending, perhaps a thought or comment related to her opinion.	The writer wrote an ending for his piece in which he restated and reflected on his claim, perhaps suggesting an action or response based on what he had written.	The writer worked on a conclusion in which he connected back to and highlighted what the text was mainly about, not just the preceding paragraph.

FIG. 1-1   Sample learning progression

Information Writing Checklist

	Grade 6	NOT YET	STARTING TO	YES!
Structure				
Overall	I conveyed ideas and information about a subject in a well-structured text. Sometimes I incorporated arguments, explanations, stories, or procedural passages.	☐	☐	☐
Lead	I wrote an introduction in which I interested readers, perhaps with a quote or significant fact. I let readers know the subtopics that I would develop later and how my text would unfold.	☐	☐	☐
Transitions	I used transitions to help readers understand how different bits of information and different parts of my writing fit together. I used transitions to help connect ideas, information, and examples, and to imply relationships such as when material exemplifies, adds on to, is similar to, explains, or contrasts. I used transitions such as *for instance, such as, similarly, therefore, as a result, in contrast to, and on the other hand.*	☐		☐
Ending	I wrote a conclusion in which I restated the important ideas and offered a final insight or implication for the reader to consider.	☐	☐	☐
Organization	I chose a focused subject.	☐	☐	☐
	I used subheadings and/or clear introductory transitions to separate sections.	☐	☐	☐
	I made deliberate choices about how to order sections and about the sequence of information and ideas within sections. I chose structures such as compare-and-contrast, categories, and claim-and-support to organize information and ideas. Some sections are written as argument, explanation, stories, or procedural passages.	☐	☐	☐
Development				
Elaboration	I included varied kinds of information such as facts, quotations, examples, and definitions.	☐	☐	☐
	I used trusted sources and information from authorities on the topic and gave the sources credit.	☐	☐	☐
	I worked to make my information understandable and interesting. To do this, I may have referred to earlier parts of my text, summarized background information, raised questions, and considered possible implications.	☐	☐	☐

FIG. 1–2   Sample checklist

goals. The Resources section of the Teachers College Reading and Writing Project's website, http://readingandwritingproject.com/resources/video-and-e-media.html (Google search term "Reading and Writing Project Multimedia") contains videos showing the use of these checklists in whole-class and small-group teaching. These videos, along with the units of study themselves, can help you imagine the many ways to use these checklists in your daily writing workshop.

• **Prompts for three on-demand assessment tasks.** These three prompts direct students to compose the best piece of writing they can—narrative, information, or argument—in a fixed period of time. The resulting pieces can then be assessed using the learning progressions and rubrics (most of these are located on the CD-ROM, some within the text). In other words, each student's on-demand writing can be ascribed a grade level ("Overall, Natasha's argument writing is at the sixth-grade level, although her elaboration meets seventh-grade standards"). Assuming you conduct a similar assessment at intervals throughout the year, you can track each student's progress over the year, starting from this baseline piece of writing.

• **Two sets of carefully selected benchmark student writing samples for each type of writing, at each grade level.** Each text was written by a student, without help, using the on-demand prompt and protocol. These benchmark texts represent what students at each grade level should be able to do within a similar on-demand context by the *end* of that grade. The two texts at each grade represent different but equivalent ways for a student to be "at standard" for that grade level. For example, one of the seventh-grade arguments is based on a topic of personal concern—wanting access to more rides at amusement parks—with evidence and analysis that stems from the writer's own experience and logic; the other seventh-grade argument writer used a number of articles she had recently read to support her position that even dangerous animals should not be killed. One of the eighth-grade narratives tells a story and weaves suspense and character relationships into the narrative details of the scenes; the other eighth-grade narrative is more like a memoir, with explicit self-reflection and essaylike passages incorporated into the storytelling.

The pieces are also selected because they are memorable: they are funny, or insightful, or demonstrate command of a topic. You and your students will enjoy them and find them worth studying. Many teachers use these texts within minilessons, conferences, and small-group work as a way to give a clear vision for specific writing goals. The pieces are not perfect! But that's part of what's interesting about this work—looking at writing that approaches, hits, and sometimes surpasses certain elements of the

ON-DEMAND PERFORMANCE ASSESSMENT PROMPT

Argument Writing

Say to students:

"Think of a topic or issue that you know and care about, an issue around which you have strong feelings. Tomorrow, you will have forty-five minutes to write an opinion or argument text in which you will write your opinion or claim and tell reasons why you feel that way. When you do this, draw on everything you know about essays, persuasive letters, and reviews. If you want to find and use information from a book or another outside source, you may bring that with you tomorrow. Please keep in mind that you'll have forty-five minutes to complete this, so you will need to plan, draft, revise, and edit in one sitting.

"In your writing, make sure you:

- Write an introduction.
- State your opinion or claim.
- Give reasons and evidence.
- Organize your writing.
- Acknowledge counterclaims.
- Use transition words.
- Write a conclusion."

Use the teaching rubrics to assess and score these pieces of on-demand writing.

FIG. 1–3   Sample on-demand assessment prompt

- **Three progressions of annotated texts in argument writing, information writing, and narrative writing, developed across grade levels.** These are not student-written texts, but are instead teacher-written demonstration texts. My colleagues and I have written these texts, which progress up the K–8 grades with essentially the same content across those grades, to show how small revisions add up incrementally to texts that meet increasing expectations. In each instance, we wrote a text as if we

standards and talking about it, but also noticing what's missing or almost there, but not quite. By middle school, the standards demand such sophisticated work for students: to navigate narrowing their topic of choice to something manageable, determine what's important enough to showcase, plan for a workable structure within the genre, then write to convey key points and elaborate with meaningful details, including outside sources. That's a lot for forty-five minutes! But it's so important because it's actually what students will often have to do—in life as well as in school.

Grade 7

The writer interested readers with a compelling anecdote and provided background information in the form of historical context.

The writer developed not just information but also an idea about the information. The author made the claim, and made it clear how the ideas and information in the text would unfold.

The writer attempted to vary the sentence structure, combining simple sentences with complex sentences.

The writer used a transitional phrase to compare/contrast. Comparisons were used as a way to explain information and the explanation was further supported by text features.

The Bulldog: A Dog Like No Other

A small dog huddles in a corner, waiting to be released into a giant arena. Though it seems difficult to believe, there was a time when dogs were bred for sport, a brutal sport called bull-baiting. The dogs were trained to clamp on to a bull's nose and to not let go until either the bull killed the dog or the dog brought the bull to the ground (Gray, 1976). Not every kind of dog would have been up to this task. The dog bread for this sport is the dog that we know today as the bulldog. In fact, that's how this dog got its name. Maybe this is also why these dogs have a reputation for being fierce. However, bulldogs are one of the most special dogs out there, for many reasons. There are no other dogs that look like a bulldog, with its characteristic wrinkles. Bulldogs do require some unique care, as does any prized possession, so owning a bulldog isn't easy, but is very, very rewarding. Finally, Bulldogs have a fascinating history, unlike that of any other dog.

I. A Unique and Varied Appearance

The English Bulldog looks like no other. It is a compact dog with a short, smooth coat and a wide head and shoulders. Bulldogs typically have **prognathism**, essentially meaning its lower jaw sticks out beyond its upper jaw. This is also called an underbite. In contrast, dogs like golden retrievers rarely have an underbite. Their top teeth stick over their bottom teeth. Though this condition is not considered attractive in humans, many people find it to be quite adorable on a small dog.

Bulldog underbite   Golden retriever with no underbite

A bulldog's eyebrows are made of thick folds of skin, and it has small black eyes. These small eyes and eyebrows with folds give it the illusion of being angry, though that's typically not the case.

FIG. 1–5 Sample annotated information writing for grade 7

Xinyu   September 16

On-Demand Narrative Writing

I frantically searched the living room for a good place to hide. "Four, five, six..." I heard Lucy count in the other room. I looked at the table, the counter-tops, the cupboards, and chairs. Nothing was appealing to me. Then it hit me the halls, I thought. She'll never be able to find me there. I tiptoed through the living room, careful not to bump into anything. Just as I was about to put my right foot down, my foot made contact with a sticky, gooey substance. I sighed, exasperated before directing my eyes to my foot. Then there, I stood in complete shock as the horror dawned upon me.

Earlier, when I arrived at Lucy's house, the first thing that attracted my attention was a yellow, glistening mouse trap that laided in the corner of the living room. "Watch your step," Lucy said as I dropped my bag on the side. It was those mouse traps where anything that made contact with it, the thing would get stuck. I bent down on my knees as I took a closer look and studied the two furry half-dead mice that were unfortunately fell into the trap. "My mother's going to throw that out later, when she comes home from work," Lucy explained to me. Lucy was 12, so she was allowed to stay home by herself. I sat down, on the other hand I was only 8 at the time.

"Come on, get up," tartly she commanded I then reluctantly pushed off my toes and jumped onto my feet, into an upright position.

Now, my right foot was glued to the mouse trap and even worse, it was on top of the two mice. I shrieked in pure terror.

FIG. 1–4 Sample of leveled student writing

were a third-grader and then improved it up a notch to write it like a fourth-grader, then a fifth-grader. After writing the same text as a sixth-grader, we improved upon it in this same notch-by-notch way so that it shows seventh-grade work. For each K–8 grade level, there is a text that matches the expectations for that grade. Teachers will find it is helpful to have a sixth-grade level text, for example, that they can improve upon to show students, say, a seventh-grade level conclusion, or structure (which can in turn also be improved upon). We've done this, for example, with a report on bulldogs (a dog that is surprisingly popular among Teachers College Reading and Writing Project staff!). We wrote a little report on bulldogs as if it were written by a fifth-grader, then revised it to reflect sixth-grade standards, then revised it again to reflect seventh-grade standards, and so on. Similar work is also included in narrative and argument. These pieces illustrate the items on the checklist—more precisely and completely than any one piece of student writing ever could—and can be used to show students how they can revise their own writing to take it from one level to the next.

• **Rubrics for scoring.** These rubrics, grounded in the learning progressions, use numbers corresponding to grade levels and give appropriate weight to each category, so that you can derive a point score for each student's work in a particular type of writing, as well as track students' progress statistically. The grade-specific rubrics (provided for each genre) can be used to assess both on-demand writing and students' published writing. While the checklists only allow a student to say "not yet" with regard to doing a particular level of work, the rubrics allow you to note whether that aspect of the writing resembles work expected for students who are two years below grade level, one year below grade level, or somewhere in between. While these scores are reductive—reducing the complexity of the work to numbers, as rubrics always do—they can be helpful in measuring growth across time, noticing patterns that will help you inform whole-class and small-group instruction, and looking at the data from select groups (your boys versus

FIG. 1–6   Sample rubric

Rubric for Narrative Writing—Grade 8

STRUCTURE

	Grade 6 (1 POINT)	1.5 PTS Mid-level	Grade 7 (2 POINTS)	2.5 PTS Mid-level	Grade 8 (3 POINTS)	3.5 PTS Mid-level	Grade 9 (4 POINTS)	SCORE
Overall	The writer wrote a story that has tension, resolution, and realistic characters, and also conveys an idea, lesson, or theme.	Mid-level	The writer created a narrative that has realistic characters, tension, and change, and that not only conveys, but also develops an idea, lesson, or theme.	Mid-level	The writer not only created a narrative with well-developed characters who change, he used the story to comment on a social issue, teach a lesson, and/or develop a point of view.	Mid-level	The writer created a narrative with well-developed characters whose interactions build tension and change over time. The writer used that story to comment on a social issue, teach a lesson, and/or develop a particular point of view.	
Lead	The writer wrote a beginning that not only set the plot/story in motion, but also hinted at the larger meaning the story would convey. It introduced the problem, set the stage for the lesson that would be learned, or showed how the character relates to the setting in a way that matters in the story.	Mid-level	The writer wrote a beginning that not only sets the story in motion, it also grounds it in a place or situation. It includes details that will later be important to the story. These details might point to the central issue or conflict, show how story elements connect, or hint at key character traits.	Mid-level	The writer wrote a beginning that establishes the situation and place, hinting at a bigger context for the story (revealing issues that have been brewing, showing how the setting affects the character, contextualizing a time in history, developing one out of many points of view).	Mid-level	The writer wrote a beginning establishing a situation, place, and/or atmosphere; foreshadowing the problem(s); and hinting at questions, issues, ideas, or themes. The writer introduced a particular narrative voice and point of view.	
Transitions	The writer not only used transitional phrases and clauses to signal complicated changes in time, she also used them to alert her readers to changes in the setting, tone, mood, point of view, or time in the story (such as *suddenly, unlike before, if only she had known*).	Mid-level	The writer used transitional phrases and clauses to connect what happened to why it happened (*If he hadn't ... he might not have, because of, although, little did she know that*).	Mid-level	The writer used transitional phrases and clauses, grammatical structures (paragraphing, descriptive phrases, and clauses) and text structures (chapter divisions, extended italics) to alert his reader to changes in the setting, the mood, the point of view, or the time in the story.	Mid-level	The writer used transitional phrases and clauses, grammatical structures to demonstrate the passage of time, to connect parts of the story, to imply cause and effect, to raise questions, and/or to make allusions (*long before, as when, just as, without realizing, ever afterward*).	

your girls, for example, or your strong writers versus your struggling writers). Looking at data in this way also makes it easier to report according to your district or state mandates.

- **Other writing performance assessments.** These assessments include an information reading/argument writing (about information reading) performance assessment that has been widely used across New York State and progressions for assessing students' engagement with the writing process.

- **A progression of sixth- through eighth-grade benchmark student samples of writing about literature.** This kind of writing bridges argument and informational/explanatory writing. A writer could take up a position about a literary text, acknowledge and refute alternative interpretations, and support his own through the use of evidence; this would be argument writing, and it's the way that our sixth- and eighth-grade units in literary essay and analytic essay are angled. On the other hand, a writer could write to analyze and explain character relationships, complex themes, and the effects of author's craft; this could be considered explanatory writing, because it doesn't take up a "position" in the same way that an argument text would, and it's how we approach writing about reading in the seventh-grade unit of study on companion books. This latter interpretation of writing about literature is one privileged by Partnership for Assessment of Readiness for College and Careers (PARCC): their rubrics for literary analysis align to the CCSS for information writing, not argument. But high school and college literature courses have often framed writing about literature as argument, and we find that it's productive for students to consider what's "debatable" in a literary text and to work to think through not just one possible interpretation, but others as well. In any event, we have included these samples as a separate progression to leave this conversation open. We have also included an example of a literary essay checklist made with teachers—modified from the argument checklist for eighth grade.

THE SOURCE OF THE EXPECTATIONS THAT UNDERGIRD THE ASSESSMENT TOOLS

You will want to know the source of the standards that are codified in these checklists, rubrics, and benchmark texts. Our intent is for them to be closely aligned with the Common Core State Standards. In some cases, there are items here that exactly match the standards listed in the CCSS for that grade. Sometimes, while still trying to preserve important uses of academic vocabulary, we have used student-friendly language to describe something. There are other times when an item in our progressions, rubrics, and checklists is entirely missing from the CCSS, and in such an instance, this item is here because we believe it is vital to writers' success with that genre. Usually, when our tools differ from the CCSS, it will be because our tools are more specific and, we hope, more operational.

In the CCSS for seventh grade, for example, it says argument writers should "provide a concluding statement or section that follows from and supports the argument presented" (W.7.1e). Our checklist says it this way: "In the conclusion, I returned to the sides of the argument and reiterated how the support for

FIG.1–7 Sample additional performance assessment

"You're going to have a chance to show off what you know about doing quick, on-the-run, intensive research and composing an argument essay. Over the next couple of periods, you'll encounter a few texts that will provide you with information and claims about the pros and cons of bottled water. It will be up to you to really analyze the information and ideas, so that you can state your own claim and justify it, using researched evidence.

"For each text, you'll have a chance to respond to prompts that ask you to identify and explain key details in the text that support central ideas. Then you'll have some time to look over your research. Then, we'll imagine that our school is hosting a debate about whether or not schools should ban bottled water. You have to decide which side of the debate to argue. You can take the position that bottled water should be banned—in which case you want to gather convincing evidence from your research. Or you can make a claim to support bottled water in school—in which case you also want convincing evidence.

"One thing to tell you ahead of time—part of what makes a convincing argument is the ability to acknowledge the opposing claim and reasons, and refute those. So no matter which side you end up taking, be alert during your research for evidence that could be used for either side of the argument.

"This period is part one of this research project. You'll have a chance to watch a video and read two texts today, and to write to explain key details that help support the different points of view on this topic. At a later time, you'll write your position paper, or essay. You'll have a chance then to look over your notes and any of the texts again."

Task 1: Respond to Video "CNN: Most Bottled Water Is Tap"

"You're about to watch a news video about the relationship between bottled water and tap water. As you watch, think about the important ideas and information in the video. After I show the video a second time, write a central idea that this video teaches us, and fill in the outline with specific examples or evidence that the video gives to support that idea."

Task 2: Respond to Article "Goodbye, Bottled Water?"

"Now you'll have a chance to study an article about bottled water. After reading this, write two reasons that the article gives for why bottled water is a problem. For each reason, write a quote from the article that explains or supports that reason."

Task 3: Respond to "International Bottled Water Association Statement"

"Now you'll have a chance to read a response from the International Bottled Water Association regarding a state attorney general's decision to allow a town to ban bottled water. Read to find the strongest evidence that the Bottled Water Association gives in defense of bottled water. Write to explain why this evidence is convincing."

Seventh-Grade Informational Reading/Argument Writing Performance Assessment

Student Booklet

Task 1: Response to "CNN: Most Bottled Water Is Tap"

Name: _____   Date: _____

This video informs us about bottled water. What is a central idea in this video about bottled water?

_____

_____

_____

What examples or specific evidence does the video give to explain or support this?

• Example or evidence: _____

_____

_____

• Example or evidence: _____

_____

_____

Lara

In the book Matched by Ally Condie, Cassia Reyes is the main character. Throughout the story Cassia has many struggles and problems. The author uses many crafts to reach her goals.

One goal the author uses is to build empathy for Cassia. Cassia met a boy named Ky Markham. They started to talk more and more each day. They got so close they fell in love with each other. But she is not about to pick who she wants to love. She was match by her best friend Xander, but she told him it's not going to work. If you do such a thing, and switch your match you could become an aberration, which is almost like an outcast. When the officials found out about their secret relationship they got into big trouble. They were also sent away for a while so they can think. But Cassia really missed Ky. On page 363 Cassia thinks to herself, "I think of him, I think of him, I think of him." Cassia is thinking this so the reader would build empathy for her. The author did this so the reader would feel the pain of loosing someone she loved. This is how the author uses many crafts to reach a goal.

Another goal the author uses is building and setting up a problem for the next book in the series. When Cassia got sent away she never stopped thinking about Ky and trying to find him. The whole time she was away she remembered things that Ky either told her or wrote her on his pictures. On page 365 Cassia remembers what Ky wrote to her, "Cassia. I know which life is real one now, no matter what happens. It's the one with you." This is setting up a problem because Ky is telling her that he loves Cassia. But they can not talk to each other or see each other because they are way to far away. Cassia really wants to see Ky and Ky really wants to see Cassia. The author makes a cliff hanger about where Ky is. Cassia wants to go on a journey to find him. The author made the end of the book like this so the problem will lead into the next book. Cassia and Ky might never see each other again but to then that like death. This is how the author used another craft to reach a goal.

FIG. 1–8 Sample Grade 7 benchmark student writing, Lara's literary essay about "Matched"

my claim outweighed the counterclaim or how my claim is the most important in certain conditions." In this instance what we say is the same—no more, but more helpful, operational, and kid-friendly.

There is no one source of authority that can say whether the benchmark pieces we've selected are actually "on standard." The pieces of writing collected in Appendix C of the CCSS—the only authoritative reference point—were often written over long stretches of time, with help from teachers and parents. The benchmark texts found in this resource represent our hypothesis for benchmark levels of at-standards-level on-demand writing. We have selected these texts by drawing on our deep knowledge of the Common Core Standards and of the exemplar texts in Appendix C, our study of texts that other organizations have since put forward as exemplars of the CCSS levels, and our own thirty years of research, publications, and work in middle school classrooms. We are confident, in any case, that the texts are at least at, and perhaps beyond, the level of the standards. Working toward these levels, then, will be helpful for you and your writers.

Of course, expectations for students' published work will always exceed expectations for their on-demand writing. The work we include here in no way shows the full capacity of what students can do when given many days (and sometimes weeks) of time to research, assess, draw on sources, get feedback, revise, rethink, and reimagine. We trust that you, our reader, understand that it is through a deep engagement in the writing process that students' abilities are stretched, that their horizons are extended. All of my other publications describe that work and brim with examples of what students can do when given opportunities to engage in the full dimension of the writing process. Keep in mind that the focus in this particular book is on students' on-demand writing—the writing work they can do independently and with automaticity when we step back and let them go.

When you first assess your students, you will probably find that their work is considerably below the level of expectation outlined in the Common Core. Don't be dismayed. I recently heard a group of people who have been hard at work developing the new tests say that the expectation is that only 20% of students will score "at standard" on the new tests when they are first rolled out. So you should not be surprised that the expectations in this assessment system may at first seem uncomfortably high. After all, most students have not yet received coherent and rigorous instruction in writing. Until the Common Core placed a premium on writing, many schools had made no effort to provide a schoolwide approach to writing or even to ensure that writing was a subject in which students received explicit instruction. And although a single year of strong writing instruction can produce impressive results, growth takes time, and it would be unrealistic to expect a seventh-grade teacher to produce seventh-grade level writers if students entered that classroom with the skills of a third- or fourth-grade writer.

While it may well take more than a single year to bring students up to par across a classroom, school, or district, we believe that the progressions in this book represent work that most students can do if they are given a sequence of skilled teaching, a coherent and rigorous writing curriculum, and a set of assessment tools such as these. If you have studied the CCSS, you have probably settled on the thought that when the day comes that your students enter your grade level having met the standards for the previous year, you'll be able to get them to standards levels for your grade. We look forward to helping that day to come soon!

You'll note that, generally, if a student needs to work on a skill in one type of writing, the student will also need to work on that same skill in another type of writing; craft moves, say, will be similar whether in narrative writing, information writing, or argument writing. In this way, the writing progressions are linked, though they are also distinct. This means that as students receive instruction and engage in writing work in one kind of writing, they will be honing their craft moves also in other kinds of writing—as long as they receive help in understanding the reciprocity between genres, as well as the time and coaching needed to transfer what they've learned from one kind of writing to the next.

Looking at Craft across Writing Types			
	Argument	**Information**	**Narrative**
6th grade	I chose my words carefully to support my argument and to have an effect on my reader. I worked to include concrete details, comparisons, and/or images to convey my ideas, build my argument, and keep my reader engaged. When necessary, I explained terms to readers, providing definitions, context clues, or parenthetical explanations. I made my piece sound serious.	I chose my words carefully to explain my information and ideas and to have an effect on my reader. I worked to include concrete details, comparisons, and/or images to explain information and concepts, and to keep my reader engaged. I incorporated domain-specific vocabulary, and when necessary, I explained terms to readers, providing context clues, parenthetical explanations, text boxes, or similar support. I supported readers' learning by using a teaching tone and a formal style, as appropriate.	I developed some relationship between characters to show *why* they act and speak as they do. I told the internal, as well as the external story. I wove together precise descriptions, figurative language, and some symbolism to help readers picture the setting, actions, and events and to bring forth meaning. I used language that fit my story's meaning and context (e.g., different characters use different kinds of language).

FIG. 1–9   This chart highlights how the craft component is connected across all three writing types. You can see how skills such as precise word choice and tone carry throughout argument, information, and narrative writing.

THIS ASSESSMENT MATCHES THE CHARACTERISTICS OF EFFECTIVE FORMATIVE ASSESSMENTS

We've built this assessment system to embody the characteristics of effective formative assessments. To do this, we paid attention to the research on factors comprising effective teaching. In the research article "Assessment and Classroom Learning" (*Assessment in Education*, 1998 (5): 7–74), the authors summarize key findings, suggesting that research indicates that improving learning through assessment depends on five deceptively simple key factors: the provision of effective feedback to pupils; the active involvement of pupils in their own learning; the adjustment of teaching to take into account the results of assessment; a recognition of the profound influence assessment has on the motivation and self-esteem of pupils, both of which are crucial influences on learning; and the need for pupils to be able to assess themselves and understand how to improve.

The approach to assessment in *Writing Pathways* will support both you and your students in taking a reflective stance, creating consistent occasions for looking backward, looking forward, goal-setting, and deliberate practice. As you move between the *Units of Study* and the resources in this book, you will find an emphasis on the following priorities:

- **Students can be active agents** of their own writing development, self-assessing their own work constantly on a day-to-day basis and reaching toward next steps. Students can see what is expected of them, can see concrete examples of texts at the next level, and can emulate examples of those benchmark texts. The assessment tools help students clarify their next steps so they can work with expediency to move forward. They can approach a new chunk in an information text or the exciting part of a story and think, "Wait, what are my goals for this part of a piece?" and then work with resolve to achieve those goals.

- The assessment tools are **aligned to the Common Core State Standards but not limited to them**. That is, when the standards are obscure, leaving teachers and kids thinking, "What? What does that mean?" this system is crystal clear, providing the Teachers College Reading and Writing Project's knowledgeable interpretation of sometimes unclear expectations. In instances when research on writing development reveals that the CCSS have neglected a key developmental step in writing, we've filled in that step. Then, too, when expectations in the CCSS arrive out of the blue without precursor steps or are embedded in the sample texts but not the bullet points, this assessment fills in a more detailed progression toward the goal of CCSS levels of achievement.

- The assessment tools **help students transfer their skills from one type of writing to another** by showing them ways expectations for the different types of writing are similar to each other. That is, although the specific nature of elaboration will be different whether one is elaborating in narrative, argument, or information writing, it is consistently true that across the three types of writing, a degree of elaboration and a variety of elaboration is required. It is also true that elaboration tends to be most important in key areas of a text—in a narrative scene that reveals a character's true motivations or relates back to the theme of the story, in the parts of an essay where the writer is trying to make an important point or rebut a counterargument, and so on. Expectations for introductions and endings, transitions, and so forth tend to be aligned across all the different types of writing as well. Conclusions, for example, are best if they relate back to the heart or central ideas in a text, whether that text is an essay, a story, or a research article.

- The assessment tools are based on the assumption that **students will usually choose their own topics for writing**, allowing them to demonstrate what they can do as writers when writing about topics they know and care about. In some schools and districts, teachers may have received the message that for a writing assessment to be reliable, every student must respond to an identical writing prompt. The problem with this is that when students all respond to the same prompt, it becomes unclear whether the assessment is of the student's writing ability or of the student's knowledge of the content contained in the prompt. Similarly, if an assessment asks students to respond to reading, conflating reading and writing, it is hard to discern if their trouble lies in the writing alone or if they simply haven't understood about the content—the reading—to write well. These writing assessments, therefore, are designed to **assess writing separately from reading**. Assessing writing about reading is described in Chapter 9 of this book.

- The gridlike design of the assessments highlights ways students engage with skills with more or less complexity, depending on their level of proficiency. This means that these assessment tools, like the standards themselves, **allow students to move ahead as quickly as possible**, while also **allowing teachers to differentiate instruction**. For example, a teacher can teach the importance of elaboration in opinion/argument writing, keeping in mind that some of his students are still at the fifth-grade level of making sure their reasons are parallel and don't overlap as well as sequenced in a convincing order, while others are working on the seventh-grade elaboration skills of including a variety of evidence and analyzing the ways that evidence builds the argument and outweighs any possible counterclaim(s).

Chapter 2

The First Step

Conducting On-Demand Performance Assessments

T O HAVE A RECORD that shows how your students have improved as writers, you won't want to delay conducting your initial assessments. Start tomorrow, before you read beyond this chapter; there's not a lot you need to know to pull this off! It is important to students and their parents (and to you as well) to be able to look back on the journey traveled, saying, "Look at where you started and contrast that to where you are now!" The sooner you collect that initial assessment, the better. Ideally, you do this on Day One of the school year. Imagine the parent-teacher conference with, say, Robert's parents. You bring out Robert's first on-demand writing, say to his parent, "This is what your son's information writing looked like at the start of the year." Then you lay his most recent writing alongside the on-demand piece, saying, "Look! *This* is what he produced just the other day!"

You will rightly hesitate over the idea that on the first day of school, you'll say, "Welcome to my class. I want to start our year together by weighing and measuring you as a writer," but frankly, thousands of teachers are doing just that. At least you'll be in good company. Then too, remember that you control the tone of this work. Shift the way you introduce these assessments, so that you describe this as giving students a chance to "show off" all they know about writing.

The truth is that the earlier in the year you assess, the lower the starting level, and therefore, the greater the display of progress. There is no more potent way to encourage future growth than to show past growth. "Look at how dramatically you are improving. I can just *imagine* what your writing will be like by the end of the year. Amazing." Author and educator Peter Johnston reminds us in his book *Choice Words* (2004) that "Once students have a sense that they are constantly learning, and are presented with evidence of that learning, teachers can ask not only about the details of their learning histories, but about the details of their futures, and the plans they have for managing those futures." By conducting an on-demand assessment as close to the start of the year as possible, and then gathering data in a similar way at other set intervals, you and your students will be able to see evidence of growth—and evidence of the effectiveness of your teaching. So don't tarry.

One more thing: the good news is that the assessment itself is not taxing to give, and at least for this first administration, at the start of the year, the results won't make you feel vulnerable. After all, the start-of-the-year on-demand pieces will reveal the *challenge* you have before you, that's all. Meanwhile the payoff for conducting these initial assessments can be immediate. You can quickly ascertain whether your planned curriculum is roughly appropriate for your students and make alterations as needed. The payoff for conducting these assessments is described in Chapter 4.

THE RATIONALE FOR CHARTING GROWTH BASED ON ON-DEMAND WRITING, NOT ON WRITING THROUGH THE PROCESS

The striking thing about asking students to work with absolutely no input from anyone during an assigned interval of time to show their best work as writers is that these on-demand writing tasks provide a crystal clear demonstration of what students have learned to do without assistance. Whereas other peoples' hands are all over the published writing that students produce—as well they should be—an on-demand narrative, information, or argument piece written in class provides a snapshot of what the student can do on her own and in a limited window of time.

It is significant that although this assessment tool is rooted in a writing process approach to writing, the assessment tools channel you to study your students' writing and your own teaching on the basis not of pieces of writing that are produced (with lots of input) across weeks of work, but on the basis of pieces that your students produce when they work on their own, on the spot.

Granted, you will presumably also assess other aspects of student work (their effort, their final publications, etc.) to generate report card grades. The combination of grades from on-demand writing (both achievement and growth, in the three modes) and grades from students' final publications (both product and process goals) will go a long way toward justifying an earned grade for each of your students. You can, of course, take other factors into consideration, as long as you make these public. For example, you could calculate into the equation a grade for the sheer volume of writing that each student does, or for the degree of hard work that student exhibits, or for a student's abilities to help other students, or for the student's revisions.

That being said, the emphasis on students' on-demand writing does convey a larger message. All the work on writing process is not just for students to learn that when they have a month to do so, they can produce an effective piece of writing. All the revision, all the conferences, all the study of mentor texts and the like culminates in students becoming vastly more skilled at flash-draft writing, as well as at working on extended writing projects. In the end, writers need to be able to rehearse, draft, revise, and edit on the spot, quickly, under time pressure—and with independence.

The emphasis on on-demand writing also says to parents, to other teachers, and to you as well, "If any of us coauthor a student's piece of writing, making it vastly better than anything the student could possibly do on his own, and if we do this by working so far outside the student's zone of proximal development that the student doesn't learn to do what we teach on his own, then even if this produces better writing, it is essentially for naught." If a teacher or parent's involvement with a student's writing doesn't lead the student to write better another day, on another piece, that involvement doesn't add up to much.

One of the cardinal rules of any responsible approach to teaching writing is that instruction must teach students in ways that affect not just today, but every day. If you simply tell a writer what to do to improve his piece of writing, saying something like, "Your piece about the afternoon you spent walking in Hudson River Park would be stronger if you described the park. When you arrive at the park, add a visual detail. Also, here, when you take a picture of the seagull on the railing, show yourself making eye contact with the bird," then the piece of writing will presumably get better. But I doubt if the student will have learned anything that he can transfer to another piece, another day.

Throughout *Units of Study in Argument, Information, and Narrative Writing*, you'll find that we support instruction in *transferable skills* and strategies. This means that instead of telling the writer to add that he made eye contact with a seagull at the park, you can teach a principle or a strategy that the writer can rely on after. For example, you might say, "I'm noticing that in this piece, although you name the setting—the park—you don't *describe* that setting. In fact, often in your writing you develop characters and plot, but forget about the role of setting. Your stories will be much richer if you remember to develop the setting. It is a good idea to scatter little descriptions of the setting throughout a piece—not just adding one big description at the beginning—and to show your main character interacting with the setting. In a personal narrative, that means you can find places in the story where you show yourself being aware of the setting. For example, when you say that you watched the seagull before taking a picture of it, you might show yourself taking in the setting, pointing out some of what you saw at that moment so that your reader can see it, too."

The first approach—telling the student to add details into a specific paragraph—improves the *writing* more than the writer. That interaction is not apt to transfer to another day and another piece. The second approach aims to teach the *writer*; the distinction is essential to effective writing instruction.

Knowing that your writers will be assessed for what they do with independence will encourage you and your colleagues to work with fervor to help students learn skills that transfer to any new work. When this assessment system is in place, it means that you and your colleagues (and your students' parents as well) are less apt to obsess over helping a student make one particular piece of writing "perfect." Instead, the emphasis shifts to helping students grow demonstrably as independent writers. These on-demand assessments become students' chance to show off what they know how to do and your chance to measure the stickiness of your teaching.

THE LOGISTICS

The schedule we suggest for these assessments is, first, at the start of the year and then again after every relevant unit of study. You and your colleagues can decide whether you want to assess in all three kinds of writing at the start of the year or to just get start-of-the-year data on the genre you teach first (presumably, narrative writing).

Remember that whatever plan you devise, it is best if all the teachers across your school agree on the same plan. Some schools start the year assessing only the genre that will be taught first. (Of course, because your students' work with any one type of writing will improve all their writing, the baseline for the other two kinds of writing will be at a higher level when you obtain that baseline later, which means less progress will be visible.) If you teach two units of study on one genre (for instance, literary essay and argument essay) and assess at the end of each unit as well as at the end of the year, then you will give four on-demands on argument writing. That may seem like a lot of days devoted to assessment, but you can be sure that students work with extra fervor on these days, and what they are doing is actually not very different than what you ask them to do during any other day. Of course, one possible downside of so much assessment is that you are more overwhelmed with the pressure to score, but as you will see later in this discussion, you and your colleagues can make the decision to use peer scoring (or self-scoring) instead of teacher-scoring for some of the assessments.

It is important to note that the Common Core specifically encourages writing in different subjects. Therefore, not all writing assessments need be confined within the time allocated to English Language Arts (ELA). The rubrics and checklists in this book can be adapted for use in any subject, and part of a schoolwide plan might be to schedule on-demands across the curriculum, so that the time spent writing the assessments is distributed across different classrooms, not taking time away from ELA during every administration. Students will benefit enormously when they hear the same (or similar) writing criteria used for all of their writing, whether it is a science lab report, a description of a conflict in history, a comparison of media in art, or a reflection about characters in a novel. History and science teachers we've worked with who have incorporated this into their assessment plans have learned a lot about how their students process and articulate the content from these disciplines; the independence and tight time frame spotlights students' own understandings and skills in ways that guided class discussions or more extended projects sometimes mask.

It is important to keep in mind that the purpose of assessment is to support growth. This means that although these on-demand assessments will be somewhat formal and need to be administered with consistency, you and your colleagues can decide to vary the plan if doing so supports students' growth. Imagine that you and the teachers across your grade conduct an assessment of students' narrative writing on the very first day of school and their work is shockingly low (this happens, trust me). You and the other teachers across the grade might meet and decide that the first on-demand, collected on Day One of the school year, may not have been a good reflection of what the students can actually do. Perhaps it showed summer rustiness. With this in mind, you and your colleagues might all decide to give students a two-day immersion in narrative writing, one you plan together so that it includes showing examples of effective narrative writing, and then you might readminister the on-demand assessment. After all, why adapt the instruction you had planned based on an artificially low assessment of what students can do, if you can actually ramp up that level through a short, intensive review?

Alternatively, after scoring a set of essays, you might decide the class needs remedial work, say, on structuring writing, and so you say to the class, "I think you have forgotten to do things you know full well how to do! I'm going to teach a one-day intensive course (we often refer to this as a boot camp), and then you will have a chance to do another on-demand assessment." You might even add a day for students to reflect on and revise their first on-demand pieces of writing before heading into writing a second round of them.

Any of these decisions will work within this system of assessment, provided that all teachers on a grade level (if not all teachers across the school or the district) conduct the assessment under similar conditions so that the assessment data can be compared. I do encourage you, however, to keep and to cherish that first bit of baseline data, even if this means photocopying the initial on-demands before allowing students to revise them. Just as a parent cherishes the souvenirs of a child's first days, first steps, first words, you and the students in your care will enjoy looking back to celebrate progress. Imagine the end of the year celebration when students display their start and end of the year work, announcing, "I used to be this kind of writer . . . but now . . ."

Many teachers find that it is powerful for students to keep their on-demands close at hand during the day-to-day writing workshop so they work with deliberateness to make sure their writing is improving. You might consider having students keep their own writing portfolios, where their work is kept as the year progresses. Visitors to the classroom, parents, students, and others can flip through these photo-album-like collections and extol the progress made from September onward. Alternatively, you might have students paste their first on-demand writing into their writer's notebooks. As the unit progresses and students' writing grows exponentially, you might encourage them to flip between their original on-demand piece and their latest entry, admiring the progress they have made and the goals they have met. This will also help ensure that the level of students' writing *does* grow. Given that students tend to pour their energy into assessments, this sets a high personal bar for writers.

PROMPTS FOR ON-DEMAND PERFORMANCE ASSESSMENTS

It is important that all students across a class, school, grade level cluster, and even school district be given the same prompt for each type of writing and that you and your colleagues agree to offer no further support to the writers. This way, the writing students produce can show what they are able to do independently in that particular kind of writing. All of the prompts are included in Part II of this book. Here, for example, is the prompt for a piece of argument writing to be used as a performance assessment:

"Think of a topic or issue that you know and care about, an issue around which you have strong feelings. Tomorrow, you will have forty-five minutes to write an opinion or argument text in which you will write your opinion or claim and tell reasons why you feel that way. When you do this, draw on everything you know about essays, persuasive letters, and reviews. If you want to find and use information from a book or another outside source, you may bring that with you tomorrow. Please keep in mind that you'll have forty-five minutes to complete this, so you will need to plan, draft, revise, and edit in one sitting."

NARRATIVE WRITING PROMPT:

Today, write the best personal narrative that you can write. Make this be the story of one time in your life, a scene or two. You will have 45 minutes to plan, draft, revise and edit. Write in a way that allows you to show off all you know about narrative writing.

In your writing, make sure you:

* Write a beginning for your story.

* Use transition words to tell what happened in order.

* Elaborate to help readers picture your story.

* Show what your story is really about.

* Write an ending for your story.

FIG. 2–1 This is a prompt many teachers use to elicit narrative on-demand writing.

To scaffold students for greater success, there are additional grade-specific instructions after this prompt. You will probably want to read these aloud and also to display them visually as a chart. We recommend the following:

"In your writing, make sure you:

- Write an introduction.

- State your opinion or claim.

- Give reasons and evidence.

- Organize your writing.

- Acknowledge counterclaims.

- Use transition words.

- Write a conclusion."

The prompts vary slightly depending on the genre that is being assessed. The opinion/argument and information prompts require giving students one day's notice. That is, for argument writing, you initiate the idea of the on-demand writing the day before the assessment actually occurs, saying, "Think of a topic or issue that you know a lot about or that you have strong feelings about. Tomorrow, you will have forty-five minutes to write an opinion or argument text. If you want to find and use information from a book or another outside source, you may bring that text with you tomorrow."

You may be tempted to alter the prompt, perhaps by making it more related to an academic subject or a text the class has read. We understand the temptation—we've done a lot of that ourselves, trust us!—and we can caution you from experience that there is a big downside to altering the prompt. You are going to want your students' work to be able to be compared to the work that third-, fourth-, and fifth-grade students did because, frankly, you can count on the fact that some of your students' texts will be at the levels of those benchmarks. Your students' work will not feel comparable to those benchmark texts if the assessment context (your prompt or the fact that the assessment is given in school, under timed conditions) changes. If your students' work is at, say, a fourth-grade level, you are going to want the students to see this themselves, because this will shock them into action, into getting better, quickly. For this reason, we encourage you to use the same prompt that has been used across all the grade levels. But, of course, the final decision is yours, and we do understand there are also reasons to tweak the assessment.

In any case, bear in mind that the Common Core emphasizes the importance of incorporating outside sources into argument and information writing in grades 6 through 8. Students must do this to meet grade-level standards. Therefore, it is important that the prompt encourage them to bring the materials and texts that will make this sort of citation possible. It is important to tell students about the upcoming assessment a day in advance, so that they can think of a possible topic and bring related texts to school with them on the day of the on-demand. If students do not have sources at home, you may schedule a visit to the school library or allow a few minutes on the computer before administering the on-demand assessment.

On the day of the assessment, after the forty-five minutes are over, collect the writing that has been done. The next chapter in this book describes the norming meeting that you will want to participate in with your colleagues before scoring the on-demands. The data gathered can offer you the chance to see where teaching must begin or continue, and it can inform not only planning for individual conferring, small-group, and whole-class instruction. It can also inform gradewide, schoolwide, and whole-district instructional planning.

QUESTIONS TEACHERS OFTEN ASK ABOUT CONDUCTING AN ON-DEMAND ASSESSMENT

My students find it easier to get started when they are given topics. Shouldn't I give them one now?

You may raise an eyebrow at the expectation that during these assessments, students will generate their own topics rather than writing on teacher-provided topics. Your hesitation may come because you think it is easier to compare and contrast lots of pieces of writing that are all written on the same topic, or it may come because you fret about whether your students will be successful at generating (and focusing) their own topics and worry that an inability to do so could derail the whole assessment. Again, your concerns are important ones, and we've certainly entertained them as well.

I think that once you have tried doing the assessments as we suggest, you'll be persuaded. The first time we asked students who had not participated in years of writing workshop instruction (where they are taught to generate focused topics) the following prompt, we were a bit uncertain what it would yield.

"Think of a topic or issue that you know and care about, an issue around which you have strong feelings. Write an opinion or argument text in which you state your opinion or claim, and tell reasons why you feel that way."

But what a haul we brought in! You should have seen us that first day, sorting through a huge pile of powerful pieces. One student's text claimed that kids shouldn't laugh at students with autism, and went on to cite examples from that student's experiences as a brother of an autistic child. Another piece was written by a Muslim student and focused on the importance of religious tolerance. Any number of students wrote with enormous intensity about animal rights, gender issues, fairness during gym—and time and again, we saw that the writer's command of the topic and investment in the topic gave the writing special power.

We came to believe that when students can select topics, this actually *levels* the playing field. If students are all asked to write on an assigned topic—say, "Should kids wear uniforms?"—the chances are great that this topic will resound for only some writers and not for others. The assignment (and the opportunity) to write about an issue that you know about and feel strongly about allows each writer to write from an equal position of strength. And there are similar reasons for granting students topic choice in information and narrative writing.

Of course, the decision to allow students to select their own topic also reflects the belief that coming up with a topic, narrowing its scope, and expressing it clearly are skills that are integral to being an effective writer. Later in life, when kids are in college, the ability to tailor tasks, to find the part of a subject on which they can write well, will be crucial.

Having said this, we are aware that some teachers alter the prompts and turn them into more specific assignments. The most important thing is that if a teacher makes a decision like that, this decision needs to be made collaboratively with grade level colleagues so that at least across a grade level, the conditions are kept constant. Ideally, all third- through eighth-grade teachers would participate in the process to rewrite the prompt, so that the writing can be equivalent across the grades. And, of course, the resulting texts will be less comparable to those in this resource. But does this assessment still work if you decide to alter the prompt? The answer is yes.

The grades 3–8 prompt lightly suggests students *may* prepare at home. Should I make mine do so, because otherwise they won't?

If you worry that merely mentioning to students who are writing information or argument on-demands that they are welcome to bring relevant information to class will fly right over the students' heads, know that you might be right. We find that by sixth grade, many students do bring in and cite source material (especially if they grow up using the checklists to self-assess and set goals). If they have been taught using the *Units of Study in Opinion, Information, and Narrative Writing, K–5*, then they know the importance of incorporating outside source material in their writing. If students have not grown up writing in the units, they may not realize the importance of this suggestion. Then too, they may simply forget, choose not to, or be unable to find material on their own. All of this will be worth noticing. As mentioned earlier, you might strategically schedule a trip to the library or computer lab on the day before the assessment, thereby leveling the playing field and ensuring that all students have had the opportunity to access materials. In the end, though, we encourage you to simply follow the instructions and not worry too much about what might happen. Students' choices mean data-in-hand for you! The fact that they don't cite sources early in the year makes it likely their writing can improve later in the year, when hopefully they do.

What do I do as students write? If they have questions or need help—do I step in?

I strongly encourage you to take a hands-off approach to students' work. If students need help narrowing a topic, structuring a text, or spelling a word, simply record that bit of data for another day and meanwhile, say to them, "Just do the best you can and keep going." Resist the temptation to confer into what the students are doing or to coach them. If the students seem to have great difficulty and produce very little work or work that is far below grade-level expectations, let that be the case. You need to know what they can do *without you*.

I also encourage you to take notes as students work, realizing you can learn a tremendous amount from this day. Plan to construct some small groups based on what you see during just this one window of time. For example, watch to notice the students who take a long time to come up with ideas, who don't find it easy to get started. On the other end of the spectrum, notice the students who don't seem to spend even an instant planning their writing. Then too, notice the students who write in a word-by-word fashion, pausing between words or between sentences. All of this will inform your teaching.

Will this writing show me all I need to know?

You may question whether the on-demand assessment reveals enough—for it won't show you what students can do when given days or weeks to rehearse, draft, revise, and edit a piece. My answer is this: no, it does not reveal all you need to know, but it reveals a lot. It will not help you assess your students' writing stamina, nor the amount of time they are willing to invest in working on a piece of writing, nor the volume of writing they produce over time, nor the extent to which they use teacher and peer feedback, nor the extent to which they initiate writing in their own lives. Plan to talk with students and study their folders, notebooks, drafts, and publications. These are crucial aspects of students' writing that this assessment doesn't address.

We are required to input all of our assessments into a computerized grading system. How do we do that with on-demand writing assessments?

The assessments are designed to be used for diagnostic purposes, so you can accurately gauge your students' strengths and weaknesses and make a plan to guide them toward improving their skills. The assessments gain what can be a toxic level of power when these scores are input into computerized systems. So we caution you against broadcasting these and especially warn you that if you do include them in a public computerized grading system, you will want to do everything you can to downplay their importance, setting them alongside other scores for effort-related results, such as "volume of writing" or "evidence that writer tries what has been taught." Even if a student is completely failing to meet grade level expectations, particularly early in the year, you may be reluctant to enter low marks into a computerized system that is visible to parents and administrators. Think about it this way: No music teacher enters the wrong notes that students sing into a computerized grading system and tells parents, "Sally only got 60% of the notes right and needs serious improvement!" Teachers of music give feedback and focus on improvement. The important thing is that the on-demand assessments guide the teaching you do and help students work with increased clarity and drive.

I grasp that this is a preassessment. What is the postassessment like, and when do I give this?

After you teach your first unit of study—after the publications are celebrated—you will close out the first unit by again issuing the exact same invitation to your students, giving them the exact same prompt. They will once again devote forty-five minutes to an on-demand writing assessment. You and the students will then be in a position to look between the preassessment and this first postassessment, noticing ways the writing has improved and ways it has not yet done so. Of course, growth in writing takes time, so you will see that certain components of a type of writing—say, the organization of their information writing—will have improved, but other components will not yet have improved. The good news is that as your teaching and your students' work shifts to focus on another type of writing, students can continue to tackle whatever needs are identified (and work in any one type of writing strengthens skills broadly). Also, of course, you will presumably teach more than one unit on any one type of writing.

No matter what your particular question may be, the deeper answer is this: You are a professional. This book is a resource only. Make the decisions that work for you and your community.

Chapter 3

The Norming Meeting and Subsequent Scoring

Developing Shared Expectations

THE NEXT STEP to establishing a system of assessment that will support school- and district-wide writing achievement is to participate in a norming meeting. So, quick, before you even read this chapter, schedule a meeting with colleagues from across your grade level—and, if yours is a small school, with colleagues from adjoining grades as well. After the meeting is scheduled, read on to learn ways to make this meeting into a powerful learning opportunity for you and your colleagues, so that you aren't just going through the motions, but you are actually reaping benefits that make a world of difference.

THE RATIONALE FOR MAKING THE NORMING MEETING A TOP PRIORITY

The norming meeting can be a big deal, so try to convince your principal to move heaven and earth to give you a good block of time—at least two hours. Food, too, helps—and frankly for this occasion, even chocolate-covered strawberries are warranted. (I know, I will be the subject of many jokes for even dreaming of this, but as the song from "South Pacific" reminds us, 'If you don't have a dream . . .'")

The ostensible purpose of the meeting will be for you and your colleagues to align, or norm, the ways you score student work so that a piece of writing given a 3 in one eighth-grade classroom will be given a 3 in other eighth-grade classrooms as well. Expectations matter more than you could ever imagine, so although the previous sentence is easy to write and to read, it actually is a very big deal. Research by Chris Hill and others suggests that chances are great that in your school, there are enormous differences between how one teacher and another at your grade level teach writing—and those differences will be reflected in your standards for assessment, as well. As each teacher gets to know the *Units of Study in Argument, Information, and Narrative Writing,* you will find that your visions for writing will begin to align. Now, at the beginning of the year, however, it is likely that they

are still quite divergent. One teacher will look at a given piece of work and think it is splendid; another will think it subpar. And teachers' suggestions for next steps, too, will often be utterly out of alignment. Chances are great that those differences reflect not just that opinions about writing are subjective, but they also reflect varying knowledge of writing instruction and qualities of good writing.

It is not surprising that a group of teachers will have varied backgrounds and different levels of strength teaching writing—but there are few things that matter more than the fact that a school needs to provide ways for knowledge to be socialized. The grand purpose for this meeting is nothing less than for you and your colleagues to begin to talk and think together about student work and about your shared expectations for that work, doing this in ways that bring you together into a community of common practice. Shared assessment systems have amazing potential for distributing different teachers' areas of expertise, so that more people know what those individual teachers know. But a shared rubric doesn't amount to a shared assessment system. The key is using that rubric (and the other tools) to promote conversations about students' progress and about ways to support that progress. It is this sort of teaching that is the hallmark of the highest-achieving schools . . . and nations. Hence the suggestion: chocolate strawberries and a luxury of time.

If you and your colleagues can work together to engage in more evidence-based teaching, and if assessment can become a way to power your whole school becoming part of a culture of continual improvement, self-assessment, and shared study, that's a very big deal indeed. This sort of teaching is the hallmark of all the highest-achieving nations. Michael Fullan has often spoken about the need to cultivate what he called "systemness"—the deliberate cultivation of a collaborative culture. Fullan notes that you see systemness when teachers speak about "our kids," rather than "my kids" (Teachers College October 2012). You see it when teachers norm expectations, look at student writing together, and share their teaching tools and knowledge.

Performance assessments are powerful—powerfully good when used well, and powerfully troublesome when used in ways that are destructive. One review of more than 250 studies that shows that formative assessments can be an important lever for raising the level of student work and can lead to lifelong learning also shows that performance assessments can undermine teacher and student confidence and commitment if they are used to compare, to judge, or to punish rather than as part of a collaborative effort to improve learning (Black and William, "Assessment and Classroom Learning," *Assessment in Education*, 1998 (5): 7–74). This norming meeting, then, needs to be seen as part of a larger effort to create a shared culture around the performance assessments. That culture needs to celebrate risk taking, asking for help when it is needed, and supportive collaboration.

There are few things that can improve the teaching at a school more than conversations such as this one, in which teachers across a grade level convene to think hard about their students' work and to develop methods of teaching and assessing that are aligned to one another and that will lift the level of that work. These conversations also help teachers who are new to the profession or less expert in the teaching of writing gain from the professional knowledge of more expert colleagues. Certain key studies reinforce this belief.

- Carrie Leana, a professor at the University of Pittsburgh, found that patterns of interaction among teachers and administrators who are focused on student learning show a large and measurable difference in student achievement and sustained improvement. More specifically, she found that **thinking about student achievement with colleagues with whom you have a trusting relationship makes all the difference.** (C. Leana, "The Missing Link in School Reform," *Stanford Social Innovation Review*, 2011 (Fall): 29–35.)

- In *Teachers Matter: Connecting Lives, Work and Effectiveness* (Open University Press, 2007, 25) and *The New Lives of Teachers* (Routledge, 2010), Chris Day and his colleagues write about their study of teacher effectiveness in one hundred schools over three years, demonstrating that there is more variation in effectiveness *among* teachers within a school than *between* schools, so **aligning knowledge and teaching practices across a grade level can have a huge impact.**

- McKinsey and Company recently issued a report, *How the World's Most Improved Systems Keep Getting Better* (M. Mourshed et al. 2010) that described this finding: as school systems got better, **the strongest source of innovation was peers working together with transparency and a sense of collective responsibility.**

- Andy Hargreaves and Michael Fullan, in *Professional Capital: Transforming Teaching in Every School* (Teachers College Press, 2012), argue that **expertise in a school needs to be circulated, to be invested;** linking together professionals who have social capital makes a world of difference.

- *Finnish Lessons* (Pasi Sahlberg, Teachers College Press, 2011), about education in Finland, and *Professional Capital*, about education in Ontario, Canada, both describe teachers devoting a great deal of time to studying student work together, coming to shared beliefs about common standards. In both these high-achieving school settings, educators spend a lot of time adapting and enriching curriculum in response to what their students do.

THE LOGISTICS

First of all, you need one norming meeting at the start of a school year, and especially, you need a norming meeting as you begin putting this assessment resource into operation. It would be great to continue to hold norming meetings as you and your colleagues shift from one kind of writing to another, but that choice is yours. If you are a sixth-grade teacher beginning the year with *Personal Narrative: Crafting Powerful Life Stories*, you will presumably hold a norming meeting that focuses on narrative. You may decide, however, that the school needs a new focus on argument writing, so you may also schedule another norming meeting to focus on that kind of writing, perhaps before beginning *The Literary Essay: From Character to Compare/Contrast*. In a norming meeting, you and your colleagues on a grade level team will review the rubric for your grade level; examine the relevant benchmark pieces; review, score, and discuss shared samples of student work to develop a common assessment of that work; and then begin reviewing and assessing your own students' work, coming to consensus views about the way you all agree to score.

This is a tall order, so be sure someone makes plans for the meeting and facilitates it. The facilitator of the meeting needs to communicate to participants that to use every precious moment well, a protocol has been established for how the meeting will run. You and your colleagues need to have collected recent on-demand pieces prior to the meeting, pieces that match the type of writing you'll study together. Each person needs to bring a folder full of the kind of on-demand writing that will be assessed. Obviously, the type of writing you study together should be the same type of writing that you are each teaching or are about to teach.

Assuming for now that you are the organizer of this grade level study group, you will want to gather a very small collection of student work that the group will study together, making sure that the collection contains at least two pieces that you believe represent roughly "at standard" level work and at least one "above standard" and one "below standard" piece. Aim to choose especially interesting (or funny) pieces, because this keeps everyone more engaged. The student's name on these pieces of writing needs to be whited out and the pieces duplicated for each person in the study group.

In this chapter, I'll describe an expeditious way the study group might unfold—and I'll continue to write as if you are leading the group. I know you may be leading from in front, officially, or from behind, unofficially, and that it is possible the group will be a class of interested parents or colleagues from across various schools rather than your grade level colleagues (if you don't yet have colleagues who are doing this work), so I'm expecting you will alter this so that it works for your context.

WAYS FOR A STUDY GROUP OF TEACHERS TO BEGIN STUDYING STUDENT WORK

You may wish to begin by heading straight into the norming meeting. However, I recommend that you consider instead beginning this process by rallying your colleagues' interest in this work before the actual norming meeting, either at the start of the meeting or during a short meeting that precedes the norming meeting. You might first put a student's piece of writing (selected from the benchmark pieces in this resource) in front of the group, working with a piece that matches the kind of writing you'll be studying and teaching. Imagine, for example, that you are working with Xinyu's writing.

You suggest people look at the writing with a partner and decide what grade level they think the piece represents—remembering this is meant as an on-demand benchmark piece, representing what all students should be able to do in forty-five minutes. You may find that some teachers are surprised that the piece is a benchmark for eighth, rather than ninth, grade. (This same sense of surprise will occur with any piece—standards are high.) As you have them take a closer look, with the eighth- and ninth-grade checklists at

I frantically searched the living room for a good place to hide. "Four, five, six..." I heard Lucy count in the other room. I looked at the table, the countertops, the cupboards, and chairs. Nothing was appealing to me. Then it hit me, the halls, I thought. Shall I ever be able to find me there. I tiptoed through the living room. Careful not to bump into anything. Just as I was about to put my right foot down, my left foot made contact with a sticky, gooey substance. I sighed, exasperated before directing my eyes to my foot. There, I stood in complete shock as the horror dawned upon me.

Earlier, when I arrived at Lucy's house, the first thing that attracted my attention was a yellow, glistening mouse trap that laided in the corner of the living room. "Watch your step," Lucy said as I dropped my bag on the side. It was those mouse traps where anything made contact with it, the thing would get stuck. I bent down on my knees as I took a closer look and noticed the two furry half-dead mice that were unfortunately fell into the trap. "My mother's going to throw that out later, when she comes home from work," Lucy explained to me. Lucy was 12, so she was allowed to stay home by herself. I, on the other hand was only 8 at the time.

"Come on, get up," testily she commanded. I then reluctantly pushed off my toes and jumped onto my feet, into an upright position.

Now, my right foot was glued to the mouse trap, and each worse, it was atop on top of the two mice. I shrieked in pure terror.

I tried to block my brain from thinking of all the germs that were hidden in the mice grey fur and how it has been infested my foot but now Lucy came running over when she heard my scream. She was about to ask me what's wrong but saw my predicament before she got her question out. She stared at me for a second before bursting out into hysterical, toyota laughter. "I told you," she gasped for air, "to be careful."

I felt my hot, salty tears dripping onto my glasses and ideas traveling down my flushed cheeks. I was so genuinely hurt and felt embarrassed that she was laughing at me.

"Okay, okay," she said calmly after she calmed down from her uncontrollable fit of laughter. Of course she led me to her bathroom and holding onto my hands as I hopped on my left leg. She sat down on the side of the bathtub as she grabbed a stool, and sat in front of me.

"Ready?" Lucy asked. I nodded shamefully. She grabbed the sides of the trap and pulled with all her might. Just as I feared, the trap wouldn't budge. She tried again but this time, more forcefully. The trap came off slowly, the mice still intact while my right foot struggled to break contact with the mice. At last, I was free. Tranquility were restored in my life once again.

FIG. 3–1 Xinyu's on-demand narrative writing—eighth-grade benchmark

hand, you can point out that this writer's use of narrative structure *is* sophisticated: the flashback to when she first noticed the glue trap is handled seamlessly, indicating a ninth-grade level of "Organization." But this characteristic alone does not make for a grade level piece overall. Staying within the category of "Structure," if you point to the eighth-grade descriptors for "Lead" and "Ending," you can notice that Xinyu's lead and ending do not "hint at a bigger context" (though mentioning that she was only eight and her friend twelve may show the beginnings of that) and do not "circle back to a central idea, issue, or theme." Within just a minute, then, you can demonstrate that the exemplar pieces convey the message: "Ready or not—expectations are increasing." This small activity can sometimes serve as a helpful wake-up call.

You could extend that first activity by suggesting people work quietly, individually, for a few minutes, to jot the answers to these questions: What are some of the big things the writer is doing well? What might be next for this writer? Then convene the group to talk about what everyone jotted. Was this easy to do, or not?

You will probably find that many of your colleagues find this harder to do than one might think. One person will mention spelling and punctuation. Another, intent on not focusing just on conventions will say "descriptive language" or point to an isolated and perhaps awkward use of high-level vocabulary. A few more comments will surface. Then there will be silence. It is often the case that when looking at pieces of writing that are fairly strong for the age group, teachers are often at a loss over how to imagine next steps. If you are going to help your students become stronger as writers, then you need to become skilled at this work.

It matters that you can look at student work and see what is next for the student. It matters that you develop a knowledge base around writing. And it matters not just that *you* can do this work, but that your colleagues and your students can as well. Looking at student writing, naming the skills you see, imagining the revisions that are needed—those are skills every writing teacher needs, and they are skills that develop when student work is read closely and discussed with specificity.

A PROTOCOL FOR YOUR NORMING MEETING

You will find that if you read research on performance assessments, it is typical for a norming meeting to follow at least a variation of the series of steps—the protocol—that I lay out here. This protocol enables the meeting to be as time efficient as possible. The protocol consists of four major steps:

Step 1: Assess one student's writing using the appropriate rubric, working as a group.

Step 2: Score other pieces of writing individually, then revise the scores by consensus.

Step 3: Assess your own students' writing individually.

Step 4: Devise a plan for analyzing on-demand writing across the grade.

For the purposes of this text, let's suppose that yours is a group of eighth-grade teachers, and you have decided to study argument writing together.

Step 1: Assess one student's writing using the appropriate rubric, working as a group.

You'll probably want to begin by putting forward a piece of writing that you have chosen because it is generally "at standard" level—but no piece will be "at standard" for every trait. You and the other teachers will also need to read through the piece of writing you decide to examine together. Say, for example, you are looking at the piece of writing shown in Figure 3–2.

Examine the student's text alongside the rubric, as a group.

After you each read the piece, you'll then inch along through it, working as a group to read an item on the rubric, examine the piece of student work for evidence, discuss the group's judgment (asking questions such as "Does this qualify as 'on-standard' or as 'developing'?"), and come to a consensus.

The group will look first at the "Overall" descriptor for the piece—the very first item under "Structure" on the rubric. For proficient level, seventh grade, this descriptor says, "The writer laid out a well-supported argument and made it clear that that this argument is part of a bigger conversation about a topic/text. He acknowledged positions on the topic or text that might disagree with his own position, but still showed why his position makes sense." Consensus will probably be quickly reached that this "Overall" descriptor for seventh grade seems to match the text, so the group will continue checking the text against the seventh-grade column. Had the piece seemed to be more aligned to the sixth-grade column on the rubric, the group might have decided to check the piece against those descriptors instead.

As a group, you will continue to look between the rubric and the student's text to see if, for a descriptor, the text is at proficient level or if it is more accurate to describe that trait of the work as matching level 1, 2, or 4. Be sure to look for (and underline) evidence of each item on the rubric, expecting this to be a slow process for the first few pieces (after which it becomes much more rapid).

Expect and embrace conflict.

Conflict is evidence that there is a disconnect in the way you and your colleagues view student work, and digging into that disconnect will help you to align your vision. For example, someone is apt to suggest that this student's lead meets the expectations for the seventh-grade descriptor, "The writer interested readers in his argument and helped them to understand the backstory behind it. He gave the backstory in a way that got readers ready to see his point." Others are apt to counter, saying, "This writer has really not done anything more than write an introduction that states a claim and tells readers how the text will unfold." They'll protest, "This lead actually matches the sixth-grade descriptor." Still others will point out that starting with a quote lifts the level of the lead, hooking the reader and providing him with the backstory. Conversation will circle around the idea that a portion of the lead might be *at* standards, and a portion of it is *below* standards for seventh grade. So the question remains how to score this.

FIG. 3-2   Sophie's seventh-grade on-demand argument piece

Vampires [Bats] could hold the key to a problem we want to solve, like aids or cancer. But if we destroy them, they are lost for eternity." Says Francisco Oliva. Animals should never be killed. They can benefit humans by helping maintain other animal populations, being loyal companions, and by allowing scientific research to commence.

To begin, different kind of animals can actually help keep humans safe by eliminating harsh populations. Such as the vampire bat does with the insect population. Vampire bats are many insects' natural predators, meaning that the bats in actuality control the insect population. The insects can be harmful and carry diseases that could hurt humans. Vampire bats aren't the only helpful creatures that do this. Raccoons do too. Without the natural doing of raccoons eating (aphid eggs) "We would be knee-deep in bugs in 20 years," says herpetologist, Michael Dorcas. If we killed these animals, it would only cause problems for us in this way.

Another reason why we should not kill animals is that they make absolutely wonderful companions. Even the most unlikely of species can make good friends. Tx example. a worker at the North American Bear Center says, "I have learned to trust Certain bears and bear families to the extent that they mostly ignore me as I walk and sleep with them at up to 24 hours at a time." The chances of being murdered are 60,000 times greater than being killed by a black bear. There is very little to be afraid of even of a bear, and that they can actually grow on humans as great companions. It would be preposterous to kill a dear friend

Animals can also be the future of scientific discoveries and research, for example, vampire bats can also be of use to science and could give scientists what they need to potentiany find the cure to cancer or even AIDS. "Who would have thought feet sponges could lead to anti-cancer drugs, that the scales of butterfly wings could help bring about better kinds of paint?" Klasse, a German zoologist said. This shows that animals can actually benefit humans in matters of life or death. If we kill these creatures, we are only hurting ourselves in the future.

Many may say that the black bear is dangerous, having killed 61 people in North America since 1900. But in reality, it is more likely to be killed by lightning, or even a swarm of bees. Black bears are very rarely ever aggressive at first glance, the only circumstance where a black bear would be aggressive is when they are defending themselves, meaning that the human would have too initiate negative contact first. Killing animals can also slow down the progression of medical research, which could only allow more people to die of insidious diseases. If we are the cause of animal species being harmed we are also the cause of our own species being harmed.

As these examples show us as human beings should not kill animals. They can double life. Scientists with capabled research, they can be life-long friends and they can even naturally get rid of harmful infections caused by their prey. Animals are important to this earth, and the ecosystems that surrounds is. It would be morally, scientifically, and utterly wrong to destroy such natural treasures, Creatures that helps us in the present, and in the future

When discussions like these come up, know that this is the purpose of the norming meeting. You *want* these issues to arise, and you want the group to come to consensus about them. As you talk through the judgments you and others are making, be ready to help your colleagues understand that just because the on-demands are written in on-demand situations (and are not as strong as the students' published writing would be), that doesn't mean that teachers should do what a mathematician would describe as rounding high. That is, although yes, the on-demands were written quickly, without scaffolds, those are the same conditions under which the benchmark pieces were written, and the progression applies to work done in on-demand situations. So excusing less-than-close execution of a descriptor on the rubric because the student's work was created under the pressures of the on-demand context doesn't make sense.

More importantly, it will be helpful if you can help your colleagues understand that it doesn't do a student any favors to inflate an evaluation. Students are then led to believe that their work is done, that they already have reached the benchmark, when in fact they haven't. If the lead is not as strong as it should be, saying so and giving the writer crystal clear next steps to improve the writing is not an affront to the writer. Chances are great that the writer can address the issue in future writing, no problem. The purpose of the assessment is to convey those next steps clearly, in ways that will allow young writers to improve.

If your colleagues find, as we did, that even the very strongest writers at a grade level still did not write with leads that lure readers to the text, then you presumably will resolve to do a better job of teaching your students to write effective introductions. Students' work reflects the teaching they have received, and patterns in that work are especially important feedback to you and to the other teachers with whom your students have studied.

Discuss the student's text critically.

To return to the discussion about the on-demand piece in Figure 3–2, "We Should Not Kill Animals," chances are good that the group will agree that this writer has a strong command of the overall argument. Discrepancy might arise, however, when discussion begins about the grade level in which this writer addresses possible counterclaims. The writer addresses one possible counterargument, but the subtopic she chooses to address (the dangerousness of black bears) is not one that the rest of her piece directly takes on. This question will address the score you will give this piece of writing for "Elaboration." Does it fit the seventh-grade descriptor ("The writer wrote about another possible position or positions—a different claim or claims about this subject—and explained why the evidence for his position outweighed the counterclaim(s)") or not? The decision of whether to score this piece of writing as a sixth-grade or seventh-grade piece for "Elaboration" may not be one your group can agree upon, but the important thing is that your group should not just gloss over the text and generate some rough approximate score. This work should entail close-in diagnostic annotating of the text. The discussion should be critical.

You and your colleagues can continue inching through this text. The important thing is that you come to a consensus so there is gradewide consistency across raters, and so you learn from one another about ways to think about student writing. If you merely skim the student's writing, shrug, and simply call out that sure, this meets the standards, you deny your students and yourselves the chance to use the assessment to ratchet up the level of student work. This tool will be helpful to the extent that you actually engage in close, evidence-based reading and to the extent that you are hard on yourselves and your students.

Step 2: Score other pieces of writing individually, then revise the scores by consensus.

After studying one text together this way, you can work with a second piece of student writing, probably another piece that you believe is approximately "on standard." Suggest people work independently to annotate and score the piece first, then talk in small groups or partnerships to see if a consensus emerges. The whole group can then chart every partnership's score to see if a consensus has already emerged. If there are components that require more discussion, the group can talk together to achieve a consensus.

Sometimes consensus isn't possible, and for norming activities, a point of difference on either side of the rating is generally regarded as acceptable, and certainly a half-point is an acceptable difference of opinion. Generally, if ten minutes of discussion don't yield something close to consensus, the piece is set aside as a "fence sitter." Don't let one point of conflict derail the whole activity. Agree as a group that if you have a conversation for more than ten minutes on one point, you will move on.

As people do this work, some general understandings will emerge. Among other things, it will become obvious that no one piece will receive all level 1 scores or all level 2, 3, or 4 scores. For a piece to be at a particular level, when you add up all the scores and use the key at the end of the rubric, the total sum of points earned must fall within the range of one of those levels.

You'll want to balance your use of time, and you'll want to make judgments about how exact you need to be in leveling. In some schools, a record of students' exact scores are collected and becomes part of important data. In others, there is no premium put on deriving a detailed numeric score, so once teachers have scored each descriptor, they estimate to determine the overall level. You'll be able to estimate, if your eye runs down the page and you see mostly 4s, that the student is at that level.

If after doing this work with a few papers of different levels, the group finds that it is often coming to a consensus, the group can consider *itself* normed, and people can now score papers individually. You may find that you occasionally want to confer about particular points or papers.

Step 3: Assess your own students' writing individually.

Once teachers from across a grade level have worked together to calibrate scores so that scoring is aligned, the job then passes to you and other individual teachers to score your own students' writing. Assuming teachers have folders full of on-demand pieces, suggest that everyone first skim through their students' work, dividing them really quickly into categories ranging from level 1 to 4 on the rubric. Suggest that this be done in a swift, cursory way, emphasizing that they will come back later to check these evaluations carefully, with the rubric in hand. This step will help them move more rapidly through the actual scoring process. Once the papers have been categorized, suggest teachers take a little time to quickly, efficiently

A quick warning about bias:

The goal when assessing student work is to assess each student, in each category, in a way that is unbiased and independent of that student's other work. There are two kinds of biases that often occur in scoring. One is when assessment of one piece of work is based on what is known about the student's other work or the student more generally. The second kind of bias occurs when your assessment of one aspect of the student's writing ends up bleeding over into (and influencing) your assessment of other aspects of the writing. When scoring alongside Stanford's Center for Assessment, Learning, and Equity (SCALE) for an assessment project in New York City, we noted that they talked often about these potential biases as "fatal flaws" and "halos." For example, a piece of student writing may be hard to decipher because of the handwriting or a lack of paragraphing. That does not make a student bad at structure or elaboration, but if the scorer is not mindful to avoid bias, the poor handwriting or lack of paragraphs can end up being a fatal flaw, biasing readers' overall judgments. On the other hand, a piece of writing might display a characteristic that gives the entire piece a sort of halo, as when the academic vocabulary so impresses readers that the structure is presumed to be intentionally complex rather than chaotic. Knowing about these sources of bias can help you to make a conscious effort to avoid bias.

---

score a few of the papers from one pile, using the rubric. The good news is that each successive paper will become much easier to score.

It's very important that teachers have time to get started on the process of assessing their individual students' pieces during the meeting, because doing this alongside each other during protected time functions as an icebreaker, getting you and your colleagues started on what can otherwise seem to be an awe-inducing task. Another reason is that you will all find that, actually, the process becomes much faster after you've worked slowly through a few pieces. One reason to provide protected study group time for teachers to score individually is that it is critical that teachers leave this meeting aware that this is not too time-consuming. This makes it worlds more likely that you and your colleagues will actually take the time to do this on your own for your entire class.

Then, too, some new issues will undoubtedly arise, and the fact that you are together means that people can talk about these issues in ways that keep work from getting stalled as well as support people's learning curve. Your hope is that your colleagues across your grade leave the meeting feeling upbeat about the work of assessing students, confident that the task won't be too all-consuming, and clear that in any case, it will prove worthwhile.

Step 4: Devise a plan for analyzing on-demand writing across the grade.

Finally, the reason to do this together is that by the end of this session, you will have a fairly accurate sense of what it will require to do this sort of scoring for all of your students, and you and your colleagues will then be able to come to a shared understanding of the approximate length of time it should take to read and score a student's paper. Try to prevent the group from insisting (or even implying) that everyone must do a perfect job at assessing every bit of student work. It is all too easy to make the process so onerous that half the teachers at your grade level opt out of the whole process. The resulting mix of guilt, blame, and misalignment can end up derailing your effort to create a professional learning community.

Instead, use the norming experience to set yourselves up to make realistic plans for future assessments and assessment meetings. This may mean that you and your colleagues may need to be willing to imagine less-than-perfect scenarios to realistically follow up with the work you've started:

- Perhaps instead of regularly assessing every student perfectly and in depth, you decide to carefully **assess the work of emblematic students** who seem to you to be above standards, a few at standards, and a few below standards. Then, for the rest of the class, rely on either quick eyeball comparisons between

- other students' pieces and the benchmark texts (and the texts you have assessed) or on peer assessments or self-assessments of the other students' work.

- You may decide that a few traits are especially important in the upcoming parts of the writing unit, so you'll agree to **examine those few traits carefully in all students' work** and to skim over (or rely on student self-assessments and partner assessments) for the others. (The "Welcome to the Unit" at the beginning of each book gives readers a sense of the major goals of the unit. Reading this section can be helpful when determining the traits you will focus on.)

- Or perhaps you will decide that this process is so important that you will work together so you and your colleagues **gain additional time to study student work.** Might one of you teach all the students across the grade in the auditorium for an hour, freeing others to spend that hour scoring? Might the school's music teacher be willing to work with all students across the grade for a few periods during one week so that you can devote additional time to scoring? Might you convince your administration that this warrants a day of a roving substitute teacher to free up each teacher at the grade for an extra hour of scoring?

KEEP THE TONE OF THE MEETING POSITIVE

As I discussed at the end of Chapter 1, chances are very good that your students will not yet produce work that is "at standards" level (or even close). That is, when you assess your eighth-graders at the start of the year, chances are great that their work won't be as splendid as you'd like to see and that it might even appear to be many years below grade level. Remember that you have not yet had the opportunity to engage these students in a unit of study, and that "summer rust" is a powerful force! The more high-stakes assessments will come in the middle of the year, after you have taught a few units, and those assessments will reflect not just last year's teaching but this year's as well. You will want to watch that this doesn't create a toxic mood among your colleagues (and that you, yourself, don't despair).

Hope, Laughter, and Candid Talk

There are ways to console yourself. First, at the start of any year, of course, your hope is that students are writing at the previous grade's end-of-year standard. Usually it takes more than a single unit of study to help students make one year's worth of progress, so don't expect that after a single unit in argument, your students' work will have increased by an entire grade level. You haven't had a chance to revisit the unit yet or to teach for transference. Then, too, it is no secret that the bar has been set high.

Laughter will help. Confess to your colleagues that you were tempted to cherry-pick the good pieces of writing from your batch and then present the very best as average. Nothing is worse than deep, dark secrets that aren't allowed to see the light of day, and chances are that everyone in the room will be worrying over the fact that students haven't performed at close to expected levels.

Candid talk makes all the difference. Once the conversation is on the table, expect some worries to emerge. Worry may be especially intense if your decision is for parents to hear about their students' levels. Will this cause them to complain about instruction? Your group may remind you of the Dr. Seuss book in which the brother and sister want to sweep Thing 1 and Thing 2 out of sight before their mother gets home—so they pass it along. In a similar way, you may notice that your group seems intent on finding someone, something, to blame. Especially if you and your colleagues are anxious about accountability, it is predictable that there will be energy invested in passing blame along. How helpful it would be for you to stop that process by saying what needs to be said: "I think, for one, that I need to learn more so I can help my kids make the progress they need to make." There is enormous power in someone saying, "I have more to learn," because for too long, schools have been places where teachers teach and kids learn. Roland Barth, however, defines a great school as a place where every person's learning curve is sky high.

Some Positive Examples

Perhaps you have not seen a positive norming meeting in action yet. You may still be skeptical. But here are a few examples of how teachers can work together with a common purpose to share experiences and resources and to meet the needs of their students and colleagues.

Picture this: at a faculty meeting, teachers across the school study the CCSS expectations for argument writing. They then meet with colleagues at their grade level to cowrite a persuasive essay on a topic that students will find engaging, a persuasive essay that reflects the expectations for that grade level. The essays written by the sixth-grade, the seventh-grade, the eighth-grade teachers (and so forth) are combined, so that each teacher has the collection within his set of resources. Across the school, teachers are able to point to one essay and say to students, "I see you are writing a bit like this. Let me show you a next step."

Or how about this? Three seventh-grade teachers observe a colleague whose students all tend to write longer, faster, and more fluently than theirs. They've joked together about how she cracks the whip, and now they want to get past the jokes to how and what she teaches. At the norming meeting, it's clear that this colleague's students get more writing done in one period. When asked, she agrees to do some demonstration teaching, doing everything she knows how to do to increase volume, all within one period.

Or even this: the sixth-grade teachers from across the school realize that many of their students are not mastering the grade-appropriate language conventions, so they form a study group on the topic. One teacher reads up on vocabulary development, another on sentence structure, a third on median punctuation, and then they merge what they've learned. They give themselves six weeks to ratchet up this aspect of their students' writing, after which they plan another assessment.

Aim for Significant, Perhaps Even Magnificent, Growth

The most important thing for you to realize is that the health of your organization relies upon you and your colleagues finding ways to respond well to challenges that you all face. One of my guiding principles in life is this: "We can't control what happens to us, but we can control our response to what happens." Paul Tough and others have made a science out of this, conducting research and writing books about the importance of character traits such as grit, persistence, and tenacity. People who do well in life develop character traits that help them deal with setbacks with resolve and determination.

So, yes, it is not easy to write well. That really is no surprise. The important thing is that each of us needs to realize that good writing is not the product of a person's DNA. Instead, good writing comes from hard work, from using strategies, from studying effective texts, from self-assessing and working toward crystal clear goals. And it comes from a community of teachers working together to become stronger at assessing, coaching, and teaching writing.

The good news is that if teachers across your school engage in a shared study of student writing—assessing together, identifying benchmark pieces together, and learning to give feedback together based on shared assessments—if you conduct informal classroom-based research projects, exchange classroom visits, and hold think tanks and study groups on the teaching of writing—then the growth in students' writing skills will be significant. It may even be magnificent.

Chapter 4

Using Early Results to Plan and Adapt the Units of Study

I N A WORLD where people rarely agree on anything, there is unanimous agreement that the biggest problem with most performance assessments is that too often, teachers conduct assessments, gather data, and then nothing is made of these data. The process of conducting the assessment is done for compliance reasons, period.

The waste is staggering. Think of what could have been done with all the minutes and hours those teachers spent preparing for and conducting the on-demand assessments, participating in the norming meetings, and scoring the student work. Think of the waste of children's time and angst as well. And then, nothing comes of it?

This is an especially big waste, because the entire fruitless process hardens a teacher against ever wanting to conduct a performance assessment again. That is, something is learned from every dead end, every broken promise.

So just as it is imperative that time is set aside for grade level colleagues to meet to get to know the rubric and the learning progression and to norm the scoring of the work, it is also imperative that there is a follow-up meeting for you and your colleagues to begin to use the data you've gathered to inform instruction.

TACKLE HEAD-ON THE FACT THAT STUDENTS' LEVELS ARE PROBABLY DISAPPOINTING

When you and your colleagues gather a week later to talk about what you saw in your students' work, it will help everyone if you lay it out on the table: Yikes. Gulp.

This will be especially important to do if the on-demands were done mid-year, because people will feel especially vulnerable at that point. Chances are great that everyone in the room will be worrying that almost certainly, students didn't perform at close to expected levels, so get that out. Remember that nothing is worse than deep, dark secrets that aren't allowed to see the light of day. Once the conversation is on the table, your group may worry together about the consequences of telling students that their work falls several grades below grade level. How can that be good for a learner's self-image? There may be an effort to find someone, something, to pin blame onto.

Before you and your colleagues get too worked up, remember a few things. First, remember that early in the year, if students are working "at standards" level, they will be working at the level that is expected for the end of the previous grade. So if seventh-graders are doing fifth-grade level work, they are *not* two years, but instead one year, below the start-of-seventh-grade expectations.

Think also about the source of these standards. Although the Teachers College Reading and Writing Project's long history of work with writers has informed the details of this progression, the main trajectory that undergirds the learning progression is the Common Core State Standards for argument, information, and narrative writing. And it is already clear that those standards have been written to sound a wake-up call, to rally young people and their teachers to aspire to higher standards. It is frequently said that if American students were tested to see how many are performing at CCSS levels today, 80% would fail. So you should not be surprised that the expectations in this assessment system are uncomfortably high. That is actually the intention behind the Common Core.

And, in fact, you no doubt felt the same thing when you looked at the CCSS for your grade. But hopefully you have also been coached to look more closely at the gap between what students are expected to have accomplished by the end of the preceding year and by the end of your year, in which case you will have realized that the amount of progress you are expected to produce is actually doable. If you have studied the CCSS closely, you have probably settled on the thought that if the day comes that your writers enter your grade level having met the standards for the previous year, you'll be able to get them to standards levels for your grade. So the thinking that you need to do now, around these on-demand writing assessments, is exactly the same thinking that you need to do about the CCSS in the first place. That is, you will probably agree that the distance your students are expected to travel between end-of-grade expectations for the preceding year and end-of-grade expectations for your year will be doable once your school as a whole has developed a systemic, schoolwide approach to supporting writers' development across all the grades.

This should make you and your colleagues feel a bit better about the fact that during your first few years using the assessments, your students won't all leave your grade producing work that is at standards level.

You may also make the decision that other teachers have sometimes made to erase all evidence of grade levels from every scrap of paper and to swear to each other to secrecy about grade level expectations until children are more within reach of those expectations.

ADJUST YOUR TEACHING BASED ON YOUR DATA

In the meanwhile, however, you and other teachers across your school will very likely be teaching classrooms of students in which many writers are working well below standards. You'll want to talk together about ways to adjust your instruction based on these assessments.

Although you will tweak and revise your units, you can also assume from the start that the units were piloted, taught, and written so that they would be able to support a wide range of writers. After all, this entire curriculum has been piloted in classrooms in the most high-need areas of New York City, as well as in the most affluent suburbs around NYC, and teachers in that entire range of schools have taught all these units using small-group instruction, conferring, and techniques of differentiated instruction to meet the needs of all writers. The minilessons are already multilevel. For example, seventh-graders are asked to "use analysis of the evidence to help readers follow the path of their argument." Frankly, my editor would be wise to remind me to keep that in mind as well—and that is also a teaching point that is often taught to fifth-graders. The units brim with examples of instruction such as that—instruction that can at the same time support writers who are working at very different places on the learning progressions.

This doesn't mean, however, that there won't be ways you need to adjust the tempo and flow of these units of study based on your data. If you have analyzed your initial assessments prior to launching your writing instruction—that is, if the sequence of units you will teach is still an open question—and if your students' skills are extremely low, I recommend that you and your colleagues turn to the introduction of the *If . . . Then . . . Curriculum* book. That introduction will suggest ways you might alter the sequence of units. Perhaps before teaching the at-grade unit in, say, argument writing, you will want to teach an abbreviated version of a more basic-level unit. That book summarizes how such a preliminary unit might go or sends you to a resource. If you do decide to craft your own unit of study, the chapter "Building Your Own Units of Study" from the accompanying *A Guide to the Common Core Writing Workshop, Middle School Grades* will be a valuable resource.

I also want to point out that if you, as well as your students, are new to this instruction, the decision to teach a unit of study by relying only on the summary of a unit such as that provided in the *If . . . Then . . . Curriculum* book and that chapter of *A Guide to the Common Core Writing Workshop, Middle School Grades* means that you will forgo the tremendously supportive scaffold of a *Unit of Study* book that details how your instruction might unfold and provides you with the coaching, support, and materials you need to teach that unit well. My advice is that if this teaching is new to you, no matter what your students' skill levels might be, for your first year of teaching, stay with the *Unit of Study* books for your grade, adjusting those units somewhat based on your assessment of your students. The only exception I'd make to this is that if you are teaching in a school that has *Units of Study* books at every grade level, consider borrowing *Units of Study* books from grade levels before yours. For example, *Personal Narrative: Crafting Powerful Life Stories* (grade 6) is a wonderful precursor to *Writing Realistic Fiction: Symbolism, Syntax, and Truth* (grade 7). *The Literary Essay: From Character to Compare/Contrast* (grade 6) is also a precursor to *The Literary Essay: Analyzing Craft and Theme* (grade 8). You may decide to teach only the first bend or two from the earlier unit as a precursor to the first bend of your own unit.

Of course, if you are already well into the first unit, it won't be an option to alter the sequence of the units, for at least the start of the year anyhow. Remember, however, that the series as a whole provides you with many resources that should help you add sessions designed especially for your students. For example, if you are teaching the eighth-grade unit *Position Papers: Research and Argument*, and some of your students aren't writing arguments that address the counterclaim, look to the seventh-grade argument writing unit, *The Art of Argument: Research-Based Essays*. There you will find plenty of tools, mentor texts, teaching points, and minilessons that can be adapted to help your eighth-graders. You can also invent minilessons yourself that address the skills students need to learn. To develop those minilessons, you can draw on your students' writing, the benchmark texts provided in Part II of this book, and the checklists and progressions that describe what you hope students will learn to do at various grade levels.

As you become more knowledgeable about the way these units unfold, you will see that in a number of units, my colleagues and I preface the unit by teaching students a two-day intensive we've come to call "boot camp," and this may be a structure you'll want to re-create at the start—or even midway—through a unit. The sixth-grade literary essay unit, for example, begins with a boot camp in which students write essays on "The Three Little Pigs" and are quickly brought up to speed on essay structure. Boot camps give students a blast of targeted instruction as well as opportunities for repeated practice addressing the skills they need to develop right away.

Usually, a boot camp is followed by students having a chance to redo their on-demand assessments. The opportunity to redo on-demand assessments seems to fuel students' resolve, and meanwhile the second round of those assessments has allowed us to see that students respond to this opportunity by learning a startling amount in short order. Meanwhile, the teaching you do in a two- or three-day boot camp at the start of a unit gets strategies and teaching points into the air and onto your teaching charts in ways that can be reinforced throughout the unit. For example, if you are horrified to discover that in their on-demand writing, many of your sixth-graders weren't writing with commas to set off introductory parts of sentences, you might decide to lead a two-day boot camp to highlight the fact that commas are not something one inserts into a piece just prior to publication; instead, using commas to set off introductory parts of sentences is an essential part of the act of scribing. Having taught the necessity of comma work during the boot camp, you can reinforce this skill throughout the unit.

Although it is entirely reasonable to plan a detour in your unit of study or to add sessions into it, I want to advise you against stretching out a unit to longer than six weeks. That is, if you do bring some supportive instruction into a unit, lop off the last bend. Always, the most sophisticated work in a unit is what comes in the final stretch. Middle-schoolers need to be finished with a chunk of work and to have the chance to get a fresh start on some new work.

NO MATTER WHAT, YOU NEED TO PROVIDE SOME BASIC LEVELS OF DIFFERENTIATION

One of the most important things to keep in mind is that always, instruction needs to begin where students are and move them along as quickly as possible. It is not just students with Individual Education Plans (IEPs) or those who are English language learners who struggle, and it is important to put concerns for the growth of these diverse learners squarely on the table. You already know that if a sixth-grader is a struggling reader, it doesn't do any good to put *The Hunger Games* in her hands. She instead needs to read books that are at the high end of what she can handle and to be supported and taught in ways that help her progress quickly up the ladder of text complexity. In writing, as in reading, a good teacher needs to ascertain a student's just-right level and teach just one level above that point, then progress expeditiously from there.

Make Sure that Conferring and Small-Group Instruction Respond to Students, Rather Than Being Tightly Connected to Your Minilesson

Perhaps, in an information text unit, a handful of your seventh-graders are writing skeletal "all-about" books. As mentioned earlier, many minilessons will be as applicable to these writers as they will be to the most proficient writers, but there will be times when the day's minilesson may be more appropriate for one portion of the class. For example, one of your minilessons might emphasize ways information writers convey complexity about a topic by bringing forward conflicting perspectives. Such a teaching point wouldn't be the most essential thing for a writer who is just grasping the idea that information texts group information related to different subtopics. When you pull a chair alongside such a writer, it will be important to address whatever is most essential for that writer. What this means is that a fair portion of teaching involves determining where a writer, or a group of writers, are in the journey toward proficiency and then teaching that student (or those students) to progress from that point onward. Always, your small-group work and your conferring will show students how to do something they can do, first with scaffolds and supports, and soon afterward with independence.

When I coach principals in ways to help teachers lift the level of their teaching, I suggest that one of the first things to look for is whether the teacher uses the small-group work and one-to-one conferring simply as a time to repeat his whole-class teaching or if he uses these as forums for responsive instruction. Ideally, conferring and small-group instruction provide you with a time to teach responsively, inventing instruction on the spot to address problems you may not even have known existed, and then some of this responsive instruction ends up becoming more widely broadcast through mid-workshop teaching points, instructive share lessons, and newly invented minilessons.

Use Writing Materials to Differentiate

You may wonder how it is possible to support all your dozens of students across several class periods, how it is possible to work at their just-right levels, while still teaching a compelling unit. One answer to this is that you can differentiate expectations in some relatively straightforward ways—and one of the most obvious of these is by providing students with writing materials that are tailored to them. When writing information texts, for example, your less experienced writers might be writing nonfiction books, complete with tables of contents, and your more experienced writers may be working on academic papers or feature articles. The latter is more challenging. Then, too, the checklists that students use to self-assess can be differentiated, and the exemplar texts that a student aims toward can reflect the level of writing that she aspires toward. Granted, you will also have some whole-class mentor texts, but there is nothing to keep each writer from having an individual mentor text as well. Differentiating the demonstration texts you use is another way to be sure your minilessons support all learners. If you have a wide range of writers in your classroom, you may want to incorporate demonstration texts at different levels so that students can see how the work is done in a piece that looks more or less like their own writing.

Plan on Making Your Minilessons Differentiated

There are a handful of very accessible ways you can make any minilesson more differentiated. Let's think, for example, about the partnership work that occurs in the midst of minilessons. You will quickly find that if partnerships are left on their own, what tends to happen is that the same student—usually the more proficient or dominant student—will take the lead. So if you say, "Turn and tell your partner how you'd suggest I revise my piece," and you give just a minute or two for students to talk about this, the dominant partner is apt to talk first, while the less dominant partner listens, nods, and follows along. There often isn't time for both youngsters to talk, so typically the stronger student does the work, and the less proficient becomes his sounding board. Because this is predictable, I generally recommend that one student be named Partner 1 and the other, Partner 2, and you can make a point of asking for one or the other to talk first, alternating this over the course of days. This means that when you say, "Turn and tell your partner how you'd suggest I revise my piece," you can add, "Partner 1, go first." If you have taken it upon yourself to decide (quietly) which member of each partnership is Partner 1 and which is Partner 2, perhaps naming the more proficient one Partner 2, and then you can make deliberate decisions about whether you want the more or the less proficient writer to do the talking at any one time. For example, if you are asking for advice revising your own writing, the first person to be able to make a suggestion is probably in the easier position, able to choose the low-hanging fruit, so in that instance, you may say, "Partner 1s go first," or "Partner 1s, you suggest a way I could revise my piece, and Partner 2s, imagine how the revision might go, writing-in-the-air what I should write on my page." Sometimes, of course, if the more proficient partner goes first, this provides the less proficient partner with a second demonstration text, making it more supportive to be the second partner to speak. Similarly, sometimes the work will be particularly difficult. You might ask for the more proficient writer to have a go, and then at the end of the minilesson, you might say, "Will Partner 1s, who didn't have a chance to try this during the minilesson, stay with me while Partner 2s, you get started on your writing?"

You can also differentiate your minilesson by giving yourself some quick ways to assess students' understandings. Certainly, when you channel students to "turn and talk" in the midst of a minilesson, you will want to listen carefully to what students say to ascertain whether or not they are grasping what you are trying to teach. You can handle this differently, asking students to write on white boards instead of talking to a partner, holding the white boards high afterward so you can quickly keep tabs on their work. Alternatively, if you want to take account of what your more struggling writers are thinking, you might call, "Will Partner 1s write-in-the-air what you'd write next, and Partner 2s, will you record your partners' words exactly, writing his or her name as well, so I can look at those later?"

Be prepared to coach into the turn-and-talk, saying something like, "Many of you are talking in generalities. Say the precise words you'd say," or "Don't forget to . . ." You can intervene at this point to provide students with a bit more support if you say aloud, "I'm hearing . . ." and then repeat what you've just heard a student or two saying that can function as another example or as a template.

Of course, after students have talked or jotted briefly in the active engagement section of a minilesson, you may want to ask a student or two to report to the class. If you want this to provide the rest of the class with a mentor text, you'll want to call on a student you overheard earlier whose response is what you are after, but if you are wanting to use this structure to keep yourself attuned to the class, you might decide to cold call, rather than asking for a signal ("Thumbs up if . . .").

If you are concerned that despite your best efforts to differentiate during a minilesson, some students may still not have gotten access to the content, you can end the minilesson by asking students to get started doing their work, and then you can use that time as an opportunity to notice youngsters who aren't able to get started. The students who need further scaffolding will become apparent to you, and you can ask them to linger in the meeting area for some follow-up instruction that you'll make more accessible. This approach is especially useful if the strategy you are teaching is particularly new or essential to the bend.

We have come to realize one thing above all in our work in assessment—these assessments say as much about our teaching as they do about our students' skills. Perhaps more. We *cannot* simply look at low scores, at students writing far below grade level, and say, "Well, these students don't have the background," or "Hmm . . . these students don't have the brains or the ethic for success." What we *must* say is "What can we do to teach these students more effectively?" and we *must* ask, "Have we granted each student in our care every possible opportunity to grow? Every possible support?" Adjusting and differentiating your teaching across all realms of your writing workshop (individual, small group, and full class) will provide your students with everything they need to have success in their writing lives, both inside and outside your classroom walls.

Chapter 5

Self-Assessment Checklists

The What, the Why, and the How

Y OU'LL BE SURPRISED TO HEAR that for members of the Teachers College Reading and Writing Project staff, this chapter is the truly thrilling one. We are over the moon with excitement to see the difference that checklists have made in writing workshop classrooms.

You are probably arching your eyebrows and asking, "Seriously? *Checklists?*" I would have reacted in just that way had I not seen the power with my own eyes. And frankly, the secret doesn't lie in the checklists, but in the manner in which you introduce them to your class.

So please, before you print off the grade-specific checklists and distribute them among your students, read this chapter and see if you can catch some of our excitement. Lucille Clifton, one of America's greatest poet laureates, once said to us, "Nurture your image of what's possible. You cannot create what you cannot imagine." This chapter aims to help you imagine that yes, classrooms of writers can actually be on fire over the use of checklists.

WHAT ARE CHECKLISTS IN THE CONTEXT OF A WRITING CURRICULUM?

Many of us use checklists in daily life to make sure we don't forget small details. In planning a Thanksgiving dinner, for example, I'll create a checklist to make sure I don't forget any of the details: Plan the menu. Buy candles for the centerpiece. Put the extra leaves in the dining table. Dig out the tablecloth.

But checklists can be used for more than simply keeping track of whether a task has been done or not; they can also be used to monitor progress toward a bigger goal. By using checklists, students in a writing workshop can review their work systematically, checking to make sure they have met certain goals in each piece of their writing. And if they fall short of meeting their goals, a good checklist can guide them in the right direction toward meeting that goal in their next revision—and in their future writing.

Argument Writing Checklist

	Grade 6	NOT YET	STARTING TO	YES!
Structure				
Overall	I explained the topic/text and staked out a position that can be supported by a variety of trustworthy sources. Each part of my text helped build my argument, and led to a conclusion.	☐	☐	☐
Lead	I wrote an introduction to interest readers and help them understand and care about a topic or text. I thought backwards between the piece and the introduction to make sure that the introduction fit with the whole.	☐	☐	☐
	Not only did I clearly state my claim, I also told my readers how my text would unfold.	☐	☐	☐
Transitions	I used transitions to help readers understand how the different parts of my piece fit together to explain and support my argument.	☐	☐	☐
	I used transitions to help connect claim(s), reasons, and evidence, and to imply relationships such as when material exemplifies, adds on to, is similar to, explains, is a result of, or contrasts. I use transitions such as *for instance, in addition, one reason, furthermore, according to, this evidence suggests,* and *thus we can say that.*	☐	☐	☐
Ending	In my conclusion, I restated the important points and offered a final insight or implication for readers to consider. The ending strengthened the overall argument.	☐	☐	☐
Organization	I organized my argument into sections: I arranged reasons and evidence purposefully, leading readers from one claim or reason to another.	☐	☐	☐
	The order of the sections and the internal structure of each section made sense.	☐	☐	☐
Development				
Elaboration	I included and arranged a variety of evidence such as facts, quotations, examples, and definitions.	☐	☐	☐
	I used trusted sources and information from experts and gave the sources credit.	☐	☐	☐
	I worked to explain how the reasons and evidence I gave supported my claim(s) and strengthened my argument. To do this I may have referred to earlier parts of my text, summarized background information, raised questions, or highlighted possible implications.	☐	☐	☐

In Part II of *Writing Pathways*, we provide a checklist for each grade level, in each of the three types of writing: argument, information, and narrative. These are really grade-specific slices of the learning progression. The checklists are designed to be used by students to self-assess their progress toward a specific grade and genre's goals. So, for instance, a seventh-grade writer can look over her argument essay and self-assess her structure, elaboration, and use of language against the seventh-grade standards.

You'll notice the checklists are written in the first person—in the "I" voice—and in student-friendly language. In the many versions of these checklists we piloted, and in our work with Ray Pecheone and Linda Darling Hammond of SCALE, we learned that using *I* increases student accountability. It's not "someone," or "a writer," who needs to have done this work. The question is, did *I* do it?

The checklists contain three columns so that a writer can check how much progress she has made toward accomplishing each goal in her writing. Has she completely accomplished her goal, doing it consistently and often? Or is she just starting to? Perhaps she hasn't begun to meet a particular goal at all. By using the checklist, the writer can see for herself how much progress she is making, and she can see what her next steps need to be.

WHY CHECKLISTS?

There is no question but that you will need to talk up the power of checklists to your students. That's not hard to do. When people are working on something complicated and important—such as heart surgery, flying a plane, or starting a school—checklists make it much less likely that they forget essential things. In his now-famous book, *The Checklist Manifesto*, surgeon and writer Atul Gawande reports on a study in which he introduced checklists into eight hospitals. Major surgery complications dropped 36%, and the number of deaths plunged by 47%. In those hospitals, checklists saved lives.

Your students will appreciate another example of the power of checklists. Tell them the story of how Captain Chesley Sullenberger and his copilot landed their broken plane in the Hudson River in 2009, pulling off the "Hudson Miracle" by landing that plane in the river after both engines were disabled. How did he and his crew do that? They remained calm and followed a checklist! *The New York Times* reported, "Captain Sullenberger was in the unusual position of both flying an airliner and working the radio; talking on the radio is normally the job of the other pilot, but in this case the first officer, Jeffrey B. Skiles, was running through an 'engine restart checklist.'" In an increasingly complex and fast-paced world, checklists make it more likely that people don't forget what they know how to do.

Checklists are especially important if the person is intent not just on pulling off a complicated project, but also on getting better at that work—on improving the odds of success, raising the rates, maximizing the progress. In such a situation, the checklist does double duty: it reminds people of what they already know how to do, and it also reminds them of what they are aiming toward. Any effort at deliberate self-improvement is more concrete if there is a scale for measuring progress. Learners are able to see and to learn from granular evidence of progress (or lack thereof). This is why athletes use stopwatches, yardsticks, and pedometers to measure their progress and set goals. This is why doctors use heart monitors and blood tests to track the latest stats on a patient.

Frankly, in the early research for our units of study series, we scorned the term *checklist*, haunted by the disparaging expression "a checklist mentality." All of that now feels long ago. Now, everywhere we turn, we see new evidence of the power of checklists. During last year's collaboration with SCALE, we learned that even their research has confirmed for them that checklists are a powerful tool—more helpful to students than multicolumn rubrics.

HOW DO YOU USE CHECKLISTS?

Although checklists are vitally important, their importance is not as curriculum but as reminders—a glorified yarn-around-the-finger. **Checklists most definitely cannot be a substitute for instruction!** If you think that adequate instruction consists of simply distributing the seventh-grade information writing checklist—which tells students that they must write introductions that explain the significance of the topic, or provide a compelling fact, statistic, or anecdote, all while making it clear what parts of the topic the text will tackle as well as how the ideas and information in the text will unfold—then you are wrong. Students will need you to teach them how to do this first, demonstrating how you go about crafting an introduction, perhaps using your own writing as a teaching text, and pointing out the steps you take to do this. They'll benefit from studying published work and the work other writers have done to collect examples of this. They will need chances to approximate doing this and to receive coaching. Only then, once they have been taught to do this, will the reminders in the checklist be important.

Because checklists *follow* rather than precede instruction, toward the start of your first narrative unit—and your first argument and information unit—of each school year, you will probably ask students to use the checklist *from the preceding year* to check whether they have remembered to do all they learned earlier. For example, early on in a narrative unit at the start of sixth grade, eleven-year-olds will be asked to use the *fifth*-grade Narrative Writing Checklist. The checklist will remind them of the qualities of narrative writing they were taught the preceding year—a move that will help to mitigate summer writing loss. This especially makes sense because the checklists represent the *end-of-year* standards for each grade level. So, at the very beginning of sixth grade, it makes perfect sense that students would be writing at end-of-fifth-grade levels.

Of course, whatever the grade level, as soon as you have taught most of the work that belongs at that grade level, you'll cement instruction by channeling students to use the new, grade-specific checklist.

Argument Writing Checklist

	Grade 8				Grade 9			
		NOT YET	STARTING TO	YES!		NOT YET	STARTING TO	YES!
Structure					**Structure**			
Overall	I laid out an argument about a topic/text and made it clear why my particular argument is important and valid. I stayed fair to those who might disagree with me by describing how my position is one of several and making it clear where my position stands in relation to others.	☐	☐	☐	I presented an argument, offering context, honoring other points of view, and indicating the conditions under which the position holds true.	☐	☐	☐
Lead	After hooking the reader, I provided specific context for my own as well as another position(s), introduced my position, and oriented readers to the overall line of argument I planned to develop.	☐	☐	☐	I developed the argument with logical reasoning and convincing evidence, acknowledging the limitations of the position and citing—and critiquing—sources.	☐	☐	☐
					I demonstrated the significance of the argument and may have offered hints of upcoming parts of the essay. I presented needed background information to show the complexity of the issue.	☐	☐	☐
Transitions	I used transitions to lead the reader across parts of the text and to help the reader note how parts of the text relate back to earlier parts. I used phrases such as *now some argue, while this may be true, it is also the case that, despite this, as stated earlier, taken as a whole, this is significant because, the evidence points to,* and *by doing so . . .*	☐	☐	☐	In addition to introducing the overall line of development the argument will take, I distinguished that argument from others.	☐	☐	☐
					I used transitions to clarify the relationship between claims, reasons, and evidence, and to help the reader follow the logic in the argument. I also used transitions to make clear the relationship of sources to each other and to the claim, such as *while it may be true that . . . , nevertheless, there are times when . . . /certain circumstances when . . . , and others echo this idea.*	☐	☐	☐

Generally, this means that approximately half to two thirds of the way through the first unit of study in a year—say, the first argument writing unit in eighth grade—you'll review the teaching you will have done thus far in that unit by introducing the checklist for what your students will be expected to be able to do by *the end of* the school year. If later units support students working not only toward but also beyond their grade level, you may find that you have done the necessary teaching so that students can assess their work using a two-column checklist, one column for their own grade level, the other for the next grade up. It is not likely that many students will have *mastered* all the standards for the grade above, but many thrive when having time to work toward these expectations.

In addition to choosing which checklist and which combination of checklists to use at a given time for specific purposes, you will also need to consider if any modifications to the checklist are necessary for your class and situation. For example, it may be that you'd like to start your students off with a checklist with only a few items on it, adding to it over time as you teach more and more. You'll find the checklists in Part II of this book (and on the CD-ROM) in their standard form.

Using the checklists on the CD-ROM, you could create a double-column checklist for an eighth-grade student working toward the ninth-grade expectations for argument writing.

Before Anything Else, Rally Students to Invest in Self-Assessing

You might start not with the checklist, but with the broader principle. "Writers," you might say. "One of our themes this year is taking charge of making ourselves stronger. That means *you* have to be the one who says, 'I want to become a better writer.'" You might add, "It can't be my job or your classmates' job to make you into a stronger writer. It needs to be *your* job. You are in charge."

You can rally your students to participate in this shared sense of self-efficacy by likening their writing work to the work that an athlete does. "In life, you do this all the time. If you want to make the basketball team, you practice and practice. If you tend to dribble the ball in a sloppy fashion, allowing people to steal it from you, you admit that to yourself and then get help from people who are skilled at dribbling. You learn ways to protect that ball and move it down the court. Then you practice, practice, practice. That's how you get better at basketball. You make it your job, your business, to get better.

If you feel that the sports analogy leaves some students out, then broaden your examples. My colleague, Kathleen Tolan, sometimes will say to kids, "Or, if your dog is misbehaving and your parents say the dog isn't working any longer, if the threat of losing that dog is too much to bear, you get yourself and your dog on a course to better behavior. You teach that dog to sit and to come and to not pull on the leash."

Don't hesitate to preach: "It all starts with you saying to yourself, 'This matters to me and I have to get better at it.' Then you assess yourself and plan your next steps. You can do that if you have a sense of what it means to do better, if you know what the next steps are."

Of course, this is a roundabout way to introduce the checklist. But the success or failure of the checklist will have everything to do with whether or not you are able to create in your classroom a learning culture that values what developmental psychologist Carol Dweck of Stanford University refers to as a growth mind-set, as opposed to a fixed mind-set, for thinking about learning. If students believe that their current level of work reflects a fixed level of intelligence or that the level of their writing shows their writing DNA, then they won't buy into the notion that the quality of their writing reflects their effort and their use of strategies. If you tell them they can write in dramatically better ways, they'll raise an eyebrow, scoff, and think, "You just don't get it. I'm bad at writing." Their response to writing that is assessed as far below standards will be to throw in the towel, to think, "I'm not creative." It won't be to roll up their sleeves to work harder. Students with a mind-set that tells them that their intelligence is a fixed quantity, something they were born with (or without), will not respond to the news that their writing is subpar by trying harder. Instead, they will assume that the level of their work reveals a weakness that is permanent, and they will respond with shame or disengagement.

What I'm suggesting, then, is that by teaching students to regard setbacks as invitations to work with new resolve, you can actually alter a student's mind-set toward learning. Dweck, for example, asks and then answers this question: "What do academically tenacious students look like?" She writes, "First, they believe that they belong in school academically and socially. . . . Second, they are engaged in learning, view effort positively, and can forego immediate pleasures for the sake of schoolwork. . . . Third, difficulty, be it intellectual or social, does not derail them." **Academically tenacious students see a setback as an opportunity for learning or a problem to be solved, rather than as a humiliation, a condemnation of their ability or worth, a symbol of future failures, or a confirmation that they do not belong.** This is true at the level of a given task and at the level of their studies in general. Tenacious students know how to remain engaged over the long haul and to deploy new strategies for moving forward effectively (Dweck et al. *Academic Tenacity Mind-Sets and Skills that Promote Long Term Learning*, 2001, 5–6).

Paul Tough, author of *How Students Succeed*, concurs, adding, "When kids believe that they can change their intelligence, they actually do better. They work harder." (The full interview can be listened to at http://www.econtalk.org/archives/2012/09/paul_tough_on_h.html; Google search term "Paul Tough How

Narrative Writing Checklist

Grade 6		NOT YET	STARTING TO	YES!
Structure				
Overall	I wrote a story that has tension, resolution, realistic characters, and also conveys an idea, lesson, or theme.	☐	☐	☐
Lead	I wrote a beginning that not only set the plot/story in motion, but also hinted at the larger meaning the story would convey. It introduced the problem, set the stage for the lesson that would be learned, or showed how the character relates to the setting in a way that matters in the story.	☐	☐	☐
Transitions	I not only used transitional phrases and clauses to signal complicated changes in time, I also used them to alert my reader to changes in the setting, tone, mood, point of view, or the time in the story (such as *suddenly, unlike before, if only she had known*).	☐	☐	☐
Ending	I wrote an ending that connected to what the story is really about. I gave the reader a sense of closure by showing a new realization or insight, or a change in the character/narrator. I might have shown this through dialogue, action, inner thinking, or small actions the character takes.	☐	☐	☐
Organization	I used paragraphs purposefully, perhaps to show time and setting changes, new parts of the story, or to create suspense for readers. I created a logical, clear sequence of events.	☐	☐	☐
Development				
Elaboration	I developed realistic characters, and developed the details, action, dialogue, and internal thinking that contribute to the deeper meaning of the story.	☐	☐	☐
Craft or Language	I developed some relationship between characters to show why they act and speak as they do. I told the internal, as well as the external story.	☐	☐	☐
	I wove together precise descriptions, figurative language, and some symbolism to help readers picture the setting and actions, and to bring forth meaning.	☐	☐	☐
	I used language that fit my story's meaning and context (for example, different characters use different kinds of language).	☐	☐	☐
Conventions				
Spelling	I used resources to be sure the words in my writing are spelled correctly.	☐	☐	☐
Punctuation and Sentence Structure	I used punctuation such as dashes, parentheses, colons, and semicolons to help me include extra detail and explanation in some of my sentences.	☐	☐	☐
	I used commas and quotation marks or italics or other ways to make clear when characters are speaking.	☐	☐	☐

Children Succeed econ talk.") It is critical, then, to keep in mind that for performance assessments to be potent, they need to be accompanied by a belief that success depends on hard work.

The larger message is that these writing assessment tools can power your students' learning if you help students to embrace the stance that accompanies them. And these assessments will be a chore for you and for them if you don't help your students to embrace that learning stance. As you put checklists into the hands of your students, expect that you are giving them power tools. These tools can bring out a new level of zealous energy and self-reflection. Expect, too, that this work will make your classroom far more collaborative than ever, because checklists enable students to teach each other in potent ways. Young writers will begin to regard each other as valued sources of expertise.

A More Detailed Look at the Checklist as a Tool for Self-Assessment and Goal-Setting

Let's get closer to some of the details of this instruction. As an example, we'll examine teaching interactions that are detailed in the *Units of Study in Argument, Information, and Narrative Writing.*

Imagine that you are peeking in on a seventh-grade classroom. It is early in the year, and students have just started working in their narrative unit of study, *Writing Realistic Fiction: Symbolism, Syntax, and Truth.* The teacher has distributed one of the checklists they came to know during sixth grade. Now she plans to channel the students to look through the entries they have been gathering in their writer's notebooks, looking to see the extent to which their writing illustrates items in the checklist from the year before. "This checklist will remind you of the qualities of strong narrative writing you worked on in sixth grade," she says. "As I read the list to you, give a thumbs up if you think this is an item you already do well."

As the teacher reads through the items on the list, a number of students give her a thumbs up for one item or another. "It's obvious there is a lot we already know about narrative writing," she says, "and that we've got quite a few resident experts in the room. Some of the items on the list, though, will be things you've forgotten to do or things you know you can improve. Those can become your resolutions, your goals. And when you get a chance to do some writing after today, you'll want to work on those goals."

Before the students do this work independently on their own writing, the teacher and students work together, assessing several of the teacher's entries against the checklist. Then the students proceed along, noting alignment and gaps between their own entries and the checklist. Instead of using teacher entries as a starting point, another option would be for students to first look at the checklist next to benchmark pieces of writing that illustrate the standards at that particular level. After they read through the checklist and study its matching benchmark text, they could then study their own work and star or highlight items on the checklist that remain as goals for them. The benchmark writing can also become a mentor text for students; they can tape it into their writer's notebook or place it in their folder for future reference.

Within a few weeks, after the teacher has reminded students of the sixth-grade narrative expectations, she will distribute a checklist that reflects the new seventh-grade standards. If students' initial on-demands showed that they will soon be ready for an added challenge (e.g., the eighth-grade standards), the teacher will plan to eventually give students a double-column checklist, with the seventh-grade narrative checklist in one column and the eighth-grade checklist in the other. This gives students a horizon to work toward as they are taught toward it.

Help Students Crystallize Visions of Good Writing by Using Benchmark Pieces, Demonstration Writing, and Checklists in Tandem

One of the most important things you can do is help students to have a crystal clear vision of the goals they are working toward. The checklists can help to name these goals, putting student-friendly language around qualities of writing that might otherwise be difficult to discuss. It will be equally as important for students to have a *vision* of what these qualities look like. As John Hattie, the author of *Visible Learning* (2008), a meta-analysis of over 800 studies of the factors that most influence student achievement, says, "Goals have a self-energizing effect if they are appropriately challenging for the student, as they can motivate students to exert effort in line with the difficulty or demands of the goal. . . . A major reason difficult goals are more effective is that they lead to a clearer notion of success and direct the student's attention to relevant behaviors or outcomes."

To give students a grip on goals toward which they are working, you will want to call students' attention to the series of leveled student writing samples that illustrate the Teachers College Reading and Writing Project's best estimate for reasonable, CCSS-aligned expectations for on-demand narrative, argument, and information writing. You'll find these, along with all the other tools we've discussed, in Part II of this book. You can also direct students' attention to pieces of writing that have been woven into the rest of the *Units of Study for Argument, Information, and Narrative Writing* series. Within the books themselves, you will find demonstration texts written by teachers to model the skills and strategies that students are learning as the unit progresses. Whether you are using a demonstration piece written by yourself or an on-demand benchmark sample from Part II of this book, your goal will be to help crystallize students' visions of what they are being asked to produce.

As the unit progresses, you'll want to keep the momentum around checklists and goal-setting going, taking time now and again to both model and ask students to assess and set goals. Use your own demonstration texts, like the one in Figure 5–1, or those provided in this book. Encourage your students to look

A Global Issue

According to the United Nations, <u>more than</u> 34 million teenage girls around the world do not attend school. There are several reasons why girls are denied an education. Sometimes girls don't go to school because of poverty, in other places, because of beliefs in the community.

When girls are denied an education because of poverty, families want all their children to attend school, but they can't afford to purchase books or school fees for the whole family. According to Camfed, a group that helps girls around the world to attend school, when poor families have to pick and choose which children get to attend school and which don't, they tend to send their sons not their daughters

These families often believe that boys have a better chance of getting a paid job after school.

In some communities around the world, people don't believe that education is a right for everyone. They may believe that a girl's place is in the home, helping her mother take care of the family, and therefore keep girls at home, believing schools won't help a girl take care of the family.

There are many ways that people actively try to deny girls an education. One way is political. <u>If a particular political party takes power, they can create rules and laws that forbid girls from attending school.</u> Not all political parties are elected. Some take power by force. This is exactly what happened in Malala's case. The Taliban took over her home town and passed laws forbidding all

girls from attending school. <u>The Taliban has been known to change local laws so that girls cannot attend school.</u> The group has closed schools and destroyed schools. "These schools were closed, so why did they also need to be destroyed?" asked Malala Yousafzai. Girls like Malala, who believe that <u>education is a right for every child, have been attacked by Taliban members.</u>

FIG. 5–1 A teacher-written exemplar used in the sixth-grade information writing unit, *Research-Based Information Writing: Books, Websites, and Presentations*

between the demonstration texts you provide and find examples of good work they can learn from. "Ah," you might say, "as I look between my writing and the checklist, I'm noticing that including varied details is an important part of informational writing at the sixth-grade level. I've made copies of some of the work I did, adding details to my writing, so that you can use it as a mentor if you'd like." Put a stack of your writing (or the sixth-grade on-demand samples) in an area in the classroom, encouraging students to take one if they too are working to add varied and compelling details to their chapters. By doing so, you are establishing an environment in which benchmark pieces of writing become personal coaches of sorts—used to help illuminate the qualities of strong writing in a particular genre and to help students envision the work they are setting out to do as writers.

Demonstrate by Using the Checklist to Assess Your Own Writing

It won't be enough to simply show students the checklists and ask them to use them. Like any other skill, self-assessment must be taught, and one very effective way to do this is through the use of demonstration. If you have access to a document camera, overhead projector, or Smart Board, use that tool to enlarge your copy of the checklist.

Introduce the checklist.

You can run your pencil down the checklist and show students how you go between reading an item on the checklist, recalling what you know about that item/indicator, and then reading your text closely, looking for evidence. "The first term I see is *Structure*. So all these items on this part of the checklist are asking about the structure of my piece. Hmm . . . What do I know about structure already? In stories, structure relates to the story being told sequentially, but we're working on information writing. So in information writing I think structure relates to whether the writing is organized into parts and sections."

Progressing, you could say, "Okay, so let's move down this checklist. The first item is *Overall*. I'm going to read my piece to see if this grade level's descriptor describes what I do, overall: 'I conveyed ideas and information about a subject in a well-structured text. Sometimes I incorporated arguments, explanations, stories, or procedural passages.'"

Continuing your demonstration, you could say, "Hmm . . . , let's see, have I done all those things?" To make a point, try letting yourself off the hook, and then self-correct. You might, for example, say, "I definitely conveyed ideas and information about my topic, and it is well structured, organized by subtopics. I'm not sure if I really incorporated other kinds of text structures, though. There isn't much in the way of argument, or even any stories for that matter. But I *do* teach information, and I think my topics and ideas are pretty well developed." Then monitor yourself, saying, "No, no, I need to be tough on myself, or I'll never get even better. I think I should say, 'Starting to.'"

Proceeding down the checklist to the item that says, "Lead," you could then read aloud, "I wrote an introduction in which I interested readers, perhaps with a quote or significant fact. I let readers know the subtopics that I would develop later and how my text would unfold." You'll ask, "Did I do that in my piece?" and turn to your writing.

According to the United Nations, more than 34 million teenage girls around the world do not attend school. There are several reasons why girls are denied an education. Sometimes girls don't go to school because of poverty, in other places, because of the beliefs in the community.

You could then say, "Hmm . . . I *do* think I interested the reader. I used a compelling fact, a statistic, to do that." Point to and then underline the statistic about how many teenage girls around the world do not attend school.

Show how to hold yourself accountable.

The work you will have done will meet only *some* of the expectations for structure that are detailed in the checklist. The whole point of your little drama will be to show that although you found that you did do *part* of what the checklist details, you also notice that you didn't do the other part. Show kids that you are exacting and demanding of yourself.

Returning to the checklist, continue to read the descriptor for a lead. "But let me see if I also let the reader know what I am going to teach in this piece of writing." Skim your piece, point out that you didn't give your readers an early lay of the land, and then circle that part of the item on the checklist, explaining why: "I'm circling this part and checking 'Starting to' because I did just *half* of this item. The part I circled is the half I still need to do."

The important thing is that you will want to make a big deal of anything you see that you have not done fully. "I'm going to remind myself of what I *haven't yet* done because that's an area in which I can improve my writing! I'll make a note of that in the margin of my piece." Then you can jot, "Tell what I'll teach" in the margin or on a Post-it®. In this way, your demonstration can help students know what it means to check a draft for evidence, to hold yourself accountable, and to reach toward mastery.

When you create a demonstration, make sure the writing you use as a demonstration text shows you have missed portions of items on the checklist. Make sure that your demonstration text positions you to model that to check off an item, the writing needs to show that item consistently, not just once in the text. For example, one instance when you reference sources doesn't allow you to check off the "Yes!" box if there is no other evidence that you draw on sources in your writing. Show students that you hold yourself to high levels of expectation and that you are happy to discover things on the checklist you *haven't* yet done, knowing these can now become goals.

Emphasize the importance of being truly honest with yourself.

Since your goal is to encourage students to do likewise, you will want to make a big deal out of the fact that you didn't just glibly say, "*Yes*, I did this. Yes, I did that." To accentuate this, you might make an aside (illustrating this by brushing invisible things away with your hand) saying, "What if I'd just checked 'Yes!' for the lead, saying, 'Oh, I did that'? You can act as if it would have been a calamity had you merely dismissed the prospect of writing with details. "If you were my partner, and I said, 'Well, I sorta did that,' what would you say?"

One youngster recently piped in, "I'd say, 'Well, actually, you only did half of this.'"

Continuing to play the part of the mistaken student who keeps trying to get off the hook, you can protest, "No, no, I *almost* always tell the reader what I'm going to teach. Just this one little time I didn't do that." Shaking your head in feigned protest, say, "I don't need to practice it more. I know how to do it, I just don't always. So I'm checking 'Yes!'"

You can fire the students up in indignation so they agree that helping each other and themselves reach for high standards is the moral thing to do. Affirm any student who says he will remind partners (and you) to aspire toward greater heights. "You are so right! I hope everyone is realizing that it is important for you, as the partner, to not just gloss over your partner's work, saying 'It's good.' You really want to study the nitty-gritty of it. Partners need to say to each other, 'Where's the evidence that you did that?' and then, 'Yes, but is that one example really *mastery*? Couldn't you work to do this more often?'"

Stay positive.

You may want to do yet more encouraging, in which case you could say, "And writers, if you find yourself in a 'not yet' or a 'starting to' stage for some items on the checklist, remember, that's *a good thing*. That's positive! That means you are assessing your writing and saying, 'I know I can get better. I have the support of my class, and I know so much about writing, and my teacher can help me with that.' And this whole year is about getting better at things. If you self-assess and find a bunch of 'not yets' for yourself, that just means you are on a course. You have work to do."

After demonstrating how a writer can self-assess by doing this with a few items, you'll want to pass the baton to students, giving them a chance to self-assess using the checklist and their own pieces of writing.

ADAPT CHECKLISTS FOR STUDENTS NEEDING SCAFFOLDS

Teachers have devised many systems for helping students who need help processing the checklists. If students are new to the concept of standards and self-assessment, being handed a full checklist can be daunting. Consider introducing one section at a time for some classes (for instance, focusing first on structure, then later on elaboration). For other students, you might slim down the number of indicators in each category and slowly introduce the rest. Most importantly, remember that the checklists are a tool for *reminding*, not teaching. If you haven't taught a skill or strategy, don't expect students to be able to assess for it. Instead, you might have them circle the ones that feel familiar and then hold small groups or conferences to introduce the others. Many teachers have found it helpful to illustrate the checklists, providing visual support for English language learners or other students who struggle. Frankly, the illustrated versions might support all students, as they are engaging and memorable! Watch students as they work with the checklists; their successes and confusions will help guide the choices you make.

Coach Students as They Begin Using the Checklist

As your students begin self-assessing with the checklists, you'll want to coach into their work. If you have given them the charge to underline or place a Post-it on the instances where they found evidence showing they accomplished something, and they mark evidence that doesn't actually fit the descriptor, you'll want to teach them to be more accurate. If kids try to excuse themselves by saying things like, "I was just being sloppy in this draft. I *usually* do this thing on the checklist," assure them while holding them accountable to what they see: "By the next self-assessment, you'll be better already!" But don't alter the facts of this assessment. Be strict with yourself."

Students who have a straight run of "not yets" will need to be moved to a lower-level checklist where they can be working toward goals that are within their zone of proximal development and where they can see demonstrable improvement. Often this reflects the teaching a student has received prior to now, which you can let the student know. Say, "You haven't been taught a lot of this, so you didn't know that was what

Opinion Writing: Structure

I not only staked a position that could be supported by a variety of trustworthy. I explained the topic/text and staked out a position that can be supported by a variety of trustworthy sources. Each part of my text builds my argument, and leads to a conclusion.

Did I do it like a sixth grader?	Not Yet	Starting to...	YES
introduction — I wrote an introduction to interest readers and help them understand and care about a topic or text. I thought backwards between the piece and the introduction to make sure that the introduction fits with the whole.			
CLAIM! reasons — Not only did I clearly state my claim, I also told my readers how my text would unfold.			
According to... For instance, In addition, One reason — I used transitions to help connect claim(s), reasons, and evidence and to imply relationships such as when material exemplifies, adds on to, is similar to, or contrasts. I used transitions such as *furthermore, this evidence suggests, thus we can say that.*			
Hmm... — In my conclusion, I restated the important points and offered a final insight or implication for readers to consider. The ending strengthened the overall argument.			
I organized my argument into sections: I arranged reasons and evidence purposefully, leading readers from one claim or reason to another.			
The order of the sections and the internal structure of each section make sense.			

Opinion Writing: Development

Did I do it like a sixth grader?	Not Yet	Starting to...	YES
facts, quotations, examples, definitions — I included and arranged a variety of evidence such as facts, quotations, examples, definitions.			
This shows how important... This proves that... — I used trusted sources and information from experts and gave the sources credit.			
I worked to explain how the reasons and evidence I gave support my claim(s) and strengthen my argument. To do this I may have referred to earlier parts of my text, summarized background information, raised questions, or highlighted possible implications.			
active, exercise, social skills, healthy — I chose my words carefully to support my argument and to have an effect on my reader.			
phrase, metaphor, analogy — I worked to include concrete details, comparisons, and/or images to convey my ideas, build my argument, and keep my reader engaged.			
This means... — When necessary, I explained terms to readers, providing definitions, context clues or parenthetical explanations.			
Experts believe · This is important because... — I made my piece sound serious.			

FIG. 5-2 A sixth-grade argument checklist with illustrations for added support or to make them more engaging and memorable

you should be doing. Keep this checklist at your elbow as you write, so you'll start doing the items on it really quickly! Pretty soon you will be acing the earlier checklist and *then* you can move to a more challenging one. We'll all be doing that. Let's mark on the calendar that Friday in two and a half weeks, we'll assess again and see if you are ready for the next checklist. Until then, work like the dickens!"

One final note. Guard against your students setting goals that are far too small to merit attention, and guard against them thinking they can meet their goals with tiny bits of effort. The story we often tell is of the writer who decided he needed more transitions, and therefore rewrote his narrative by using five carets to insert the phrase "a little later" into five places within his draft. One way to make the goals bigger than a tiny item on the checklist is to cluster a few related items—for example, chances are good that writers who have trouble with transitions may also have trouble with structure in general. Chances are that writers who have trouble with elaboration are also writing short, underdeveloped pieces. So you can talk up related goals that snowball alongside the original goal.

Help Students Set Writing Goals by Helping Them Focus Not Just on What, but Also on How They Write

Once you have recruited your class of students to set goals for themselves, you'll want to make sure that their day-to-day work is different because of those goals. You can teach students to think not only about the content of their writing but also about how to write in such a way that they meet their goals and make their writing as strong as possible.

Demonstrate how to set goals and make plans to meet them.

To demonstrate to students the way I use an item from the checklist as a goal, holding it in mind as I write, I created a draft for the occasion. Because the class was working in a narrative writing unit at the time, my draft was a story as well. I said to kids, "The personal narrative I'm working on right now is the story about the time my younger sister and I ignored my dad's directions and wound up destroying the garden. My draft already tells what happened that day. I did a good job telling the actual events of the story. I'm not quite done yet, so before I go any further, I need to think about my goal. Let me look at the goals I've marked on my checklist so I have some reminders." I then picked up the narrative checklist that I had used to self-assess my on-demand piece, noticing that for "Elaboration" I had marked "Starting to."

I mused aloud. "Hmm . . . the checklist for elaboration says, 'I developed realistic characters, and developed the details, action, dialogue, and internal thinking that contribute to the deeper meaning of the story.' Did I do that in my draft? Well, I definitely developed my characters. I think I've painted a pretty clear picture of my sister, and especially the kind of guy my dad is. And I used dialogue to help push the action of the story. I guess because I still sort of need to figure that out. So if I want to meet this goal, check off 'Yes' and not 'Starting to,' now I need to think about the deeper meaning I want to convey, and then of course how to make that happen throughout the draft. While I do this, will you please look between your draft and one of your goals just as I'm doing, and will you think about the work you will do to meet your goal? You can talk to your partner about your thoughts."

After students talked for a bit, I told them that I would work on crafting strategies for elaborating on the deeper meaning of the story by finding a mentor text and an expert that could help me. "I'm also going to reread Jim Howe's story 'Everything Will Be Okay' to see if that mentor text can help me. I'm also going to see who in this class is especially good at elaboration and get help from that person, too."

Then I said to the class, "Do you see that I'm making plans not just for *what* I will write and also not just for *how* I will write—but for the steps I'll take to accomplish my goals?"

The point is that when people strive to write better, they think not just about what they'll write, but also about *how* that writing will go, and they can use tools like checklists to help them ratchet up their writing.

Teach students how to set worthwhile goals.

Of course, you will want to make sure students are setting goals that feel worth working toward. As they create personal goals you might say, "If you didn't write with footnotes, you need to decide whether that should be a major goal or if it is something you can start doing in your writing tomorrow, something that you just need to remind yourself to do. If some of the things you didn't do were only because you forgot, you should start doing them today. Be stricter with yourself, and maybe ask a partner to remind you. On the other hand, if something on the checklist was something you need more support with or maybe something you could learn more about in a small group—for example, improving your discussion of citations—then you could create a major goal sheet and put those items on it." That is, not every single "not yet" and "starting to" may necessarily make its way onto a student's goal sheet.

Celebrate the goals.

Most of your students will likely still have a whole armful of big and important goals. You'll see that many items on the checklist are actually part and parcel of each other, and it would be hard to tackle one without tackling the other. Celebrate the goals. Make a very big deal of them. Allow students to decorate their checklists or doodle along the sides. Just as you worked hard to help students take ownership over their writer's notebooks, you'll want to help them feel a sense of pride and ownership over their checklists and goals.

This may sound like all fluff and no substance, but it's more important than you realize. It is a very big deal if self-assessment yields goals and if that process is celebrated and transparent. This makes it far more likely that students will actually note what they haven't yet done in their writing and that they'll think about what they need to work on, talk about it, and actually aspire toward meeting those goals. It is tremendously important that your classroom regards achievement as obtainable by all and as the result of hard work, perseverance, and help from others, not as something that comes from one's DNA.

Show how to create the conditions for success.

Think, for a moment, of what you do when you set that New Year's goal to get healthy or to exercise regularly. If that goal is going to amount to anything, you know it needs to alter your lifestyle. To make that more likely, you announce your goal to everyone and even give people permission to help you meet the goal. You arrange your life differently so that you have a chance of success. You buy new running sneakers. You start tracking your progress. And most of all, you recruit others to join you.

One way for writers to give themselves lots of practice with the new regimen, the new goals, is for them to reread writing they'd previously thought was completed, this time looking for whether they could revise it yet again in ways that reflect their goals. For example, if a student needs help with endings, she can revise the ending of every piece she has written, all year long. This gives that youngster lots of repeated practice putting her goal into practice and allows her to develop some proficiency. One of the nice things about such an invitation is that if the student is looking back on work she created months ago, she'll usually find it very easy to revise that work. After all, she will have grown considerably in the interval since the original text was written. This makes it likely that the effort to revise will result in a substantially improved draft, which of course is reinforcing for the student.

Students can also decide to work toward their new goal by getting in the habit of regularly assessing that aspect of their writing. That is, if a student is working on transitions, he can develop a rating system for evaluating the transitions he uses each time he writes and get into the habit of shifting between writing and rereading, keeping an eye on his transitions while he rereads.

Set higher goals for students needing more challenge.

If you have students who need more challenging goals, suggest writers look at the exemplars and checklists that are a notch or even two notches above the one that mostly fits their writing. That is, the strong seventh-grade writer working on endings for information writing may aim not only to produce endings that are *adequate* for his grade, but to become a "professor of endings" and to become famous for his endings. You could allow this student to peek ahead and see what endings are like in the work of kids a grade or two (or three) ahead, so that he has crystal clear, ambitious goals and has words to describe what he will see when studying published conclusions.

He'll find, for example, that while the seventh-grade goal is to craft a conclusion that reinforces the main points of the piece, making it a cohesive whole, all while highlighting the significance of the main points, by eighth grade, the expectations for conclusions are higher. Eighth-grade writers are expected to do many of the same things but *also* build up the significance of their points, suggest implications, as well as allude to potential challenges. By ninth grade, the information writer must work even harder with his conclusion, using the ending of his piece to *strengthen* implications, suggest possible applications, and allude to *multiple* perspectives or challenges.

A version of this work could be within reach for a seventh-grader, and of course, you'll have students who would love to climb up the ladder of expectations, revising a piece so it is better and better, notch by notch, and then teaching others to do the same. You can have conferences with these students, with these goals in mind, during which you can offer them the teaching they'll need, the techniques writers use, to reach those standards.

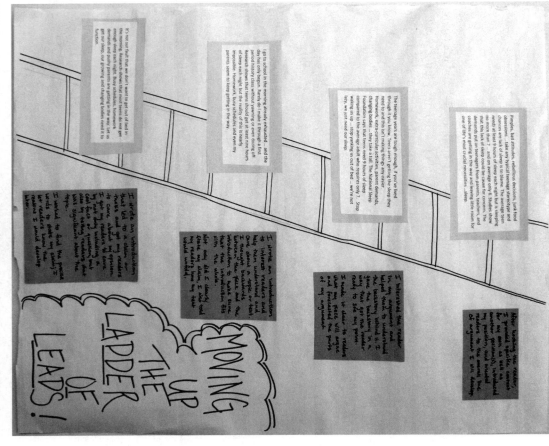

FIG. 5–3   A chart such as this can provide examples of how to lift the level of leads.

Make goals a big deal.

One way to make a big deal out of goal-setting is to set up each student to create a wall-sized timeline of her goals. On a long scroll of paper, each student hangs her on-demand writing in chronological order, alternating the drafts with intermittent goal sheets. When visitors come to the classroom or on parent-teacher conference days or on Meet Our Goal celebration days that you set up, each student can help a visitor "walk along the pathway of the student's learning." If you do this with your class, one of the interesting things you will find is that goals for one type of writing tend to apply also to other types of writing. For example, a student whose goal is to work on elaboration in narrative writing will often find that he can also gain from working on elaboration in information and argument writing. This allows for a continuity of goal-driven work across a sequence of writing units.

Many teachers find it helpful to encourage students to create a "Goals, Plans, and Reflections" section at the back of their writer's notebook, where they collect material and tools related to their goals. If a writer decides that she can work more on leads in her argument writing, she might, in this section of her writer's notebook, tape duplicated copies of a few leads that she especially admires and then annotate them to detail what exactly the mentor writers have done. Then, alongside that, she might "mirror-write" matching leads. If she has a page or two of her notebook designated for work on leads, she could also list the specific strategies she aspires to use and add the page numbers from her notebook to show where she has used those.

While students work on their self-assessments and their goal sheets, say, "Let's make these public, so that you can study what other writers have designated as work they can do well and work they need to work on. You might look over at one of your classmates' goals and say to yourself, 'Hey, he needs help on something that I can do well. I can help him with that.' Or 'He sits at my table. We can work on this together.' Hold yourself accountable to not just improving your own work, but to also supporting the work of others. Say, 'If I have a skill, it's my responsibility to help my classmate who needs help with it. That's how I'll be a good member of this writing community. So, who can I support?'"

COACH STUDENTS IN USING THEIR GOALS WITH PURPOSE, TO IMPROVE

It will also be important to help students think about how their use of time changes once they have deliberate goals in mind. The goal is to improve student agency, so students learn to work for long stretches of time toward goals they have decided matter. We've found it's possible to explicitly coach students toward agency. You might say, for instance, "It is time for you to get started on today's writing time, but before you go, will you think, 'What goals will I be working on?' Once you've brought your goals to mind, will you ask yourself, 'What do I need to have out in my work space to help me accomplish what I want to do?' Think about your writing space as a workbench in your garage. If you set out to accomplish a goal at that workbench—to build a birdhouse—you need your tools nearby. It's the same with writing."

You will need to tell students that it's not only their work space that will look different because they are working toward goals—the actual pages on which they are writing will also look different as well. When writers hold themselves accountable to meeting certain goals, they are not apt to spend writing time just writing, writing, writing, and their pages reflect their new work habits. Let's say that a writer is working on transitions, and after writing a paragraph she realizes that the transitions she's used make her piece sound sort of dull. Perhaps, for example, she thought she was doing right by adding in *first* and *next* and *after that*, but more recently she is interested in handling transitions with more finesse. She may devote a page or two of her notebook to collecting more artful transitions: "The sky was just growing dark when . . . " "It was dark out, and some stars were twinkling when . . . " Then she might tape a flap on top of each existing transition, rewriting the first efforts. There may be draft one, draft two, and draft three of these transitions. This means that a writer's volume of writing will be a bit different than before.

After your students work for ten or fifteen minutes, you could use voiceovers to remind them to work in goal-driven ways to deliberately get better at the goals they have set. You might say, "Writers, can I stop you? I just stopped by Rob's desk to ask what he was doing, and he said he was rereading his writing and asking, 'Am I accomplishing my goals?' Rob's got a great idea. Right now, would you each stop and ask that question? 'Am I accomplishing my goals?' Reread to see, and if you're not, ask, 'What tools can I use to do so?' You can use your mentor text or lists around this classroom or your partner or someone else near you to help. Right now, make plans for what you will do."

Of course, this is just one image of this kind of instruction; your classroom will have its own culture and feel. No matter what, though, have in mind that your goal is for students to learn to work hard. In Malcolm Gladwell's *Outliers* (2011), when he looked at the conditions that led to extraordinary success, the unifying factor was that someone gave the student an opportunity to work hard. Peter Johnston, in *Choice Words* (2004), also reminds us to cultivate a language of independence over a language of obedience. All of this adds up to helping students see what it means to take charge of their own writing growth.

If Students Are Only Doing Minor Revisions, Address This Directly

When you look at students' efforts to ratchet up the level of their work, you may find that they are all doing extremely minor revisions—using carets to add a word, using little fragments of torn Post-its to add a descriptor. If your students seem to think revision is just tinkering, you'll want to address this immediately. It's essential that students engage in meaningful revision, the kind that generates lots of new, stronger writing. You want students to see as much potential for revision from assessing their writing and using checklists as you do.

Perhaps you'll go to one table where this is going on. "Gaby, I notice all these little broken up bits of a Post-it all over your draft, with a word or two written on each fragment. What's going on?" you might ask. She will presumably explain, "I'm revising," or "I'm doing that . . . " and she'll point to an item on the checklist. You could then counter this with "What you're doing is not revising. You are tweaking your writing, fixing up little mess-ups. This is work that a writer does, but usually it's the very last thing a writer does—before releasing the piece to readers. It's tidying up for the company. It is a long way from revision."

If you say this so that others at the table overhear it—which is always a good idea—and then you turn to look at the work others are doing, you'll probably see that Gaby is not alone. You can ask one of the others, "What are you doing?" When my colleague did this recently, the students at the table readily said, "I guess I'm fixing it up." One of them covered his paper, and my colleague pointed out, "It's nothing to be ashamed of. Put it out, loud and proud like Cooper just did." Then she asked the kids to grab a ream of paper from the writing center so they could get ready for revision, not fixing up.

One way to fire kids up for major revision is to suggest they look around at what others are doing and "copycat" whatever they like. "Steal it," you can say. "Copy it! If someone's got a lead and you think it would work great in your story, just rewrite it, plugging in the name of your character, the way the sky looked for your character, the action your character was doing."

Another way to fire kids up to do ambitious goal-driven work is to point out that anything on the checklist is just the start of a goal. Imagine a student is aiming to write a lead that shows what is happening, and where. He reviews his lead and finds no mention of setting. He now has two choices: he can do the minimum—add the setting into the start of the story—or he can become a master of setting, weaving it throughout his story, making a ladder of drafts to show more and more sophisticated ways to add setting. Help young writers understand that making any one thing better affects the whole draft. If writing a good ending requires that the writer build on the main points of a text, then it is incumbent on her to make sure there *are* main points and that these are highlighted throughout the text. You'll want students to say things like, "A little diddly repair won't seriously improve my writing." One student, for example, added transitions to her piece by just adding *also* in three places. Tell about that student as a way to rally your students to aim for much bigger revisions.

It is through all of this work that students' skills will continue to develop. When I work with teachers I often say to them, "If your students' writing skills are not visibly, dramatically improving after a few weeks of instruction, you are doing something wrong." When you provide students with constant opportunities to write, and when you actively and assertively teach into their best efforts, their development as writers will astonish you, their parents, the school administrators, and best of all, the students themselves. Powerful writing instruction produces visible and immediate results: the stories, petitions, speeches, and essays that students produce become far more substantial and significant, revealing the young authors' ideas in ways that make parents, community members, and the students themselves sit up and take notice.

Coaching students into holding high expectations for their own work and to working hard to meet these is no small goal, and it is obviously extremely difficult teaching. Yet is it not worth every ounce of energy we can muster?

Chapter 6

Tracking Data

On-the-Run and Formal Record-Keeping Systems

WHILE YOUR STUDENTS devise goals and systems for keeping track of their progress, you will want to do the same. Of course, this will be exponentially harder for you than for them because you need to keep track of goals for all your students, as well as for yourself. Who was it who likened teaching students to leading a school full of minnows? In today's world, you not only need to lead that school of minnows, but you also need to keep accurate records of each minnows' progress!

If you are anything like the teachers I know best, you are probably constantly on the prowl in search of more efficient and helpful systems for record keeping. You have probably tried your hand at half a dozen systems and found to your dismay that not one of them turns you into the hyper-organized person you long to be. I know that for myself, no system keeps me from having little Post-its adhering to every surface of my life, as well as new notes in my cell phone, each containing a very special reminder of something that needs to be done sometime, somewhere, somehow. There's no foolproof system. Record-keeping systems are as individual as the teachers who create them. What works for one teacher will not work for another, and all record-keeping systems are like relationships: they take work.

DEVISING A RECORD-KEEPING SYSTEM FOR YOURSELF

There are some goals that I recommend you aim toward when devising a plan for yourself. An effective record-keeping system will allow you to:

- Hold yourself accountable to teaching in ways that have traction.

- Collect and consolidate large-scale data, so you can see patterns and trends across a class (or all your classes) to teach whole-class and small-group instruction in response.

- Track an individual writer's progress, seeing evidence of growth (or lack thereof), so your upcoming work with that writer can be informed by what you see and so that writer knows you are attending to his progress.

- Help writers track their own progress toward goals by teaching them to record what they are learning, what they are working toward, and achievements they've made.

HOLD YOURSELF ACCOUNTABLE TO TEACHING IN WAYS THAT HAVE TRACTION

Writing makes learning visible. One of the most powerful things about teaching writing is that you are able to make a covenant with students. You can say to them, "I'll teach you some things, and if you try these things and work hard, your writing will become visibly better before your eyes—and it will become better in just a few weeks." The results will be evident between the preassessment and the postassessment, and they'll be evident just as you turn through the pages of a student's work.

That pledge ensures not only that your students will learn in leaps and bounds, but it also ensures that you will as well, because there will be times when you teach, and the results come in just as you hoped. Bingo! The kids' work improves before your eyes. Sure, there will be some students who need reteaching, but still, there will be times when the results for most of your students provide concrete evidence that your teaching worked. Continue on course. Then again, there will also be times when your teaching doesn't yield the expected results. Your students' writing stays equally mired in the same problems. In that case, you'll need to respond.

First, check those expectations. Remember that no one week of teaching will allow all students to master a skill. If you teach a lesson on structuring and you see visible progress, but many of your students are still not at grade level standards, you can still feel great about the results of your teaching. Your intention is not for students to improve miraculously so that overnight, they all perform at grade level standards. Your goal is progress, and that progress should be visible. That's all. And sometimes there won't be progress. The good news is that when you look at the results, when you study your students' work, you will be given the feedback you need to improve that portion of your teaching. Perhaps the results aren't there. Then you know you messed up, or we, your curricular guides, messed up. So you will alter something: reteach with more power and fidelity, tweak your methods, choose different examples, speed up or slow down. You will, in any case, do something differently, and again, you'll keep your eye on the results.

For this cycle of continuous improvement to happen, the first and most important thing is that you need to regard your students' progress (or lack thereof) as feedback on your teaching. This means that if your students' literary essays are not structured well, instead of thinking, "My students are really dense about structure," or "This curriculum doesn't teach structure," you need to say to yourself, "I haven't taught structure well enough yet." Then you need to think about how to alter your instruction. A word of caution: don't feel that you need to engage in perfect assessments to harvest this benefit. You can formally assess just a sampling of students and still harvest the sorts of insights I am discussing, especially if you have 150 middle school students under your charge.

COLLECT AND CONSOLIDATE LARGE-SCALE DATA SO YOU CAN SEE PATTERNS AND TRENDS AND TEACH IN RESPONSE

Collecting on-demands from all your students at regular intervals across the year will not be the hard part of these assessments. After all, the writing that your students do on an assessment day won't be very different than the writing they do on any other day.

The challenge, instead, will revolve around scoring the work from students in cases when you are teaching writing to 150 or more middle-schoolers! This is not a problem that I can solve, but I can share with you solutions that others have devised. In some schools, the decision is made that teachers will take it upon themselves to carefully and personally score a random sampling of students' on-demands, while also channeling all students themselves to self-score and peer-score using the checklists and/or rubrics. Because students never know which papers the teacher will score and because teachers are especially looking for improvement over time, there will be fewer reasons for students to inflate their scores at any one point in the year (if they do, it could look as though their writing abilities actually lag as the year unfolds). Of course, if scores are used in punitive ways, this system is less apt to be effective. A final option is for you to score quickly, eyeballing student work in relation to the benchmark texts. While this might be a good option after you have internalized this assessment system, it is not what we recommend for your first year or two working with these assessments, because there is much to be learned from a diligent and exacting process of annotating texts to score with precision.

In any case, once you have gotten scores for all your students' work, you will want to consolidate the scores so that you can look across them and see patterns that can inform your teaching. Although it is time-consuming to do this, some teachers find it helps to create a chart with all of the traits that have been assessed across the top, and with students' names running down the side of the chart. Then they can go back and fill in the score each student's writing received for each trait.

The important thing is that you will want to mine your collection of scores to find students who would benefit from similar sorts of support. For example, you might locate four students who especially need help with something—say, structure—as shown by lower scores in many of the traits that reveal that skill. (In this instance, the lead, transitions, ending, and organization all contribute to the category of structure.) Meanwhile, you might also decide that many of your students could use help with spelling and punctuation. In this fashion, you divide students into a few groups.

Depending on the number of students in your care, you might find it helpful to use an Excel spreadsheet and a color scheme including red, yellow, green, and blue. In this color scheme, red is below expectations, yellow is approaching, green is meeting, and blue is exceeding. Type student names down the left-hand column, allowing three to four rows for their data entry points for the year. Next to their names, create a date or month column to track when the assessments were completed. Then list the categories assessed (leads, transitions, etc.) across the top of the spreadsheet. When your spreadsheet is complete, add a filter to the top row with the categories. This will enable you to group your kids for small-group instruction.

It will be important to devote some of the workshop time to need-based groups, and you may decide to keep a few groups consistent over a stretch of time. Your data can set you up to do this. For example,

Conferences:		Week of:

Structure

- **Overall:** An important moment / reads like a story
- **Lead:** What, where + clues to the problem
- **Transitions:** Time words–same (meanwhile), flash back/forward (early that morning, later that day)
- **Ending:** Closure connects to main part of story and to what character said, did, or realized
- **Organization:** Paragraphs: separate by parts or time, when a new character speaks
- **Organization:** Make some parts longer and more developed

Development

- **Elaboration:** description, action, dialogue, thinking to develop characters, setting, & plot (esp. heart)
- **Craft:** Show why characters did what they did– include their thinking & responses
- **Craft:** Slow down the heart of the story – add precise details and figurative language
- **Craft:** Use objects or actions as symbols of meaning
- **Craft:** Vary sentences to create pace and tone

Language Conventions

- **Spelling:** Use knowledge of word families & rules
- **Punctuation:** Commas used to set off intro parts or to show talking directly to someone

Other:

Partnerships: Giving feedback by asking questions

Name:	Name:	Name:	Name:
Date:	Date:	Date:	Date:
Compliment:	Compliment:	Compliment:	Compliment:
Teach:	Teach:	Teach:	Teach:
Next steps:	Next steps:	Next steps:	Next steps:
Name:	Name:	Name:	Name:
Date:	Date:	Date:	Date:
Compliment:	Compliment:	Compliment:	Compliment:
Teach:	Teach:	Teach:	Teach:
Next steps:	Next steps:	Next steps:	Next steps:
Name:	Name:	Name:	Name:
Date:	Date:	Date:	Date:
Compliment:	Compliment:	Compliment:	Compliment:
Teach:	Teach:	Teach:	Teach:
Next steps:	Next steps:	Next steps:	Next steps:

Notes:

FIG. 6–1 Sample recording sheet to record student scores from on-demand pieces

if you decide that you will work with a group of writers who need help with organization/structure and also with another group of writers, this time those who need support with higher-level elaboration and development, you might set up a folder for each of those groups, making sure those folders house copies of the on-demand work and the rubric for each student in each group. You can also put into each folder some special mentor texts or scaffolds you develop to help with the particular aims of that group. This will make it easy for you to show students examples of what they have done in their writing, as well as how they can improve.

Another advantage to students working in groups is that on one occasion, you might rally members of a group to help one writer review his work and set goals, doing this work with one group member in such a way that all the members of that group get help doing similar work.

On another occasion, you might channel all the members of the group to look between their initial on-demand writing and the piece they've just written to check that they are improving in whatever goals they've decided to tackle. Of course, most of these needs will not be genre-specific, so members of a group can also look at their goal—say, organization—across several different kinds of writing. These folders would, of course, also house notes you take or observations you make, records of the small-group instruction and of the work writers do in class, so that you can easily recall what you taught and also hold students accountable to actually doing what they agree to try.

One challenge arising from combining your notes into small-group folders is that they won't then be filed in individual writers' folders. Presumably, after the small group has met for a short sequence of times, the group will be disbanded, at which point you'll need to figure out a way to get at least some record of that group work into each of the members' individual records. (No one said this is easy!) Some teachers have used apps for iPads to address this. The Confer app lets you assign students to skills, and then it groups them into small groups and records your notes. Evernote is also a good system for this because you can create a note for each student, photograph his work with your iPad, and then the app automatically tucks this into that student's note.

LOOK BACK AT AN INDIVIDUAL WRITER'S PROGRESS TO SEE NEEDS AND EVIDENCE OF GROWTH

In addition to creating systems that will allow you to see and record the needs of groups of writers, you'll want to have a place to record research and work with individual writers. Again, you will need to decide what is workable, given the size of your student load. No matter what, you will want to be sure that students keep complete collections of their writing, including their sequence of drafts, presumably in a portfolio. Some teachers that are carrying an especially large number of students require that students assume responsibility for a major portion of record keeping, with students recording pointers learned and the plans made after each conference or small group. Those teachers can then look back on the students' records when reminding themselves of prior teaching, studying the notes on a conference or a small group alongside the evidence of the work the writer has been doing. Of course, if students lose their writer's notebook, complete with all those records, that becomes a big problem. Many teachers make binders or folders with a section for each student. And then there are those who keep all of their notes on their iPads or computers—Evernote and Notability are great for that. Whichever way you choose, you will want to be sure that this system enables you to look back at a writer's progress often, so that you can help your writers do this as well. You want writers to get into the habit of expecting that you will follow up on their goals, holding them accountable for actually working toward those goals and improving their writing.

You may find that conferring record sheets can be useful in many ways. They can function as cue cards, reminding you of things you hope to teach writers. If you sometimes aren't quite sure what to notice or teach toward in a student's writing, you can look at where the student is in the learning progression, and record in the margins of your conferring record sheet the work that the student should be tackling. Then, if nothing emerges out of a conversation with the writer, you can use the cue sheet as a reminder of possible topics to address.

When designing your conferring record sheets, you'll need to include enough content from the appropriate checklist to remind you of what you need to teach. Of course, your goals extend beyond the checklist; you are also teaching into writing process, into writerly life, and into social structures that support writing. So you'll also need to make enough room to jot down your observations for a number of students. We've provided you with a few examples of ways you can organize your conferring record sheets, but you may wish to adapt and change them to suit your particular needs.

Because a record sheet like this allows for records of multiple conferences and small groups to be laid alongside each other, it is possible to look across notes, rereading and considering the progress of the writer. You can see the notes about several conferences or small-group meetings at a glance. Another benefit is being able to identify what areas you most frequently address with the writer and what areas tend to be overlooked. For example, you might notice that you've had three conferences about structure with a writer but only one about habits. The writer might need work with structure, but of course, you could support that work through a conference about the writer's process. ("Do you tend to reread your writing and notice your structure, comparing it to the structure of the benchmark text? That would help you.")

7th Grade – Excerpts from Checklist descriptors	Naomi	Juan	Serena	Aidan	Michael	Leicia
Lead — Interested reader / Gave back story / Get reader ready / Clear position / Forecast parts	✓ / • position is unclear	Missing back story / ✓	weak lead	✓ / ✓	used a statistic to support a claim	very interesting interal di! / ✓
Transitions — Linked parts of argument / Made clear whether claim/counterclaim / Ex: *as the text states, this means, another reason, Some people may say, but, nevertheless, on the other hand.*	• repeats same transition words / • no Counterclaim	✓ / ✓ / very clear!	only used "this means" / ✓	Strong transitions / ✓	✓ / ✓	the transition words are strong, but do not link to next idea
Ending — Reinforced and built on main points – made piece cohesive / Reiterate supports, restate points or highlight significance	✓ / ✓	✓ / • does not retiedate	Feels robotic	left reader thinking!	no originality - just repeats word-for-word	✓ / ✓
Organization — The parts arranged purposefully from claim – counterclaim or reason or piece of evidence to another. / Topic sentences, transitions, and formatting (where appropriate) to clarify the structure of the piece and to highlight main points.	attempted / needs work	✓ / no topic sentence in paragraph 2	✓ / somewhat	missing evidence for Counterclaim / ✓	references counter claim movement which conflicts to his structure	evidence does not match up with claim / ✓

Conferring notes for Argument Essay – 7th Grade   Class: 701

FIG. 6–2   This example shows one way you can organize your conference notes by using a conferring record sheet.

HELPING STUDENTS DEVISE RECORD-KEEPING SYSTEMS FOR THEMSELVES

It is not only the teacher who needs to look back on a writer's work and see progress—or lack thereof. Students, themselves, need to be able to do this. Checklists can help students monitor their progress toward goals they have set for themselves, but it is also important for them to monitor their progress toward goals that you and they settle upon through the process of a one-to-one or small-group interaction. If writers are going to be accountable for actually living up to the goals that are settled upon, it is important that those goals are recorded, the aspirations set onto the page.

One way that some students set up such a system for themselves is to designate the final portion of their writer's notebook as a "Goals, Plans, Reflections" section. Allow your students the freedom to invent wonderful ways to demark such a section. Some will simply fold down a page about three-quarters of the way through their notebook, and others will find their own ways to create a boundary. Some students staple their checklist into their notebook as the first page for this section, attaching pictures or illustrations to make it celebratory.

Usually the first portion of this "Goals, Plans, Reflections" section is a reflective piece of writing in which the writer thinks about the collection of goals that he has adopted and his plans for meeting those goals. Talk to the writer about the ways in which you organize your life to support your efforts to live up to a goal. You might say, "I have this ongoing goal to follow a healthier diet by eating more vegetables. One thing I do is keep cut-up veggies and hummus at the very front of my fridge. When I feel the urge to snack, I can grab those quickly, before I am tempted to eat something less healthy. Writers also need to make plans for how to keep their goals in mind as they write." Perhaps one writer decides to write on the top of every page of his entry, "Don't forget to write with periods and paragraphs!" and institutes a habit of doing a quick reread whenever he reaches the end of a page. Of course, periods and paragraphs wouldn't be the writer's only goal, so his other goals will also have accompanying plans. That writer, then, will write all of that into the start of this goal-keeping section.

If your students have a "Goals, Plans, Reflections" section of their notebook, you can use this section as a place to record your conferences and small groups. Depending on your students' ages, you might ask them to write their own records of conferences or you might do this yourself. The important thing, either way, is that students then jot down the page numbers of their notebooks or portfolios on which they've done some of the planned work.

In a conference, of course, it will be critical for you to skim through this goals and plans section of a student's writer's notebook, using it (and the writer) as a tour guide through the work the writer has done. As students tell you how their work is going, you will also want to hold in mind the work you asked the writer to do, the writer's own goals, the previous efforts to meet those goals, and so forth.

Of course, this system has a few limitations. The first is that you will only be able to look at this section when you have a student's notebook or portfolio in hand. Often teachers decide to collect all students' writer's notebooks or portfolios every Monday night (or a particular table full of writer's notebooks every Monday night) so then, as they look through this record of a writer's deliberate practice, they can think about the week ahead.

Whatever system you and your students invent, you can be sure of one thing: you will need to revise it! Your needs and purposes will change, and your systems for collecting data will need to change as well. If your record-keeping system hasn't changed for a while, focus on what information you are getting through it—and ask whether that is still the most pressing information. If not, what information do you need, and in what form can you collect it? Has a colleague already figured this out? If so, what has she tried? With this information, you will be off and running, reinventing and re-collecting, ready to interpret what you've collected to tailor your teaching more exactly to what your students need.

Chapter 7

Teaching Informed by the Learning Progressions

Y OU MAY KNOW the experience of sitting beside a young writer, listening to the student explain what he's been doing while scanning his paper and thinking, "What am I supposed to say?" You know you wouldn't be earning your keep if you simply say, "This is dandy. Thanks for sharing." As you half-listen, your mind races frantically, trying to see, hear, notice *something* that sparks an idea about what you can say to be helpful.

All the talk about catching teachable moments and thinking on your feet works well for teachers who feel as if they are experts in the teaching of writing. Malcolm Gladwell's (2007) bestseller, *Blink*, explains that it is a mark of expertise to be able to make judgments in the blink of an eye. However, the reverse is also true: making judgments quickly is less easy work for people whose expertise lies elsewhere. If you and your colleagues have never received much help in the teaching of writing, it can be challenging to look at a student's text and to know the traits worth noting. And the catch is that you and your colleagues need to teach writing long before you have become experts at doing so. The ability to grasp what a writer is trying to do and to see how to help the writer do that work better (or to tackle something else that is even more important) represents the epitome of effective writing instruction. But this work is not easy, and developing the expertise to do this well takes time.

It helps to know that judgments and diagnoses do not come out of the clear blue sky. Instead, both come from knowing that there are learning progressions that undergird a writer's development. When you give feedback, your goal is to teach the *writer*, not the writing. Before you can give that feedback, you need to place the writer's current work and skill set (what the writer is doing) somewhere on a learning progression. When you give the writer feedback or suggest next steps, you are helping the writer go from where she is on a learning progression toward whatever you believe might be next steps for that writer.

There are, of course, many learning progressions other than those that are central to this book. For example, with experience and instruction, students' writing processes develop, and there is probably a progression that undergirds that growth. Students' spelling develops along a progression. I suspect there is a progression of skills that inform students' abilities to read mentor texts, seeing those texts as exemplars. There may even be a willingness-to-show-initiative progression. It would be a mistake to think that all of a writer's development can be reduced to the three learning progressions that are at the core of this resource.

Still, those three learning progressions are critically important to your writers' development, and they can also help you and your colleagues grasp some deep, fundamental truths about ways to give young writers feedback. It is a big deal for you to grasp that to coach a writer toward next steps, moving the writer from where she is now to where you believe she can get to next, you need to think about that writer's place on a trajectory.

ORIENT YOURSELF TO THE LEARNING PROGRESSIONS AND TO THE PRACTICE OF ANALYZING STUDENT WORK

Before thinking about ways to bring the learning progressions to your efforts to give students feedback, take a bit of time to orient yourself to whatever tool you will use. Say you are using the Learning Progression for Information Writing. Lay it before you and choose a category to focus on. Let's imagine you are a seventh-grade teacher and choose "Elaboration." Begin looking at the grade 6 elaboration category in information writing, then look at the same category for grade 7 and finally grade 8, each time asking, "What is new at this level?"

You'll immediately see a trajectory of learning you'll want to set students along. For instance, in sixth-grade information writing, students might simply incorporate relevant facts, quotations, examples, and other

Growing Elaboration Skills in Information Texts across Grades		
Grade 6	**Grade 7**	**Grade 8**
The writer included varied kinds of information such as facts, quotations, examples, and definitions.	The writer included varied kinds of information such as facts, quotations, examples, and definitions. She analyzed or explained the information, showing how the information fits with her key points or subtopics, including graphics where appropriate.	The writer brought out the parts of the topic that were most significant to his audience and to his point(s).
The writer used trusted sources and information from authorities on the topic and gave the sources credit.		The writer analyzed the relevance of his information and made sure the information supported the major concepts.
The writer worked to make his information understandable and interesting. To do this, he referred to earlier parts of his text, summarized background information, raised questions, or considered possible implications.	The writer consistently incorporated and cited sources.	The writer incorporated trustworthy and significant sources, and explained if and when a source seemed problematic.
	The writer worked to make her topic compelling as well as understandable. She brought out why it mattered and why the audience should care about it.	

FIG. 7–1 This excerpt from the Learning Progression for Information Writing shows how the skill of elaboration is expected to develop from one grade to the next.

evidence to elaborate on their topic. By seventh grade, however, it is expected that these students don't just include varied kinds of information, but they also explain and analyze that information. That is, students must write to show how the information they are citing fits with the key points or subtopics they are writing about. By eighth grade, informational writers at this level are more discerning about the source information they include, incorporating only information that relates to the most significant and key aspects of their topic. Looking across levels can help you assess where students are, and this can inform the teaching you'll do next.

After naming the key differences across a strand of the progression, you may find yourself asking, "What exactly does that look like?" "What does it look like when the writer not only included details and facts but analyzed them?" It's important to know that no one writer will do everything that the progressions call for, but looking at an exemplar or an "up the ladder" text, in conjunction with a checklist, can help you solidify a vision of this work (a vision you'll later share with students). Look at either of the two pieces of that kind of writing per grade level that have been selected as benchmarks. Look also at the teacher-written "up the ladder" annotated texts (Annotated Writing Developed through the Progressions) for that kind of writing. You will find these in Part II of this book.

In the end, taking a bit of time to orient yourself to the progressions, on-demands, and benchmark pieces will pay off in leaps and bounds. Not only will you have a clearer sense of the trajectories of writing that undergird the particular genre you are teaching, but you'll be equipped with teaching points and examples to use during conferences and small-group teaching. Once you've done this work, you are ready to bring these progressions to bear on your teaching.

CONSIDER YOUR METHOD OF INSTRUCTION

Commonly Used Methods of Instruction

- Demonstration
- Explanation and example
- Guided practice
- Inquiry

Grade 7

The writer interested readers with a compelling anecdote and provided background information in the form of historical context.

The Bulldog: A Dog Like No Other

A small dog huddles in a corner, waiting to be released into a giant arena. Though it seems difficult to believe, there was a time when dogs were bred for sport, a brutal sport called bull-baiting. The dogs were trained to clamp on to a bull's nose and to not let go until either the bull killed the dog or the dog brought the bull to the ground (Gray, 1976). Not every kind of dog would have been up to this task. The dog bread for this sport is the dog that we know today as the bulldog. In fact, that's how this dog got its name. Maybe this is also why these dogs have a reputation for being fierce. However, bulldogs are one of the most special dogs out there, for many reasons. There are no other dogs that look like a bulldog, with its characteristic wrinkles. Bulldogs do require some unique care, as does any prized possession, so owning a bulldog isn't easy, but is very, very rewarding. Finally, Bulldogs have a fascinating history, unlike that of any other dog.

The writer developed not just information but also an idea about the information. The author made the claim, and made it clear how the ideas and information in the text would unfold.

I. A Unique and Varied Appearance

The English Bulldog looks like no other. It is a compact dog with a short, smooth coat and a wide head and shoulders. Bulldogs typically have **prognathism**, essentially meaning its lower jaw sticks out beyond its upper jaw. This is also called an underbite. In contrast, dogs like golden retrievers rarely have an underbite. Their top teeth stick over their bottom teeth. Though this condition is not considered attractive in humans, many people find it to be quite adorable on a small dog.

The writer attempted to vary the sentence structure, combining simple sentences with complex sentences.

The writer used a transitional phrase to compare/contrast. Comparisons were used as a way to explain information and the explanation was further supported by text features.

Bulldog underbite

Golden retriever with no underbite

A bulldog's eyebrows are made of thick folds of skin, and it has small black eyes. These small eyes and eyebrows with folds give it the illusion of being angry, though that's typically not the case.

FIG. 7–2 A teacher-written annotated text for seventh-grade information writing

---

Before heading into a conference or small group with the learning progression in tow, you may want to consider the methods of instruction that are available to you. In this series, Chapter 7: "Inside the Minilesson" in *A Guide to the Common Core Writing Workshop*, provides you with a comprehensive overview of the four methods that are most often used for writing instruction.

Demonstration. The predominant form of instruction in writing is demonstration. Using demonstration, you model and narrate the step-by-step process a writer undertakes to do the work. If you want to teach a writer to use comparisons in her informational writing, for example, you might say, "Today I want to teach you that one way information writers give details about a topic is by creating comparisons." Then, you'd demonstrate, showing the student how you do this in your own writing. If your students have not already studied the seventh-grade bulldog piece, you might demonstrate the work you do to make your piece (the sixth-grade bulldog piece) better, showing, in particular, the process you use to rewrite the opening introduction from one that doesn't contain comparison into one that does. "Hmm . . ." you might think aloud in front of the student. "I want to show that even though bulldogs look kind of mean, they are really great pets. I wonder if a comparison might grab my reader's attention? What could I compare a bulldog's looks to?" I'd eventually find my way to the answer, which as you can see from the seventh-grade version of this story, means comparing bulldogs to a curmudgeon. You could then show the student how you craft a sentence using that comparison.

Explanation and example. Rather than demonstrate, you might instead decide to use the explanation and example method. Rather than having students watch as you demonstrate the entire process, you'd simply explain what you hope to accomplish (to use a comparison to grab readers' attention and help them envision a bulldog's face). Then you would show them the example that the writer of the sixth-grade bulldog piece used. After both the demonstration and the explanation and example method, you'd help students to try the same in their writing, coaching them until you feel they are ready to work independently.

Guided practice. Then, too, you might teach through guided practice. In this method, you walk students through the process of using a strategy. You guide students so that they have an instructive experience that they wouldn't have had on their own. As you engage students in the activity, you use clear, efficient prompts to coach them along.

Inquiry. Finally, you might consider teaching through inquiry. This method is particularly effective when you have a strong student sample that students can mine and learn from. Rather than directing students to one particular strategy, you'd be more likely to pose an inquiry question. For instance, you might say, "This writer has done some interesting things. For instance, she is particularly strong at helping us to see that bulldogs are not only brave, but loving animals. Let's look closer at her writing and try to figure out how she did this." In this example, students are left to figure out what the writer has done and how they could do similar work.

No matter which method you choose, you'll want to make sure you have the tools you'll need to teach clearly and efficiently. The assessment tools that accompany this book will provide you with all you need.

The Power of One-to-One Conferring as a Method of Instruction

The writing workshop was once known as "the conference method of teaching writing" because of the central role that conferring plays in any writing workshop. Don Murray, the Pulitzer Prize–winning writer who is regarded as "the father of writing process," once did a study to determine which of his eighty students felt they learned more in his two-hour graduate courses and which thought they learned more in ten-minute writing conferences. Murray wondered whether the students' preferences would differ based on their gender, their experience level as writers, or their success in the course. Interestingly, what he found was that none of those extenuating circumstances mattered. The students all felt the ten-minute writing conferences were the most valuable form of instruction.

In one-to-one conferences, you move students along trajectories of skill development, like those laid out for you in the learning progressions that accompany this book. Teaching writing requires that you provide students with feedback, and that feedback will be far more potent if you first listen to student intentions and assess their work, and then give the feedback face-to-face, rather than trying to shoehorn the feedback into a scrawled note at the end of the paper. Then, too, the feedback is most potent if you give it when writers are in the midst of writing and rewriting, rather than after they've declared a piece done. If you pull a chair alongside a writer as she works on her lead, for example, and then discuss what she is aiming to do and the strategies she is using, that writer will be able to incorporate your suggestions immediately, on that piece of writing. Of course, the real goal is for that writer to apply that feedback to other drafts, produced on other days.

Working one-to-one with a student creates opportunities for you to provide tailored instruction in response to what you see the student doing, rather than simply giving the student a summary of your whole-class minilesson or of the day's work expectation. Ideally, conferring and small-group instruction provide you with a time to teach responsively, inventing instruction on the spot to address problems you may not even have known existed previously. Don't be surprised if you find yourself wanting to broadcast some of this responsive instruction more widely, through mid-workshop teaching points, instructive share sessions, and newly invented minilessons.

Let's consider a specific example. Perhaps, in a personal narrative unit, a handful of your sixth-grade students are writing chronological stories that seem to lack depth. As mentioned earlier, many of your minilessons will be as applicable to those students as to your most proficient, but there will also be times when the day's minilesson is more appropriate for more proficient writers. For example, one of your minilessons might emphasize that writers manipulate time to bring forth meaning—slowing down moments that reveal something integral about a character or the series of events. This teaching point *could* be a minilesson for all of your students, but it won't resonate with students who have not yet decided what, exactly, they want to convey through their story. For these students, the most essential teaching will be

CONFERENCE WITH A MIDDLE SCHOOL STUDENT USING THE CHECKLIST

Let's look specifically at an example of how the checklists can help inform and clarify your teaching in a conference. I pulled my chair alongside eighth-grader Nate as he worked on the first draft of a literary essay about *It's Kind of a Funny Story* by Ned Vizzini. While he worked, I looked back on my notes from prior conferences with him, reminding myself of the work we'd been doing together. I scanned his writing notebook, too, quickly evaluating his writing and checking to see that he had been working on the skills and strategies I'd taught him. The last time Nate and I had a conference, we worked on citing specific and relevant details to support his argument. His current writing showed evidence that he had, indeed, been practicing this work. In fact, I immediately noticed that Nate had cited an abundance of evidence to support his idea that art brings mental stability to the main character of the novel, Craig.

I looked at Nate's writing against the eighth-grade Argument Writing Checklist and considered my teaching possibilities. In his introduction, Nate introduced the idea that Craig's drawings "symbolize his mental stability, and how he copes with stress." Nate then provided evidence to support this idea, citing examples from the text where Craig talks about how drawing makes him happy and gives him relief from the problems in his life. However, I immediately noticed that Nate did little to unpack and explain these quotes to the reader. Yes, Nate stated an idea and provided evidence, but he didn't work to analyze that evidence or show how it supports his claim. Curious about Nate's intentions, I asked, "What are you working on as a writer?" Nate explained to me that he was trying to prove this idea about art as a symbol for Craig's well-being, and that a big part of this work was mining the text for quotes that show Craig's positive relationship with art. "I found a lot of evidence to back up my theory," Nate said, "so now I'm drafting my body paragraphs. The first paragraph is about how art helped Craig when he was younger, and the second paragraph is about the role it played when he went to the hospital." I glanced at the eighth-grade checklist, focusing on the expectations for elaboration.

By eighth grade, argument writers are expected to not only incorporate "trustworthy and significant sources" (in this case, textual evidence), but to analyze those sources. Specifically, students are called upon to analyze "the relevance of the reasons and evidence for [their] claims . . ." and help the reader "to follow [their] line of argument."

helping them to determine the message, lesson, or emotion they most hope to convey in their personal narratives. When you pull a chair alongside these writers, it will be important to address whatever is most essential for them—and this may or may not connect to that day's whole-class teaching. What this means is that a fair portion of teaching involves figuring out where a student, or a group of students, are in the journey toward proficiency, and then teaching that student (or those students) to progress from that point onward. Always, your small-group work and your conferring will show students how to do something first with scaffolds and supports, and then, soon afterward, with independence.

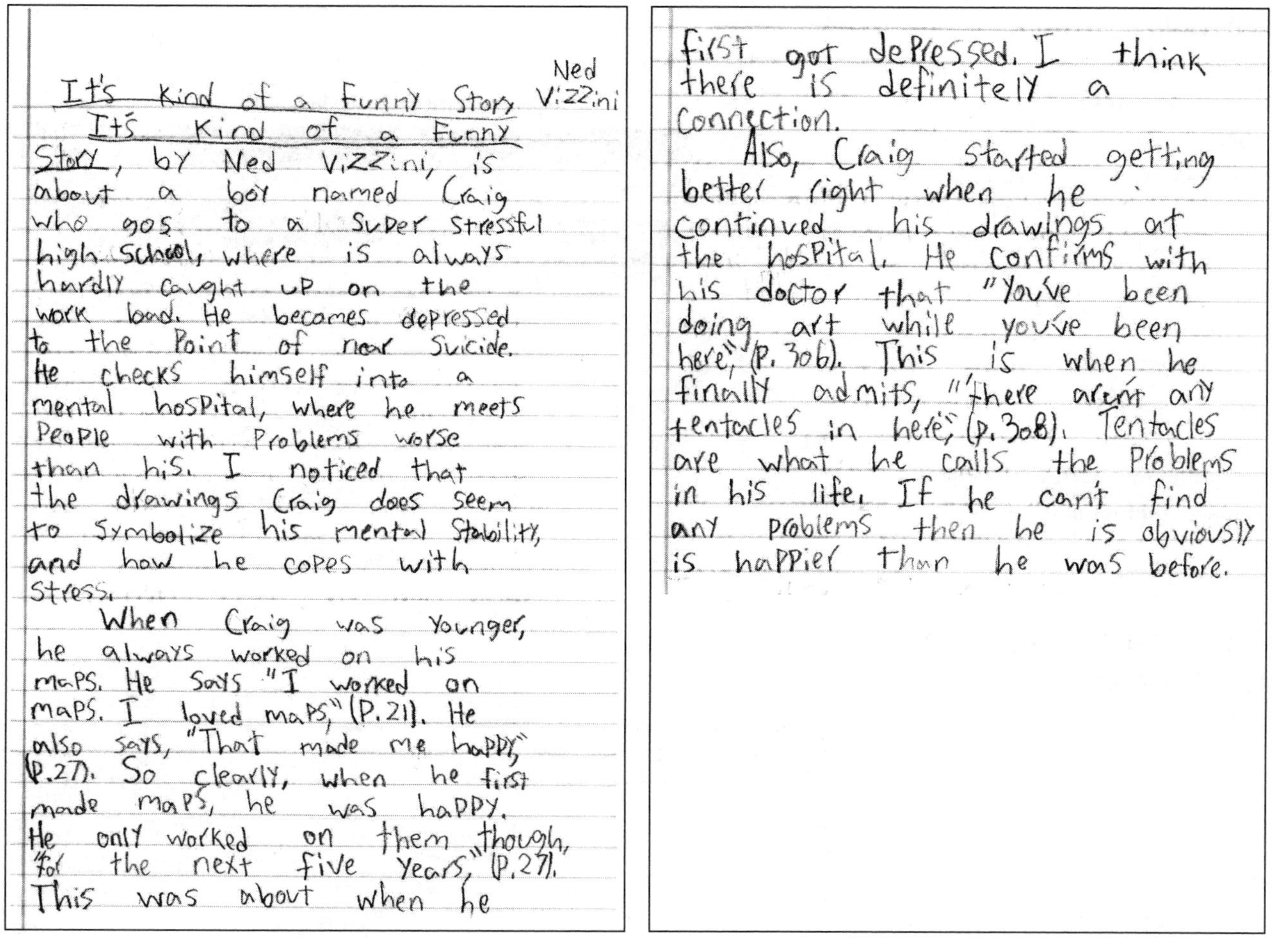

It's Kind of a Funny Story   Ned Vizzini

It's Kind of a Funny Story, by Ned Vizzini, is about a boy named Craig who goes to a super stressful high school, where is always hardly caught up on the work load. He becomes depressed to the point of near suicide. He checks himself into a mental hospital, where he meets people with problems worse than his. I noticed that the drawings Craig does seem to symbolize his mental stability, and how he copes with stress.

When Craig was younger, he always worked on his maps. He says "I worked on maps" (P.21). He also says, "That made me happy" (P.27). So clearly, when he first made maps, he was happy. He only worked on them though, for the next five years "(P.27). This was about when he

first got depressed. I think there is definitely a connection.

Also, Craig started getting better fight when he continued his drawings at the hospital. He confirms with his doctor that "You've been doing art while you've been here" (p.306). This is when he finally admits, "there aren't any tentacles in here" (p.308). Tentacles are what he calls the problems in his life. If he can't find any problems then he is obviously happier than he was before.

FIG. 7-3   The beginning of Nate's essay draft

Bingo! I had found the teaching that felt perfectly suited to Nate and his intentions as an argument writer. After complimenting Nate on the work he had done with text citations, I laid the checklist between us and turned his attention to the Elaboration section. We read it over together, and I explained the implications that this set of standards might have on his writing. "Nate, as I looked over the argument checklist, I zoomed in on elaboration as a place where you might be ready to take some next steps. You've already done this bit about incorporating sources," and I pointed to the places in his essay where he had quoted directly from the text. "You and I know that each of these quotes are meant to support your idea that drawing comes to symbolize mental stability for Craig. But part of your job as an argument writer is to make the connection between your evidence and your claim clear for your reader. You can't just plop in a quote and hope that readers will understand why it is there. Instead, you need to explain and analyze the quote, pointing out the specific ways in which it supports your argument. Let's try a bit of this together using your first body paragraph."

Beginning with Nate's first quotes about Craig's love of mapping, we practiced adding onto the citations with an analysis of their meaning and an explanation about how the quotes relate back to the overall point Craig is trying to make. To support this work, I prompted him lightly with phrases like, "This proves . . ." and "This is relevant because . . ." Soon enough, Nate was ready to revise his work, adding in the elaboration we had rehearsed orally. When I felt Nate was ready to proceed independently, I reminded him once more of the teaching point and left him with a copy of the checklist with his new goal circled.

Before we pause to extract transferable principles from this conference, let's step into one more classroom and quickly conduct another conference with a sixth-grade writer.

CONFERRING WITH A MIDDLE SCHOOL STUDENT USING A LEARNING PROGRESSION AND BENCHMARK TEXTS

Let's imagine another scenario in which the checklists inform instruction. This time, notice how I helped a sixth-grade student learn from benchmark pieces that incorporate the kind of work this student had yet to tackle.

As I drew a chair alongside Simone, I noted in my conference records that the last time I had talked with her, she had shared her intention to include more varied, concrete, and specific evidence in the body paragraphs of her essays and to make any revisions in the margins of her paper. Before we even started talking, I noticed that she had done just that. I asked her what she was working on, and she explained her work to me, pointing out how she had even added a variety of evidence to her essays, including facts, quotations, and definitions. I complimented her on doing that work and for keeping track of her goals and her progress toward them in a special section of her notebook she'd dedicated to this purpose.

As Simone showed me the varied evidence she was now putting into her essays to support her reasons, I noticed that the link between the evidence and her support was not entirely clear, which was also the case with other students' writing. I'd already decided to address this in a whole-class lesson soon and considered raising it here, in a way that might produce a story for the upcoming lesson.

Argument Writing Checklist

Grade 8

	Structure	NOT YET	STARTING TO	YES!
Overall	I laid out an argument about a topic/text and made it clear why my particular argument is important and valid. I stayed fair to those who might disagree with me by describing how my position is one of several and making it clear where my position stands in relation to others.	☐	☐	☐
Lead	After hooking the reader, I provided specific context for my own as well as another position(s), introduced my position, and oriented readers to the overall line of argument I planned to develop.	☐	☐	☐
Transitions	I used transitions to lead the reader across parts of the text and to help the reader note how parts of the text relate back to earlier parts. I used phrases such as *now some argue, while this may be true, it is also the case that, despite this, as stated earlier, taken as a whole, this is significant because, the evidence points to, and by doing so . . .*	☐	☐	☐
Ending	In the conclusion, I described the significance of my argument for stakeholders, or offered additional insights, implications, questions, or challenges.	☐	☐	☐
Organization	I organized claims, counterclaims, reasons, and evidence into sections and clarified how sections are connected.	☐	☐	☐
	I created an organizational structure that supports a reader's growing understanding across the whole of my argument, arranging the sections to build on each other in a logical, compelling fashion.	☐	☐	☐
	Development			
Elaboration	I brought out the aspects of the argument that were most significant to my audience and to my overall purpose(s).	☐	☐	☐
	I incorporated trustworthy and significant sources and explained if and when a source seemed problematic.	☐	☐	☐
	I analyzed the relevance of the reasons and evidence for my claims as well as for the counterclaim(s) and helped the reader understand what each position is saying. I made sure all of my analysis led my readers to follow my line of argument.	☐	☐	☐

Knowing that this is a hard concept to teach, I turned to the column in the elaboration section of the Learning Progression for Information Writing, where Simone had focused her work, and saw that a next step might be to teach her how to unpack, or discuss, the evidence she had gathered.

This was both within her reach and the kind of teaching point that would set her up for next steps. Rather than illustrating the point by doing this work for Simone, demonstrating by "writing" aloud to show her how she might unpack the evidence in her first body paragraph, I opted to teach using example and explanation. By making this decision, I knew that I would leave her with challenging work and the ensuing sense of confidence that comes from tackling such work.

I pulled out a benchmark piece of student writing—one that was a level higher than the sixth-grade level at which Simone was working—and explained to her how the author of the benchmark piece did the unpacking work that Simone still needed to learn to do. Specifically, I pointed out that the author had analyzed and explained her supporting information, showing how it fit with the key points she was making. I also gave Simone another benchmark text to study on her own, so that she could identify other instances where this writer had done what she, herself, had been trying to do.

I reminded Simone of the prompts that writers use to unpack their evidence, which were recorded on a chart the class had been using during reading time. I suggested that she retrieve one of the small copies of the chart I had placed in an envelope at the bottom of the chart. Many teachers place envelopes containing copies of the charts they make, at the bottom of each chart in their room. Their students know that they can take these small charts and store them in their own notebook or in the "Goals, Plans, Reflections" section at the back of their notebook. The particular chart I referred Simone to contained prompts such as "This shows that . . ." and "The important thing about this is . . ." and "This connects back to my idea that . . ."

I considered suggesting that Simone do this unpacking work on all the essays she'd written during the unit, and I knew I might suggest that later. But I decided for now, instead, to channel her to regard unpacking evidence as just one part of a larger endeavor. I pointed out that what she was actually doing was making her essays more idea-based, more thoughtful. And I suggested that once she was done with this, a future step might be to reexamine her introduction and conclusion, making sure they each highlighted for readers why the idea she was positing was so important. I pointed out that when she was ready to tackle this work, the benchmark pieces of writing I'd given her and the checklists, with their descriptions of more advanced beginnings and endings, would be useful resources to get her started.

PRINCIPLES OF CONFERENCES THAT MOVE STUDENTS ALONG A TRAJECTORY IN A LEARNING PROGRESSION

You may have had conferences like these, or you may be setting out this year to do more conferring in your classroom. In the conferences with Nate and Simone, the checklists, learning progressions, and benchmark texts undergirded the conference, but they didn't do all the work for me. If you think carefully about what I did, you'll spot a few things I believe are key principles to any conference that draws upon the learning progressions.

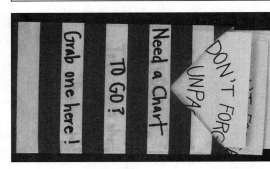

FIG. 7–4   This class chart about unpacking evidence also includes a pocket with small copies of the chart that students can keep in their notebooks as a reminder to include evidence in their writing.

Follow good practices of conferring well.

First and most importantly, both the conferences continued to follow a pattern. Let's look at the conference with Simone as an example, but we could look at either one. I did not approach Simone with the checklist in hand and set to work, checking off what she had and had not done, and then proceed to tell her what the checklist required her to do next. Instead, I followed some theories about conferring well. I began by asking, "What are you working on as a writer?" and by researching her progress myself. I took in information on several aspects of her writing, noting volume, structure, and the amount and kind of elaboration. I mulled over all this and especially took note of the goals she'd been aiming to accomplish. Then I responded by complimenting her in a way that I hoped was instructive and, in this instance, extended that compliment into a teaching point that came both from the checklist and from a close study of her as a writer.

Carefully analyze student work and assessment tools.

Second, although at first glance these conferences "come from" the checklists and learning progressions, in reality, they came from my attentive study both of the students' work across time and of the assessment tools themselves. For Simone, it was fairly straightforward to see that the work she'd already done represented a step forward on the learning progression, and I knew that supporting those steps would set the stage for me to help her progress a bit farther in the same progression. That conference was easy. There was low-hanging fruit because she'd done one part of this work and not the next part. Voila! I had my conference. Nate presented a similar situation. He had set his sights on the incorporation of evidence—an important and worthwhile goal—but needed help understanding that evidence requires analysis to be truly compelling.

With some students, when I coach toward mastery, I notice what the writer has just accomplished and then suggest we tour the writer's work to see if he is doing that item on the checklist repeatedly. Has this new work become part of the writer's usual repertoire? "Mastery," I point out, "doesn't come from just doing something one time! Far from it." I will often suggest a writer look not only to see whether he did a particular kind of work, but also to see whether he is doing that work repeatedly, and has gotten better at it through practice.

My point, then, is that although the checklists and learning progressions are powerful tools, they are what you make of them. It is crucial that you (1) recall all you know about participating in a good conference, letting the assessment tools be resources you draw upon, but not letting them take over the conference. It is also crucial that you (2) read the items on the checklist and your students' work with great attentiveness and teach toward mastery.

Avoid the checklist mentality.

The third principle is this, and bear with me: your conferences using checklists should actively help students avoid "the checklist mentality." In all of life, it is the case that powerful tools can be used in ways that are powerfully good or powerfully bad, and this is certainly true of the checklists that you put into your students' hands. Those checklists, if used mechanically, not thoughtfully, can make a piece of writing antithetical to everything that the writing process represents. Instead of focusing on meaning and audience and craft, writers can work solely for the goal of complying with a checklist. Horrors!

I saw this, for example, when I drew close to Sam and asked him to tell me about his writing work. He explained that he'd written an entry—a page-long information text about economic inequities, and that he was now "revising" it. I was tickled to hear that he'd no sooner finished an entry than he'd turned around in his tracks to reread what he'd written. I asked to see his efforts. When I peered at the work, all I could see were five or six sentence-long inserts peppering the page, each of which said the same thing: "This shows things aren't equal." Huh? The additions added very little. Sam explained that he'd used the checklist to assess his writing. He'd seen that he needed to relate his information to his claim, and he was almost finished making his way down the entire page, referring back to the claim after each drop of information.

Of course, Sam isn't alone. There is something about a checklist that can make a person think the entire goal is to get yourself into a position so that as soon as possible, you can scroll down that checklist going, "Check! Check! Check!" So I talked with Sam about how these checklists are meant as sources of goals that writers can use to make their writing *worlds* better. I pointed out that Sam was right that in information texts, it is important not only to include information, but also to *unpack* that information, and that doing so often involves analyzing ways the information relates to central ideas that are being forwarded in the text. Then I suggested that getting strong at doing this particular work—and any work—involves studying exemplars, using the insights gleaned to try this work again, getting feedback, then trying again. We talked about how Michael Jordan tried to take his weak jump shot and make it a strength—and how Sam could do the same. He could tackle the challenge of analyzing the chunks of information he had chosen to include in his texts. Soon afterward, Sam zealously studied several nonfiction articles and then created lists of all the ways that the authors of those texts could set him up for success.

Principles of Conferences that Move Students along a Trajectory in a Learning Progression

1. Begin by looking back at old conference notes, checking to see what was taught previously and how the student is advancing toward those prior goals.

2. Research your student's work, asking questions like, "What are you working on as a writer?" and studying the student's work yourself.

3. Don't limit your research to one area—gather information about what the student is doing as a writer in many areas of the progression.

4. Compliment the student in a way that will allow her to do *more* of what she is doing well. This includes praising successful work, naming it clearly, and showing the student an example.

5. Use checklists for grades above and below the students you are working with, to target your instruction to the student in front of you.

6. Incorporate the use of checklists into what you already know about good conferring.

7. Avoid developing a "checklist mentality," wherein students narrow their work as writers to simply comply with the checklist. Help students see checklists as a source of goals writers can use to grow in substantial ways.

8. Guide students to understand the reasons behind each aspect of the checklist, for example, *why* a writer would add dialogue.

USING THE ASSESSMENT TOOLS TO TEACH THE PROCESS OF SELF-IMPROVEMENT

The examples I've shown so far will help you imagine one way you can use learning progressions, checklists, and the leveled student- and teacher-written pieces to move students along in their skill development. But you can also use these tools to teach your students independence and to help them find motivation and energy for writing.

For example, you may feel that during writing time your kids work almost as if on autopilot, aiming to produce the expected page or booklet a day. It may seem to you that the only strategies kids actually draw on without your nudging them to do so are the strategies they use to generate content, to come up with something to say. And it may seem to you that this is part of a larger pattern of your kids being more concerned with producing enough writing than they are with making sure their writing is improving in dramatic, palpable ways.

You may for a time, then, decide that a goal for all of your conferring will be to recruit students to work with zeal toward an effort to deliberately improve themselves as writers. If you do so, you might decide that one of your hopes will be to spread the mantra, "Try again, try again, try again." To make self-improvement efforts the hottest thing in town, you might suggest in many conferences that writers find someone else who is strong at something they're trying to do, and then suggest they ask that writer to mentor them, showing them instances when he's done that work. As part of this, teach writers that when they are trying to learn from another author's technique, it is perfectly fine to "echo-write," or use someone else's writing as a model for your own. For example, in a conference you can show writers that you can borrow from what someone has written, just changing the words into your own words but maintaining the sentence structure. You could say, "If Simone has unpacked the evidence in her essay in a way that you want to do as well, you can echo-write. You can note how many sentences she has for information, how many sentences for unpacking the information, and you can either emulate or even borrow the phrases she uses to shift from providing to discussing evidence. Of course, you will substitute your book and your ideas." You could add, "Seek out Simone as a professor of unpacking evidence. She can confer with you and give you pointers."

In your conferences and small groups, you can emphasize that a writer's notebook needs to be regarded as a workbench, as a place to use all of your tools, trying things one way, then another way, until you write something just right. You might remind students that you've been saying this, and then say, "But earlier, when I watched you working, I noticed many of you didn't have your tools on hand. One of the defining features of a workbench is that the tools are all nearby. If you're working on getting better as a writer—not just producing the same ol' stuff—then you need tools!

"So, writers, like you, I'm going to write some new opinion entries in my writer's notebook. Because I want these entries to be a lot better than the ones I wrote earlier this year, I'm not just going to pick up my pen, think up an entry, and then let my pen fly, hoping for the best. Instead, I'm going to take the time to set myself up, so that this piece of writing is apt to be the best I've ever done in my whole life.

"The first thing I get out is the Argument Writing Checklist. I'm going to make sure that I'm holding myself accountable to *all* these goals, so I'll put the checklist right beside me as I write. Then the next thing I'm going to have out is the benchmark text that is sort of my goal. I also want to get small copies of some of the class charts, and I am going to turn them into checklists that I can follow as I work on my essay."

Then you can point out that once you have your tools on hand and you have a goal, the work involves trying something, trying it again, and trying it again. In the conference with Simone I described earlier, chances are that she'll rally around the challenge I gave her, finding a way to unpack the evidence in her essay body paragraphs. But if I don't teach otherwise, she'll do that job and think she is done. So it is important to be ready to remind students that when Michael Jordan wanted to get good at jump shots, he didn't just do one and then check it off his checklist. No way! He did literally thousands of jump shots. He studied people who did them well. He studied his own jump shots. He pushed himself over and over to do better, better, better.

After showing students the way you use your writer's notebook as a workbench, trying something over and over until you get it right, you can look over students' efforts to do the same. What you will see as you watch students work is that their tendency is to do something once and then just tweak that effort with the teeniest, tiniest revisions imaginable. Say to those students, "Try this. Stop. Draw a line under the work you just did. Now, try it again, in another part of your writing, or in another, totally different way. This has got to be hard work. Ask yourself, 'How will I make this even better?'"

On the next round of conferences, you can push students a bit more. You might pull up next to a student and say, "Is this really your best? What do you think? I think you can do better. Look, right here in your published piece, you tried out this same strategy and it worked so well. I don't see that in the piece you're working on now. I know you can do better than this."

Over and over you will want to push your young writers to think and care about how they write, not just what they write. You will say things like, "Remember, to hold a reader's attention—to get that reader to keep reading your story—you have to pay attention not just to *what* you write but to *how* you write. So as you try this again, think more. Craft purposefully. Ask yourself, 'Am I writing in a way that will get my reader to want to keep going?' If you're stuck, all around you are resources. You have charts full of reminders you can draw upon. You can find passages in books that inspire you. You can use checklists that detail ways to get better, and consult benchmark texts that illustrate those expectations, and you can work with other students whose work you can reference—and whose techniques you can try out in your own writing. Get going!"

SUSTAINING STUDENTS' DEVELOPMENT THROUGH SMALL-GROUP WORK

Think about the times in your life when your learning curve was sky high. Chances are good that you didn't learn alone. You may have been part of a team, a work group, a seminar group, a study group, a think tank, a research project, or a staff. There are lots of ways to work in learning relationships with others. No matter the configuration, chances are good that you didn't outgrow yourself by working alone.

There are many reasons to teach your students by leading small groups. First, this is the only way you will be able to reach many students, often. Think about the amount of feedback students are accustomed to when they play video games. They tilt their handheld, they push some buttons—and then bing, bing, bing!—the feedback comes, right then and there. If your teaching and your feedback are only reaching kids every two weeks or so, that's just not enough. You'll have the data right at your fingertips telling you that there are a few students in your class who have begun using metaphor and could profit from thinking about the risk of writing with mixed metaphor. Instead of working with each one of them individually, repeating yourself each time, you can opt instead to convene them in a small group.

Many teachers seem to worry about small-group instruction. "I haven't planned how it will go," they tell me. But the truth is that you can lead a small group in a fashion that is very similar to the way you lead a one-to-one conference.

You will recall that after looking for a moment at Nate's work, I supported the way he'd begin to do something—and encouraged him to do it in a more sophisticated way. That's a fairly easy conference to lead—and an equally easy small group. You could tell a small group of students that you noticed they had places in their books where they used quotes from texts to prove their point, and to illustrate that you could show them an example of where Nate had done so. You could say to the members of the small group, "Could you locate quotes from your own writing where you've attempted to argue the validity of the claim you are making?" After the members of the group have located those places and shared them with each other, you could tell them—as I told Nate—that including evidence isn't enough. Instead, writers need to analyze that evidence, explaining to readers how it relates to and supports the argument at hand. You could ask all the members of the group to start with one quote and think about how they'd explain its relevance to their reader. Then, as I did with Nate, encourage them to orally rehearse their elaboration with each other.

Presumably, as students work in these small groups, you might at times suggest they work with each other in partnerships. So in the small group described above, students could work in pairs to rehearse their elaboration before writing. Here are a few suggestions to help you lead these groups effectively.

Although some of your small-group instruction will resemble the teaching point and guided practice portion of a conference, it is important for you to think broadly about small-group work that can support students' progress toward goals they set—or you help them to set. Don't imagine that all these groups are variations of one-to-one conferences, done to scale.

For example, suppose a group of your seventh-graders are writing essays that already resemble the seventh-grade benchmark texts and you want them to experience some enrichment, yet you need to spend some time helping kids who are struggling. Why not convene that small group that is already working at grade level standards and challenge them to try their hand at writing like eighth-graders? You could give them the benchmark text for the grade above and a tiny portion of the checklist for that grade, perhaps printing that portion of the checklist so that the relevant items on it are printed onto teeny-tiny labels, and you could suggest the group study the benchmark, annotating it with those labels when they see that text exemplifying those traits. Then you could suggest they work together to revise one of their

Making Your Small-Group Work Effective

- Plan to begin these small groups by talking for a minute or two, and then give students five or six minutes to work (alone or in pairs) as you circle among them, coaching into one writer's (or one partnership's) work after another. Then talk to the whole group for another minute, before you leave to work with the next small group. Allot the vast majority of the time for students to work and you to coach into their work.

- During the initial talk to the members of the small group, direct. You have called them together because . . . why? Chances are good that you'll be saying, "Because I think your writing will get a lot stronger if you . . ." That is, don't mince words. You are teaching them about ways to improve, about next steps. Out with it.

- When you coach into students' work, you will usually use lean prompts to provide running commentary or quick guidance that influences their work, often said into an ear as the writers keep working. "That's it, keep writing, don't stop." "Remember to be detailed." Aim for your commentary to lift their level of work a notch but not for it to solve all the problems you can possibly find.

- When you coach into group members' work, remember that you are teaching toward a goal or two—and pursue that goal. Don't be sidetracked by every other possible goal. You aren't trying to make the writing perfect; you are trying to help the writers practice more skilled work on the one trajectory you've chosen to address.

- If you refer to a mentor text, try to be sure it is already familiar to the writers. Now is not the time to introduce a brand-new text.

- Encourage the writers to do whatever new thing they are doing not just once, but repeatedly. This may mean doing that work on a series of pages or in a series of paragraphs, but it may also mean that the writers do that work in one text, then return to other, already completed, texts to do that same work while revising those texts.

essays—jointly—making it show the relevant characteristics of that eighth-grade benchmark. Afterward, of course, they could each work independently to revise one of their own essays in the same fashion.

Then again, you could work entirely differently with those seventh-graders who are already working at standard. You could tell them that one of the ways to really know a skill deeply is to be able to teach that skill to someone else. Partner them up with classmates and ask them to figure out ways to teach those classmates to do the work they've learned to do. You could also suggest that youngsters make teaching tools to remind themselves and others of what they've learned—starting with using snippets from their own essays as illustration. One sixth-grader recently reported to her mother, a teacher in the school, "Today I called a small group on conclusions and worked with them. They're coming along pretty well."

Alternatively, you could let your seventh-graders know that the checklist is actually far from complete. There are lots of qualities of effective essays that are not included on the checklist. You could provide them with a small stack of essays, written by published authors, and ask them to study those essays and to agree on a few characteristics of those published essays that they think should be added to the checklist, and then suggest they revise their work to reflect those characteristics.

Small groups can be equally effective for students whose work is well below grade level standards. You could ask those students to act as mentors to teach others what they know, but in this instance, they may be teaching younger students. For example, if some of your middle-schoolers are writing information texts that aren't as well structured as they need to be—with paragraphs and pages that contain information unrelated to the subtopic—you might suggest that a few of those students work as mentors to help younger students at the nearby elementary school learn how to organize their first efforts at writing chapter books. There is no better way to learn something deeply and well than to be asked to teach it to others. These middle-schoolers could reread the younger students' writing, notice instances when information is misplaced, and consider ways to help their young charges reread critically. They could search through nonfiction books to find some simple ones that have a very clear structure, bringing those books to their tutees.

Another option would be to encourage these students to help each other make tools to remind themselves and each other of the particular goals they've adopted. If their goal is to reread their drafts to check their structure, for example, they can make little reminder signs to attach to the bottoms of their pages or placards to prop up on their desks.

Rufus Jones, the great American Quaker, once said, "I pin my hopes on the small circles and quiet processes in which genuine and reforming change takes place." I've often shared that quote with teachers, reminding them to band together with colleagues to outgrow their own best teaching. But the truth is that small circles and quiet processes are as necessary for students as they are for you and me.

Chapter 8

Supporting Transference of Learning across the Content Areas

TEACHING FOR TRANSFER. What does this phrase really mean? *Teaching for transfer* means teaching so that students are able to apply what they've learned to a range of new situations—and it is critically important. The goal of instruction must always be to help learners bring a set of skills into the whole of their lives, not just to the exact same kind of writing under the exact same conditions under which they first learned it. For kids, that most certainly involves bringing writing and reading and thinking skills across the divide that separates the writing workshop from social studies, science, and reading. It is critical that students leave writing workshop, backpacks and books in hand, knowing they carry a wealth of skills that can be applied to new writing situations: to the informational reports they'll be asked to write about force and motion, to explanatory writing in math, to essays about the death penalty or the Emancipation Proclamation.

Although it seems obvious that students should be applying their writing skills to content areas, educator Grant Wiggins points out that learners typically will not use all their prior learning or even necessarily recognize how the new situation could call for prior learning. Although students don't naturally transfer skills from one setting to the next, you can teach them to do this in relatively short order. And the payoff for bringing writing skills across the curriculum is not just that students' writing in those other disciplines will become better. It's also that their knowledge of those other disciplines will become deeper (D. Reeves), and their skills and knowledge of effective writing will become deeper, more flexible, and more expert. In fact, brain research has shown that if people repeat the same learning tasks but do them under different conditions, their learning goes up. You know this for yourself: when you are able to draw on the same knowledge and skills in different situations, to put your knowledge or skills to work in a variety of ways, those skills become deeper. If you want your students to master writing, then a surefire way to do this is to help them transfer their writing skills into other domains.

So, it will be critically important for you to use the same checklists, learning progressions, and benchmark writing samples to support students' writing, whether it is during the writing workshop or writing across the curriculum. This also means collaborating with the colleagues that share your students across the day. Does the social studies teacher know what students are learning in writing, so that he can cue students to applying those skills? Consider planning for gradewide meetings in which you share the appropriate writing checklists and charts you used with your content-area counterparts. The chart that once taught students to organize argument essays in writing workshop can now hang in the social studies classroom, helping students prepare for debates related to historical topics. The checklists students used to assess their essays can now be used, in a similar fashion, to self-assess the content-area essays they craft. By quite literally carrying the teaching tools from one classroom to the next, we show students the ways their writing skills are applicable across the domains.

It will be important to stress to content-area teachers that the intent is not for social studies or science to *become* writing workshop. You can be sure that they have sets of plans and curricula they use and love, and asking them to switch that around to teach *your* curriculum would be unreasonable. Instead, emphasize the idea that this is not about teaching, but about transference and reinforcement. That is, by simply asking students to take a stance and write a quick essay in social studies, you have strengthened their argument writing skills *and* given them the opportunity to think more deeply about the content. By asking students to write a narrative from the perspective of a red blood cell, detailing its experiences as it travels the human body, you help them to improve their narrative writing skills, all the while requiring an abundance of research and in-depth understanding of the content. Essentially, it is a win-win situation for all educators involved!

USING THE LEARNING PROGRESSIONS, CHECKLISTS, AND ON-DEMANDS TO TRANSFER WRITING SKILLS INTO THE CONTENT AREAS

As mentioned above, one easy way to get this work started is to use the same checklists to assess writing, whether it is produced in one subject area or another. You will find that new insights rain down on you and your colleagues once you begin to do this. Your first step might be to have students do a quick-write in the content areas. If you are the teacher, you'll plan for this. If not, you'll want to coach your colleague through this process. You'll want to create a situation that is comparable to on-demand writing in the writing workshop. First, consider what students know well. You won't want to research or the acquisition of new knowledge to get in the way of their writing (similar to the way you ask students to write about topics of personal expertise during informational and argument on-demands), so think of a topic that students have already studied.

Let's suppose for a moment that in social studies, students have been studying Westward Expansion in the United States. You (or your colleague who has been teaching this content) might ask students to lay their texts and other resources before them, open their notebooks, and you might say, "Consider the following question: Did settlers have the right to travel west and conquer new land from the Native Americans as they did? Write an essay defending your claim." You might hang the same chart of reminders you did for the argument on-demand, reminding students to write an introduction, state their claim and reasons, and so on. This needn't only be something done in social studies. Consider science and the recent reclassification of Pluto from a planet to a dwarf planet. Perhaps you ask students, if they have studied this, to produce an argument explaining their point of view on this. Should Pluto remain categorized as a planet? Ask students to defend their opinion, address counterclaims, and cite the resources they've read throughout their argument. The next-generation science standards place a premium on writing evidence-based arguments, as do leaders in history education who advocate for teaching history not as a long catalog of facts but as an interpretation.

For now, let's imagine that you decide to look between students' on-demand essay writing and an essay they've been asked to produce in social studies. If you teach both these subjects, this process will be easy enough to coordinate. If not, you'll want to set aside a time for you and the social studies teacher to collaborate and study student work.

The second step is for you and your colleagues to look between the on-demand writing from the writing workshop and the social studies class on-demand. In our example, you would compare on-demand writing samples from the ELA classroom with the samples of argument writing students did about Westward Expansion in the United States. Use the learning progressions and checklists to measure students' mastery of skills in both writing contexts. Then ask this question: "To what extent have these students transferred their skills as argument writers from language arts to social studies?" If students have not been asked to do this before, it is possible that you will see a disparity in quality between the work done in the two different contexts. Study the differences between the work students did in the two different areas of the curriculum. Are there reasons you can pinpoint that might account for any disparities? What are the most common issues you see? Collecting this sort of data will be essential as you consider the teaching that remains and the writing skills that remain unused.

Next, consider asking the students themselves to look between the writing they produced in those two different settings. It will be especially helpful if you give students checklists, learning progressions, and charts from the unit to rely on, so that they can check to see what they did and didn't do in each context. You might go further and decide to collect the data on this in a more systematic way and to track improvement over time, or to at least engage every student in this sort of self-assessment and tracking of improvement. Chances are good that improvement can be buckle-your-seat-belt dramatic, so this is a good area for students to be involved in tracking their own progress. Watching themselves improve is a great incentive for students to increase their efforts—and helps turn students from believing that intelligence (and writing ability) is fixed, toward believing that intelligence is the result of hard, strategic, informed work.

BRINGING CHECKLISTS AND GOALS FROM ELA TO IMPROVE CONTENT-AREA WRITING

If you set students up to contrast their writing work in ELA and in social studies and science, they will often come from this work saying, "Wow! I do all these things in my writing workshop on-demands that I don't do when I'm writing in social studies or science!" It will be a natural next step for you to ask them what they intend to do about that gap. Again, this will require a bit of coordination between you and your content-teaching counterparts if students are learning social studies and science in a classroom other than your own. Students will generate lots of ideas, and all—or most—of them will be terrific. They'll suggest they bring copies of their on-demand ELA writing into the social studies and science classes so they remind themselves that their writing should always be at least that good. They'll suggest they use the same checklists to assess their social studies and science writing as they use to assess their work done in writing workshop. They'll suggest they set goals for themselves when writing across the curriculum, spend time planning (even just a few minutes), look at mentor texts—the works!

Of course, the payoff for doing this won't just be that young writers begin to apply the same standards to their content-area writing that they apply to their language arts writing, not that they begin to bring their goal-driven, reflective stance across the day. The payoff is that you, your colleagues, and your students will all end up bringing teaching and learning methods and conversations across the curriculum.

Before long, before the social studies teacher asks his burgeoning historians to write their ideas about, say, whether they would have been a Patriot or a Loyalist, that teacher will remind them that this will be a bit of argument writing. "Prepare for this writing by thinking for just a minute about what you know about that type of writing." It will make a world of difference when students preface their writing in social studies and science classrooms by glancing at one of the examples of argument or information writing we've provided. It will also make a world of difference that when these students write during science, they have the checklist for argument writing, or information or narrative writing, nearby. There is no doubt that students' first-draft attempts to argue for a theory of gravity will be far better for this effort to support transference. And, of course, the same can happen whenever youngsters are given the opportunity to write information pieces in any discipline.

AN EXAMPLE OF TRANSFERENCE FROM ELA TO SOCIAL STUDIES

Over time, you will see that the qualities of good writing from a student's work in language arts also shine through in the writing that student does across her day. And best yet, you will see that a student's work in one type of writing were written in one class period by a student on the cusp of middle school. The Legos piece is an on-demand informational piece written in ELA by Jack. The social studies piece was written long after Jack's teacher, Kelly Boland Hohne, had begun explicitly teaching for transfer and asking students to bring their checklists across the curriculum. Students drafted their social studies piece with the checklist and also with their on-demand informational piece (for Jack, his Lego text) at hand.

In the two pieces of writing that follow, notice the way that the student's style shines through whether he is writing about his favorite hobby or writing a flash-draft in a social studies unit. Both of these pieces of writing were written in one class period by a student on the cusp of middle school. The Legos piece is an on-demand informational piece written in ELA by Jack. The social studies piece was written long after Jack's teacher, Kelly Boland Hohne, had begun explicitly teaching for transfer and asking students to bring their checklists across the curriculum. Students drafted their social studies piece with the checklist and also with their on-demand informational piece (for Jack, his Lego text) at hand.

Legos: A Lasting Legacy

Legos are not just toys. When you build with Legos you make machines. You use your mind. You get lost in the Legacy of Legos.

Getting Started

When you build with Legos you want to start by sorting out the pieces you have. Some people like to sort by color. It's better to sort by what kind of piece it is. Look at them carefully so that you end up with pieces that go together. That way, when you need four pieces that are exactly the same, you can find them quickly.

Color matters less than shape and size. Some pieces are special pieces, with hooks, or wheels or windows. Keep track of these pieces and don't lose them. The wheels will roll away if you tip over their container and you'll never find them again. Same with the tires. Also, pets like to play with Lego pieces, so put your cat or dog in another room. Otherwise just when you want a tire, it will be chewed up.

Building Alone or with Others

It's important to decide if you want to build by yourself or with a friend or with someone in your family. Once, I was building a Lego starship from Star Wars. "Hey, I'll help," my dad said. He sat down on the floor, and reached for the pieces. Snap! Snap! Snap! "Look, it's all done," dad said, handing me the starship. "Great, thanks" I mumbled. Inside, though, I was infurriatted. I've never played with that starship. This year, though, I got the Star Wars Death Star for Christmas. A Death Star is a huge space station, like the one that Darth Vadar used in Star Wars 3. "Will you help?" was the first thing I asked my dad. Its got 3,802 pieces. Theres plenty for both of us to do.

To Keep or to Destroy

One of the hardest desisions is wether or not to take apart a Lego object once you've built it. Picture this: the Death Star is built. All 3,802 pieces are in place. It gleams beside your bed at night. It dominates your room during the day. Everyone who comes over admires it. Do you really want to take that it apart? I doubt it. But if you build a little star ship, after a week, take it apart. You need the pieces to build something else. And it's fun to destroy stuff.

Growing Old with Lego

Legos are not just toys, and there not just for kids. You can visit LegoLand, for instance, and you'll see what adults can build with Legos. You can go to California, or look at their website, to see what you can build with Legos. They can build an Egyptian temple! Youll never be too old for Lego.

When you look at Jack's on-demand writing about Legos from ELA, you can see the traction of instruction. Look at the sixth-grade Information Writing Checklist, and notice what he does independently.

Overall, the piece takes a clear teaching stance. The lead is slim but focused. There is a clear organizational structure. In fact, the organization is not just logical but compelling in how it leads the reader from getting started to getting old with Legos. The sections each make sense and fit with the organizational plan. There are transitions within sections and across sections. Jack tucks in storytelling effectively and brings over storytelling craft, including dialogue and vivid imagery and a sense of drama. Jack also explains expert vocabulary, such as Death Star. As you move down the checklist, you can see clear evidence that this student is demonstrating the skills that were taught in the unit of study and beyond.

Next, when you compare Jack's ELA on-demand to a piece he wrote in social studies, you'd look for evidence that Jack carries some of these skills over. Are the cuing systems and reminders the teacher uses having any effect? Let's look at Jack's early social studies draft, drawing from the research he had been doing in class on castles in the Middle Ages. On this day, the teacher suggested they do a flash-draft, getting down what they know so far about the topic and organizing their writing so that it would make sense to their reader. Writers were explicitly reminded to do their best informational writing, and to have the charts, checklist, and writing done during ELA at hand.

Castles

Castles in the Middle Ages were not like the castles in fairytales. They were built for defense, and they were cold and uncomfortable. Castles are fascinating because of their engineering, not because of their luxury.

Attack and Defense

When attackers began their attack, they would try to take the castle quickly, using all their manpower. They might try to mine under the gate, or use battering rams or catapults. For the defenders, it was awful. Picture this: you could hear, inside the castle, the <u>undermining</u> (undermining was when they tunneled under the floor and into the walls) that was going on. Chip, chip, chip! You would hear the constant sound of the building being chipped away. Who wouldn't cower in fear!? At any moment the undermining might be set on fire, causing the castle to collapse. Morall would decrease especially as it got darker, and hungrier, and dirtier. Eventually there would be no light to see by, as the siege went on. The attackers would use <u>trebuchet</u> or catapults, to demoralize the defenders. Sometimes attackers would use the trebuchet to shoot the heads of their prisoners into the castles.

Information Writing Checklist

Grade 6	Structure	NOT YET	STARTING TO	YES!
Overall	I conveyed ideas and information about a subject in a well-structured text. Sometimes I incorporated arguments, explanations, stories, or procedural passages.	☐	☐	☐
Lead	I wrote an introduction in which I interested readers, perhaps with a quote or significant fact. I let readers know the subtopics that I would develop later and how my text would unfold.	☐	☐	☐
Transitions	I used transitions to help readers understand how different bits of information and different parts of my writing fit together. I used transitions to help connect ideas, information, and examples, and to imply relationships such as when material exemplifies, adds on to, is similar to, explains, is a result of, or contrasts. I used transitions such as *for instance, such as, similarly, therefore, as a result, in contrast to, and on the other hand.*	☐	☐	☐
Ending	I wrote a conclusion in which I restated the important ideas and offered a final insight or implication for the reader to consider.	☐	☐	☐
Organization	I chose a focused subject.	☐	☐	☐
	I used subheadings and/or clear introductory transitions to separate sections.	☐	☐	☐
	I made deliberate choices about how to order sections and about the sequence of information and ideas within and across sections. I chose structures such as compare-and-contrast, categories, and claim-and-support to organize information and ideas. Some sections are written as argument, explanation, stories, or procedural passages.	☐	☐	☐
Development				
Elaboration	I included varied kinds of information such as facts, quotations, examples, and definitions.	☐	☐	☐
	I used trusted sources and information from authorities on the topic and gave the source credit.	☐	☐	☐
	I worked to make my information understandable and interesting. To do this, I may have referred to earlier parts of my text, summarized background information, raised questions, and considered possible implications.	☐	☐	☐

Castles usually had only one entrance, which was often marked by the moat and drawbridge. The drawbridge would connect those inside the castle to the outer world. If the drawbridge were drawn up, attackers couldn't get into the castle.

Comfort

Castles were cold, dirty, and messy! They didn't have any heat, only big fireplaces, which were very smoky. All the heat was right near the fireplace. In the great hall, they would hang tapestries to try to keep the rooms warmer—but it was still freezing. Living in a castle in the Middle Ages was nothing like it is for the princes and princesses in Disney. It was war, discomfort, and tragedy. There was disease lurking everywhere. Always, everywhere, it was dirty.

There was poop too to get rid of. Yuck! If it didn't rain, citizen's "number one" and "number two," would just sit there. It would stink up the place and gong farmers would have to clean up all the poop. They would often spread disease.

Castles were cold and dirty and actually, pretty awful to live in. But they kept you safe!

Glossary

Undermine: when attackers would take mining tools and would literally mine under the castle. They would erect wooden props to hold up the ceilings—and then they would set these on fire and retreat.

Siege: a campaign in which attackers completely surround a castle to cut it off from outside supplies or rescue.

Trebuchet: a tall catapult with a net sling on the end, for slinging rocks or severed heads.

I've read—

Castles
Castle Diary
Life in the Middle Ages: The Castle
http://www.medieval-castles.org/

You could assess for transference by laying the pieces side by side and looking for places where the writer does the same kind of work in each piece. For example, Jack uses embedded anecdotes and images to enliven his writing. In the "Legos" piece, he tucks in a small moment about his father building his starship and another vivid image of the Death Star gleaming in his bedroom. In the "Castles" piece, Jack creates a vivid image of the castle walls being chipped away, with an invented small moment that brings the reader inside this scary moment. The storytelling that Jack probably learned in a narrative unit, practiced in fiction, and then learned to tuck into information writing, is showing up in his information writing now in social studies, to great effect. This teacher should shout, "Hooray!" There is significant transference here.

READING-WRITING CONNECTIONS: USING WRITING CHECKLISTS TO BUILD CLOSE READING SKILLS

The learning progressions that are foundational to your writing workshop and to your students' writing in the content areas will also pertain to your students' reading, as well. When students read their own writing with the checklists in hand, annotating their writing for evidence of ways they've used transitions to show the passage of time, for example, or written an ending that links back to the central ideas in the story, what they are doing is not just writing work. They are also doing reading work—analytic close reading of texts.

The second band of reading standards in the Common Core all ask students to read texts, attending to the language, literary devices, structure, and point of view of the stories they are reading. (Let's think about reading literature for now, but this is also true for reading information texts.) Students are expected to be able to think about the choices authors have made, wondering how the craft of the writing (not the content of it) promotes the central ideas in the story. When you first ask students to do that—say, to read *The Fault in Our Stars*, or *Wonder*, or *Speak*, attending to the choices the author made and thinking about those choices in relation to the central meanings—there is a kind of pause as the students wonder, "What, exactly, does this reading work look like?"

You may be unsure of the answer yourself. It's not that you don't know what this reading work looks like when you engage in it as an adult. This was the sort of interpretive reading you were taught to do in high school or college English courses when you read *Hamlet* and wrote essays about why Shakespeare used this or that metaphor. But it is less easy to imagine how one gets young adolescents to do that sort of intellectual work—and to do it in ways that feel authentic.

If you look to the Common Core for help, you won't find it. The document was written for professionals, and it was written in the discourse of the university, not the middle school classroom. You need to translate that discourse into talk that your students can understand. Here is where the checklists can help.

While you might struggle to teach a student to notice the "connotative meanings of words," or the "structure of texts" when reading *Bad Boy: A Memoir* or *New Moon*, from The Twilight Series, you could ask students to reread their own writing and think about whether they have used carefully selected words in their story. You could even go further and help them to grasp that words have different connotative meanings, making it important for them to choose words with connotations that match their intended meaning. Then you could ask students to reread and think whether they have elaborated upon the important parts of their draft and summarized the less important. The reading and thinking work that writers do as they scrutinize their own writing in relation to their intended meaning puts writers well on the way toward learning to be analytical readers of literature and other texts.

You might even want to suggest that students reread published stories with their own narrative checklist in hand. This will allow them to revisit those published texts with lenses they already know as writers. The writing checklist is a checklist of craft, structure, and meaning, and it can help students unpack authorial choices in the published texts they read.

This method of analyzing published texts through the lens of the checklists is not only for literature. It can also help students transfer their writing skills in nonfiction into close reading of nonfiction. The writer who rereads her own information piece, assessing how her information is organized and conveyed, is much more likely to notice organizing structures in a published text she reads. The reader who has learned to convey technical vocabulary in various ways, and assess her own control of that skill in writing, is more likely to notice and accumulate technical vocabulary in the texts she reads. The writing checklists have turned out to be very helpful for focusing close reading skills.

Chapter 9

Designing Reading–Writing Performance Assessments

BECAUSE THE COMMON CORE STATE STANDARDS call not only for high levels of reading comprehension and writing, but also for the combination—high levels of writing about reading—many school districts are looking for ways to assess reading and writing together. In this chapter, we'll show ways you can extend the performance assessments described throughout this book so they also allow you to assess how well students approach a text, knowing that they will be asked to write from or about that text in an on-demand assessment. You'll see that the principles informing the reading-writing assessments remain the same, as do most of the goals for students' writing. The inclusion of reading adds a new dimension, however, and poses new challenges.

We've created a performance assessment system that began as a Teachers College Reading and Writing Project endeavor, centered around extending our writing assessments so they could also be used to assess writing about reading. This endeavor eventually became a project that has been informed also by SCALE (Stanford's Center on Assessments for Learning and Equity), ETS (Educational Testing Service), NCREST (National Center for Restructuring Schools and Teaching), the NYC Department of Education, and the United Federation of Teachers. We've included examples of the resulting performance assessments in Part II of this book. Other examples are available on the Teachers College Reading and Writing Project website (readingandwritingproject.com). You are welcome to use these at no cost, and can do so knowing they benefit from input by many knowledgeable people.

From the start, we knew no single performance assessment could assess all the reading or the writing standards. It is appealing to find a way to assess many things at one time, and we agree with Doug Reeves and Mike Schmoker in *Focus: Elevating the Essentials to Radically Improve Student Learning*, who suggest teachers home in on the standards they want to assess, selecting ones that have leverage across many disciplines and that are critical for success in upcoming grades (2011). But we have always known that an attempt to conflate reading and writing assessment will have "costs" as well as benefits.

When a student doesn't do well, for example, how is the teacher to know whether the problem came from the student's inability to read the text or her inability to write well about it?

SELECTING THE READING LEVEL YET ALLOWING FOR DIFFERENTIATION

Nevertheless, we began by creating a performance assessment for grades 4–8 to assess students' ability to read informational texts and write text-based arguments. For students to write an argument that draws on central ideas and key details in information texts (College and Career Readiness reading anchor standards 1–3), those texts need to inform a discussion about a question or issue. The information texts students read should push them to take a position, to argue for a claim. This meant that we needed to collect short texts that pose conflicting, yet compelling, ideas. That would push readers to take a position, drawing on the texts to do so.

You will recall that when assessing writers, we must be able to see if a student is able to do work well above her grade level. This means that we wanted to compile a text set that allowed sixth-grade readers to do work at the eighth-grade level. For example, although weighing the credibility of sources is above sixth-grade expectations, we wanted the text set to allow for the possibility that the reader could demonstrate the skill to do so. To allow for this, the text set we compiled needed to contain enough information about the sources so that readers could conceivably critique those sources.

Remember, the central challenge in developing these assessments is that the assessment tends to conflate reading and writing. That is, to assess CCSS levels of reading, it is important for students to be asked to read a grade level complex text. On the other hand, if a student cannot read that text, then he will also not be able to do the writing on that assessment, even if his writing skills are actually well above grade level. In other words, if the student cannot read that level of text, the assessment fails to provide a window onto his abilities to write. And the entire point of a performance assessment is to gain a window onto what students can and cannot yet do.

We studied what others have done when conducting assessments that conflate reading and writing, and we've found that oftentimes, others have attempted to resolve this challenge by providing large amounts of scaffolding to students, usually through extensive whole-class and small-group work on reading. In many performance assessments, students work in small groups to create T-charts or other forms of notes that set them up for their writing about reading. They discuss the topic together before writing about it. This way, students who can't independently read the texts are at least able to produce some writing based on their co-constructed notes.

For us, it is absolutely a priority that teachers keep an eye on what their students can do *independently*, so that instruction supports and extends students' true abilities. We think it is less than helpful when the performance assessment disguises the true issues—such as students' inability to read texts. Therefore, the commonplace solution of embedding the performance assessment into a whole sequence of class work—and therefore allowing students to rely on classmates' comprehension and note-taking rather than their own—was not an option for us.

We imagined two possible solutions. One was to develop a ladder of assessments that each contain grade-specific text sets and writing prompts, with the idea that a teacher will use running records or some other record-keeping system to estimate which of these leveled texts is apt to be appropriate for any given youngster. This allows students to work within their zone of proximal development and to move toward more demanding text sets after mastering more accessible ones. The other solution, which is the one we in fact devised, involved making text sets that contain not only grade-specific texts, but also texts that are either well below grade level and/or are videos. Ultimately, we decided to include one text that was below grade level and accessible, as well as one text that was at grade level, so that we could monitor which texts students used in their writing—and so that all students had an entry point for the writing task. We also used digital texts such as videos for readers who needed special amounts of help, with the intent that digital texts would make the assessment more inclusive, engaging, and useful for some English language learners and other novice readers of English. (When these assessments have been given to scale across New York City schools, some schools didn't have the technology to show videos, so this component of the performance assessments has sometimes been changed so that teachers read aloud a text instead.)

Remember, meanwhile, that we also wanted to be sure that each text offered different perspectives on a controversial topic. In sixth grade, for example, students encounter a text set containing a video, an easier print text, and a more difficult print text, with each offering not only different information, but also different points of view on whether or not pets should be allowed in classrooms. The video explains how dogs reduce stress in the classroom. One article provides many reasons for keeping pets in classrooms, while the other article takes a clear stance against it. These texts (or the titles of the books) are available on the Teachers College Reading and Writing Project website (readingandwritingproject.com).

DECIDING ON CONTENT, CONCEPTS, AND CURRICULUM

Another decision we wrestled with was whether or not it would be helpful to embed the task in grade-specific content. Should seventh-graders, for instance, write about a social studies topic that is common to many seventh grades? In our work with schools across the nation, we see a great variety in the social studies and science curriculum content. Nonetheless, there are some topics that almost every city and state adopts in each grade. More problematic, however, was the discrepancy between students' knowledge base that would factor in if we assessed their abilities to embed information from texts on topics they already know into their writing; students who had studied a given topic especially deeply, with a particularly skilled teacher, would appear to be more capable than those who had received a less intensive curriculum. For this reason, we focused on texts and tasks that were not apt to be central to content studies in a school and yet were still representative of the discipline. For example, seventh-graders who are working with our *Units of Study in Argument, Information, and Narrative Writing* learn about competitive sports for kids within an argument unit of study and, for a portion of the unit, write to defend the many pros, cons, and nuanced issues related to this topic. Alternatively, in a performance assessment available to teachers on our website (www.readingandwritingproject.com), students are channeled to read and then write about bottled water and whether or not it is a better option than drinking from the tap. At the end of Part II of this book, you will find a sample on-demand performance assessment prompt for writing and reading. Whether within a unit of study or for a one-day assessment, we found that it is often helpful to isolate a topic, thus isolating students' reading and writing skills more clearly.

Of course, it has also been important to make the work as engaging and motivating as possible. ETS has done extensive research that shows that too often, assessments intended to test higher-order skills are really testing engagement and stamina. If kids aren't engaged, they perform poorly, and this produces a false assessment of their skills. In the on-demand writing assessments, students were able to select their topics, thus increasing the likelihood of engagement and comfort with the topic. We didn't have that option in this instance. Instead, we chose texts, issues, and questions for the performance assessment that our experience showed us students would find engaging. We found that gross topics did the trick, as did ones that students knew a bit about (but didn't necessarily have entrenched views on). We also found that topics that might appeal to certain students (such as sports) would give an unfair advantage to those with deep prior knowledge. Therefore, we only selected sports-related topics that allowed closer to equal access for all students, such as the issue of concussions in contact sports and pressures around competitive sports.

To increase engagement and also to illuminate learners' abilities to transfer and apply skills to real-world situations, we created a scenario that would position students to envision their audience and purpose. For sixth-graders, for example, the task is to imagine that the principal of your school is deciding whether or not to allow pets in classrooms. Students are asked to "imagine that you are writing an essay to send to the principal, clearly stating one side of this argument in a convincing way and supporting that claim with strong evidence you've gathered in your research."

MAKING THE ASSESSMENTS PRACTICAL TO ADMINISTER

As we set out to decide on the parameters of the task we'd ask of students, we immediately recalled the advantages we've seen from having streamlined and efficient writing performance assessments—the on-demand tasks we ask of students at the beginning and end of each unit. This allows us to conduct those assessments repeatedly, thereby keeping an eye on growth over time, which is essential to inform instruction. From the start, our intention was to keep this assessment as similar to the writing assessment as possible, and certainly to make it brief. However, because the task must involve reading texts at varied levels and representing different sides of an issue as well as writing an argument, we knew from the start that this would require at least two class periods. As an aside, let me acknowledge that some people imagine an ideal performance assessment might be a long-term project that grows out of a month or two (or an entire school year, with a few checkpoints). Although long-term projects are important and deserve to be assessed and celebrated, it is problematic when they are regarded as reflections of students' independent abilities. In grades K–6, certainly, if not at every grade, long-term projects are presumably the result of lots of teacher and peer support. If performance assessments are being used as reflections of teachers' abilities to teach, then certainly there is a risk that teachers will become overly invested in raising the quality of these projects, helping students produce work that is well beyond anything they can do on their own. Such performance assessments could influence writing instruction so that it aims merely to raise the level of a given piece of writing—without teaching the writer anything lasting. For these reasons, it was important to us to design writing-about-reading performance assessments that could be accomplished in two or three class periods.

Our goal right from the start was to create a lean assessment so that teachers would be more likely to insert it into their pacing charts without stress. The most major revision we made between the first and second year of innovating these performance assessments focused on pacing and efficiency. In the first year, because we wanted a range of texts, students read three to five texts (or were read several). Most grade levels included a video as one text. Teachers reported back, however, that the assessments were taking more than two periods to give and that students had more information than they really needed to write well—and more than teachers could assess easily.

Two revisions came from this research. The first was to eliminate asking students to create a written summary of each text, and to ask them instead to answer more pointed questions that directly addressed the relevant reading standards—in this case, standard 1 in reading informational texts, which asks that, by middle school, students are able to cite the evidence that supports explicit and implicit interpretation of the text. The advantage to this was that it took students less time to produce, and was also easier for teachers to score. The loss was that no longer could teachers determine what level of text students struggled to summarize; however, we have other, better reading assessments to assess that skill.

The second revision was to cut back on the number of texts students encountered and the length of each so that the entire assessment would take no more than eighty to ninety minutes (two class periods). Otherwise, we'd be assessing stamina more than anything else, and also it would be too burdensome for the teacher in the pacing of the year. After all, we wanted teachers to be able to give this assessment twice to monitor progress.

We also needed to revise the directions we gave students based on the writing they produced after each completed task. For example, we once asked them to write about a subject they cared about—and every student selected one of the "subjects" they were studying at school! Another time we provided a word bank of literary terms and suggested that students use some of these terms to describe the craft that the author of the text used, and students treated this like a Mad Libs game, stringing together random terminology into nonsensical responses. For a long while, our directions led students to produce writing that was not a fair sample of the work we knew they could do. It took countless revisions to home in on a prompt that reliably set students on course to produce the work samples we need to assess their development.

DESIGNING YOUR OWN PERFORMANCE ASSESSMENTS

There is much to be learned from piloting performance assessments in nonfiction reading and writing such as these. So that you can begin your own work at a higher level, here are two key principles that we learned from what is now four years' of research and innovation, research that included taking multiple drafts of assessments through pilot studies, assessing student work in grade level and cross-grade think tanks, revising texts and tasks to study results, looking at rubrics with experts such as Ray Pechone, and studying the skill set needed for writing arguments with experts such as Deanna Kuhn from Columbia University and colleagues from CBAL (Cognitively Based Assessment of/for/as Learning) at ETS.

- Presumably, you will be assessing skills that have enduring importance—that are important in the fall and in the spring, in one grade and in another. As you develop the performance assessment, answer the questions "What evidence will show that students have learned the essential skills/knowledge?" and "How good is good enough?" The thinking that you will do will involve the backward-design approach, in which you conceptualize an end goal. This goal should be one that you believe is worth teaching toward.

- Once you begin to think about what good work entails, you'll quickly find yourself thinking about how to engage students in doing this work so that you have work enough to assess. Before you fall headlong into that work, pause to think about the form that your performance assessment will take. The questions revolve around the degree of standardization and the length of time involved.

STUDYING THE RESULTS OF PERFORMANCE ASSESSMENTS

Once you've scored a piece of writing with a reading–writing rubric, you've only just begun the interpretive work necessary to determine next steps for the student. Really, you have a new set of questions: Did the reading get in the way of the student's ability to write with voice and authority, thereby weakening the lead and conclusion? Did the need to pull quotes from the reading interrupt the student's interpretation of the provided text as a whole? These are predictable questions that will demand putting this assessment next to other examples of the same student's work, as well as working with the student in a small group or conference to further confirm where the breakdown was, and then quickly moving to strengthening that area.

Study the work that these performance assessments yield to ask your own questions. Do you decide to have inquiry groups in your school on this topic? Are you considering teacher performance? Do you want to know how students are doing with these skills before the state test? Do you want to compare this kind of writing across content areas?

Although some people continue to support the "let a thousand flowers bloom" approach that was popular in the 1980s, increasingly there is widespread agreement that if the goal of performance assessments is to lift the level of teaching and learning, one of the most important ways for this experience to be as educative for teachers as possible is for it to channel teachers and students into shared conversations about student work. Through those conversations, some teachers come to realize that others are comfortable with entirely different levels of work. It is helpful for teachers to give students a common task on performance assessments, and then, even more importantly, to assess students based on common expectations.

Once you have carefully examined and studied the results of your performance assessments—and after those shared conversations about student work—you can begin to use these results to develop and adopt a curriculum with confidence, based upon what the evidence shows you. You will have the information you need about what students have yet to master and how to begin addressing their needs.

As Michael Fullan has pointed out, the problem with education today isn't resistance to change, but the existence of too many changes, uncoordinated with existing systems and with one another, implemented in superficial or ad hoc ways—a frenzy of efforts made in the hopes of finding some sort of magic solution. The truth is, there is no simple program to install that will be that magic solve-all, but the solution is well within your grasp. If used with persistence, dedication, and honesty, the tools in this book will help both you and your students self-assess, collaborate with other learners, learn from feedback, and work collectively toward clear and challenging goals. By engaging in this persistent cycle of teaching, observing, and thoughtful response, you will have found that magic solution—a process of continuous improvement in education.

The Assessment Tools

All the assessment tools are also provided on the CD-ROM, including some additional materials for grades 3–5 and 9.

Learning Progression for Argument Writing

STRUCTURE

	Grade 3	Grade 4	Grade 5
Overall	The writer told readers his opinion and ideas on a text or a topic and helped them understand his reasons.	The writer made a claim about a topic or a text and tried to support her reasons.	The writer made a claim or thesis on a topic or a text, supported it with reasons, and provided a variety of evidence for each reason.
Lead	The writer wrote a beginning in which she not only set readers up to expect that this would be a piece of opinion writing, but also tried to hook them into caring about her opinion. The writer stated his claim.	The writer wrote a few sentences to hook his readers, perhaps by asking a question, explaining why the topic mattered, telling a surprising fact, or giving background information. The writer stated his claim.	The writer wrote an introduction that led to a claim or thesis and got his readers to care about his opinion. The writer got his readers to care by not only including a cool fact or jazzy question, but also by telling readers what was significant in or around the topic. The writer worked to find the precise words to state his claim; he let readers know the reasons he would develop later.
Transitions	The writer connected his ideas and reasons with his examples using words such as *for example* and *because*. He connected one reason or example using words such as *also* and *another*.	The writer used words and phrases to glue parts of her piece together. She used phrases such as *for example, another example, one time,* and *for instance* to show when she wanted to shift from saying reasons to giving evidence and *in addition to, also,* and *another* to show when she wanted to make a new point.	The writer used transition words and phrases to connect evidence back to her reasons using phrases such as *this shows that . . .* The writer helped readers follow her thinking with phrases such as *another reason* and *the most important reason.* She used phrases such as *consequently* and *because of* to show what happened. The writer used words such as *specifically* and *in particular* to be more precise.
Ending	The writer worked on an ending, perhaps a thought or comment related to her opinion.	The writer wrote an ending for his piece in which he restated and reflected on his claim, perhaps suggesting an action or response based on what he had written.	The writer worked on a conclusion in which he connected back to and highlighted what the text was mainly about, not just the preceding paragraph.

Learning Progression for Argument Writing

STRUCTURE

Grade 6	Grade 7	Grade 8	Grade 9
The writer explained the topic/text and staked out a position that can be supported by a variety of trustworthy sources. Each part of the text helped build her argument, and led to a conclusion.	The writer laid out a well-supported argument and made it clear that this argument is part of a bigger conversation about a topic/text. He acknowledged positions on the topic or text that might disagree with his own position, but still showed why his position makes sense.	The writer laid out an argument about a topic/text and made it clear why her particular argument is important and valid. She stayed fair to those who might disagree with her by describing how her position is one of several and making it clear where her position stands in relation to others.	The writer presented an argument, offering context, honoring other points of view, and indicating the conditions under which the position holds true. The writer developed the argument with logical reasoning and convincing evidence, acknowledging the limitations of the position and citing—and critiquing—sources.
The writer wrote an introduction to interest readers and help them understand and care about a topic or text. She thought backward between the piece and the introduction to make sure that the introduction fit with the whole. Not only did the writer clearly state her claim, she also told her readers how her text would unfold.	The writer interested readers in his argument and helped them to understand the backstory behind it. He gave the backstory in a way that got readers ready to see his point. The writer made it clear to readers what his piece would argue and forecasted the parts of his argument.	After hooking her readers, the writer provided specific context for her own as well as another's position(s), introduced her position, and oriented readers to the overall line of argument she would develop.	The writer demonstrated the significance of the argument and may have offered hints of upcoming parts of the essay. The writer presented needed background information to show the complexity of the issue. In addition to introducing the overall line of development the argument will take, the writer distinguished that argument from others.
The writer used transitions to help readers understand how the different parts of his piece fit together to explain and support his argument. The writer used transitions to help connect claim(s), reasons, and evidence and to imply relationships, such as when material exemplifies, adds to, is similar to, explains, is a result of, or contrasts. The writer used transitions such as *for instance, in addition, one reason, furthermore, according to, this evidence suggests,* and *thus we can say that.*	The writer used transitions to link the parts of her argument. The transitions help readers follow from part to part and make it clear when she is stating a claim or counterclaim, giving a reason, or offering or analyzing evidence. These transitions include terms such as *the text states, as, this means, another reason, some people may say, but, nevertheless,* and *on the other hand.*	The writer used transitions to lead readers across parts of the text and to help them note how parts of the text relate back to earlier parts. He used phrases such as *now some argue, while this may be true, it is also the case that, despite this, as stated earlier, taken as a whole, this is significant because, the evidence points to,* and *by doing so.*	The writer used transitions to clarify the relationship between claims, reasons, and evidence, and help the reader follow the logic in the argument. The writer also used transitions to make clear the relationship of sources to each other and to the claim, such as *while it may be true that, nevertheless, there are times when/certain circumstances when,* and *others echo this idea.*
In the conclusion, the writer restated the important points and offered a final insight or implication for readers to consider. The ending strengthened the overall argument.	In his conclusion, the writer reinforced and built on the main point(s) in a way that made the entire text a cohesive whole. The conclusion reiterated how the support for his claim outweighed the counterclaim(s), restated the main points, responded to them, or highlighted their significance.	In the conclusion, the writer described the significance of her argument for stakeholders or offered additional insights, implications, questions, or challenges.	In the concluding section, the writer may have clarified the conditions under which the position holds true, discussed possible applications or consequence, and/or offered possible solutions.

	Grade 3	Grade 4	Grade 5
	STRUCTURE (cont.)		
Organization	The writer wrote several reasons or examples why readers should agree with his opinion and wrote at least several sentences about each reason. The writer organized his information so that each part of his writing was mostly about one thing.	The writer separated sections of information using paragraphs.	The writer grouped information and related ideas into paragraphs. She put the parts of her writing in the order that most suited her purpose and helped her prove her reasons and claim.
	DEVELOPMENT		
Elaboration	The writer not only named her reasons to support her opinion, but also wrote more about each one.	The writer gave reasons to support his opinion. He chose the reasons to convince his readers. The writer included examples and information to support his reasons, perhaps from a text, his knowledge, or his life.	The writer gave reasons to support his opinion that were parallel and did not overlap. He put them in an order that he thought would be most convincing. The writer included evidence such as facts, examples, quotations, micro-stories, and information to support his claim. The writer discussed and unpacked the way that the evidence went with the claim.
Craft	The writer not only told readers to believe him, but also wrote in ways that got them thinking or feeling in certain ways.	The writer made deliberate word choices to convince her readers, perhaps by emphasizing or repeating words that made readers feel emotions. If it felt right to do so, the writer chose precise details and facts to help make her points and used figurative language to draw readers into her line of thought. The writer made choices about which evidence was best to include or not include to support her points. The writer used a convincing tone.	The writer made deliberate word choices to have an effect on her readers. The writer reached for the precise phrase, metaphor, or image that would convey her ideas. The writer made choices about how to angle her evidence to support her points. When it seemed right to do so, the writer tried to use a scholarly voice and varied her sentences to create the pace and tone of the different sections of her piece.

ARGUMENT: LEARNING PROGRESSION, 3–9 (continued)

Grade 6	Grade 7	Grade 8	Grade 9
		STRUCTURE (cont.)	
The writer organized his argument into sections: he arranged reasons and evidence purposefully, leading readers from one claim or reason to another. The order of the sections and the internal structure of each section made sense.	The writer purposely arranged parts of her piece to suit her purpose and to lead readers from one claim, counterclaim, reason, or piece of evidence to another. The writer used topic sentences, transitions, and formatting (where appropriate) to clarify the structure of the piece and to highlight her main points.	The writer organized claims, counterclaims, reasons, and evidence into sections and clarified how sections are connected. The writer created an organizational structure that supports a reader's growing understanding across the whole of his argument, arranging the sections to build on each other in a logical, compelling fashion.	The writer created a logical and compelling structure for the argument so that each part builds on a prior section, and the whole moves the reader toward understandings.
		DEVELOPMENT	
The writer included and arranged a variety of evidence such as facts, quotations, examples, and definitions. The writer used trusted sources and information from experts and gave the sources credit. The writer worked to explain how the reasons and evidence she gave supported her claim(s) and strengthened her argument. To do this the writer referred to earlier parts of her text, summarized background information, raised questions, or highlighted possible implications.	The writer included varied kinds of evidence such as facts, quotations, examples, and definitions. He analyzed or explained the reasons and evidence, showing how they fit with his claim(s) and built his argument. The writer consistently incorporated and cited trustworthy sources. The writer wrote about another possible position or positions—a different claim or claims about this subject—and explained why the evidence for his position outweighed the counterclaim(s). The writer worked to make his argument compelling as well as understandable. He brought out why it mattered and why the audience should care about it.	The writer brought out the aspects of the argument that were most significant to her audience and to her overall purpose(s). The writer incorporated trustworthy and significant sources and explained if and when a source seemed problematic. The writer analyzed the relevance of the reasons and evidence for her claims as well as for the counterclaim(s) and helped readers understand each position. The writer made sure all of her analysis led readers to follow her line of argument.	The writer brought out the aspects of the argument that were most significant to the audience and to the purposes. When appropriate, the writer acknowledged limitations or critiques of sources—perhaps evaluating sources' reasoning or suspect motivations. The writer angled and/or framed evidence to clearly and fairly represent various perspectives, while also maintaining a clear position.
The writer chose his words carefully to support his argument and to have an effect on his reader. The writer worked to include concrete details, comparisons, and/or images to convey his ideas, build his argument, and keep his reader engaged. When necessary, the writer explained terms to readers, providing definitions, context clues or parenthetical explanations. The writer made his piece sound serious.	The writer used words purposefully to affect meaning and tone. The writer chose precise words and used metaphors, images, or comparisons to explain what she meant. The writer included domain-specific, technical vocabulary relevant to her argument and audience and defined these when appropriate. The writer used a formal tone, but varied it appropriately to engage the reader.	The writer intended to affect his reader in particular ways—to make the reader think, realize, or feel a particular way—and he chose language to do that. The writer consistently used comparisons, analogies, vivid examples, anecdotes, or other rhetorical devices to help readers follow his thinking and grasp the meaning and significance of a point or a piece of evidence. The writer varied his tone to match the different purposes of different sections of his argument.	The writer intended to make the reader think, realize, or feel a particular way—and chose language to do that. In addition to using other literary devices, the writer may have used allusions. The writer varied the tone to match the purposes of different sections of the argument, as well as to develop and overall impact.

May be photocopied for classroom use. © 2014 by Lucy Calkins and Colleagues from the Teachers College Reading and Writing Project from *Units of Study in Argument, Information, and Narrative Writing* (firsthand: Portsmouth, NH).

	Grade 3	Grade 4	Grade 5
CONVENTIONS			
Spelling	The writer used what she knew about word families and spelling rules to help her spell and edit. The writer got help from others to check her spelling and punctuation before she wrote her final draft.	The writer used what he knew about word families and spelling rules to help him spell and edit. He used the word wall and dictionaries to help him when needed.	The writer used what he knew about word patterns to spell correctly and he used references to help him spell words when needed. The writer made sure to correctly spell words that were important to his topic.
Punctuation and Sentence Structure	The writer punctuated dialogue correctly with commas and quotation marks. While writing, the writer put punctuation at the end of every sentence. The writer wrote in ways that helped readers read with expression, reading some parts quickly, some slowly, some parts in one sort of voice and others in another.	When writing long, complex sentences, the writer used commas to make them clear and correct. The writer used periods to fix her run-on sentences.	The writer used commas to set off introductory parts of sentences (*At this time in history, . . .*). The writer used a variety of punctuation to fix any run-on sentences. The writer used punctuation to cite her sources.

Grade 6	Grade 7	Grade 8	Grade 9
CONVENTIONS			
The writer used resources to be sure the words in her writing were spelled correctly, including returning to sources to check spelling.	The writer matched the spelling of technical vocabulary to that found in resources and text evidence. He spelled material in citations correctly.	The writer spelled technical vocabulary and literary vocabulary accurately. She spelled material in citations according to sources, and spelled citations accurately.	The used accurate spelling throughout, including cited text and citations.
The writer used punctuation such as dashes, colons, parentheses, and semicolons to help him include or connect information in some of his sentences. The writer punctuated quotes and citations accurately.	The writer varied her sentence structure, sometimes using simple and sometimes using complex sentence structure. The writer used internal punctuation appropriately within sentences and when citing sources, including commas, dashes, parentheses, colons, and semicolons.	The writer used different sentence structures to achieve different purposes throughout his argument. The writer used verb tenses that shift when needed (as in when moving from a citation back to his own writing), deciding between active and passive voice where appropriate. The writer used internal punctuation effectively, including the use of ellipses to accurately insert excerpts from sources.	The writer used sentence structure and verb tense purposefully (i.e., using fragments to emphasize key points, using present tense to create immediacy). The writer used punctuation to emphasize connections, to strengthen tone, and to clarify and add complexity.

ON-DEMAND PERFORMANCE ASSESSMENT PROMPT

Argument Writing

Say to students:

"Think of a topic or issue that you know and care about, an issue around which you have strong feelings. Tomorrow, you will have forty-five minutes to write an opinion or argument text in which you will write your opinion or claim and tell reasons why you feel that way. When you do this, draw on everything you know about essays, persuasive letters, and reviews. If you want to find and use information from a book or another outside source, you may bring that with you tomorrow. Please keep in mind that you'll have forty-five minutes to complete this, so you will need to plan, draft, revise, and edit in one sitting.

"In your writing, make sure you:

- Write an introduction.

- State your opinion or claim.

- Give reasons and evidence.

- Organize your writing.

- Acknowledge counterclaims.

- Use transition words.

- Write a conclusion."

Use the teaching rubrics to assess and score these pieces of on-demand writing.

Name: _____ Date: _____

Rubric for Argument Writing—Sixth Grade

STRUCTURE

	Grade 4 (1 POINT)	1.5 PTS	Grade 5 (2 POINTS)	2.5 PTS	Grade 6 (3 POINTS)	3.5 PTS	Grade 7 (4 POINTS)	SCORE
Overall	The writer made a claim about a topic or a text and tried to support his reasons.	Mid-level	The writer made a claim or thesis on a topic or text, supported it with reasons, and provided a variety of evidence for each reason.	Mid-level	The writer explained the topic/text and staked out a position that can be supported by a variety of trustworthy sources. Each part of the text built her argument, and led to a conclusion.	Mid-level	The writer laid out a well-supported argument and made it clear that this argument is part of a bigger conversation about a topic/text. He acknowledged positions on the topic or text that might disagree with his own position but still showed why his position makes sense.	
Lead	The writer wrote a few sentences to hook her readers, perhaps by asking a question, explaining why the topic mattered, telling a surprising fact, or giving background information. The writer stated her claim.	Mid-level	The writer wrote an introduction that led to a claim or thesis and got his readers to care about his opinion. The writer got his readers to care by not only including a cool fact or jazzy question, but also by telling readers what was significant in or around the topic. The writer worked to find the precise words to state his claim; he let readers know the reasons he would develop later.	Mid-level	The writer wrote an introduction to interest readers and help them understand and care about a topic or text. She thought backward between the piece and the introduction to make sure that the introduction would fit with the whole. Not only did the writer clearly state her claim, she also told her readers how her text would unfold.	Mid-level	The writer interested readers in his argument and helped them to understand the backstory behind it. He gave the backstory in a way that got readers ready to see his point. The writer made it clear to readers what his piece would argue and forecasted the parts of his argument.	

May be photocopied for classroom use. © 2014 by Lucy Calkins and Colleagues from the Teachers College Reading and Writing Project from *Units of Study in Argument, Information, and Narrative Writing (firsthand:* Portsmouth, NH).

ARGUMENT: TEACHING RUBRIC—SIXTH GRADE (continued)

STRUCTURE (cont.)

	Grade 4 (1 POINT)	1.5 PTS	Grade 5 (2 POINTS)	2.5 PTS	Grade 6 (3 POINTS)	3.5 PTS	Grade 7 (4 POINTS)	SCORE
Transitions	The writer used words and phrases to glue parts of his piece together. He used phrases such as *for example*, *another example*, *one time*, and *for instance* to show when he was shifting from saying reasons to giving evidence and in *addition to*, *also*, and *another* to show when he wanted to make a new point.	Mid-level	The writer used transition words and phrases to connect evidence back to her reasons using phrases such as *this shows that . . .* The writer helped readers follow her thinking with phrases such as *another reason* and *the most important reason*. She used phrases such as *consequently* and *because of* to show what happened. The writer used words such as *specifically* and *in particular* to be more precise.	Mid-level	The writer used transitions to help readers understand how the different parts of his piece fit together to explain and support his argument. The writer used transitions to help connect claim(s), reasons, and evidence and to imply relationships, such as when material exemplifies, adds to, is similar to, explains, is a result of, or contrasts. The writer used transitions such as *for instance*, *in addition*, *one reason*, *furthermore*, *according to*, *this evidence suggests*, and *thus we can say that*.	Mid-level	The writer used transitions to link the parts of her argument. The transitions help readers follow from part to part and make it clear when she is stating a claim or counterclaim, giving a reason, or offering or analyzing evidence. These transitions include terms such as *as the text states*, *this means*, *another reason*, *some people may say*, *but*, *nevertheless*, and *on the other hand*.	
Ending	The writer wrote an ending for her piece in which she restated and reflected on her claim, perhaps suggesting an action or response based on what she had written.	Mid-level	The writer worked on a conclusion in which he connected back to and highlighted what the text was mainly about, not just the preceding paragraph.	Mid-level	In the conclusion, the writer restated the important points and offered a final insight or implication for readers to consider. The ending strengthened the overall argument.	Mid-level	In his conclusion, the writer reinforced and built on the main point(s) in a way that made the entire text a cohesive whole. The conclusion reiterated how the support for his claim outweighed the counterclaim(s), restated the main points, responded to them, or highlighted their significance.	

ARGUMENT: TEACHING RUBRIC—SIXTH GRADE *(continued)*

	Grade 4 (1 POINT)	1.5 PTS	Grade 5 (2 POINTS)	2.5 PTS	Grade 6 (3 POINTS)	3.5 PTS	Grade 7 (4 POINTS)	SCORE
STRUCTURE (cont.)								
Organization	The writer separated sections of information using paragraphs.	Mid-level	The writer grouped information and related ideas into paragraphs. She put the parts of her writing in the order that most suited her purpose and helped her prove her reasons and claim.	Mid-level	The writer organized his argument into sections: he arranged reasons and evidence purposefully, leading readers from one claim or reason to another. The order of the sections and the internal structure of each section made sense.	Mid-level	The writer purposely arranged parts of her piece to suit her purpose and to lead readers from one claim, counterclaim, reason, or piece of evidence to another. The writer used topic sentences, transitions, and formatting (where appropriate) to clarify the structure of the piece and to highlight her main points.	
							TOTAL:	
DEVELOPMENT								
Elaboration*	The writer gave reasons to support her opinion. She chose the reasons to convince her readers. The writer included examples and information to support her reasons, perhaps from a text, her knowledge, or her life.	Mid-level	The writer gave reasons to support his opinion that were parallel and did not overlap. He put them in an order that he thought would be most convincing. The writer included evidence such as facts, examples, quotations, micro-stories, and information to support his claim. The writer discussed and unpacked the way that the evidence went with the claim.	Mid-level	The writer included and arranged a variety of evidence such as facts, quotations, examples, and definitions. The writer used trusted sources and information from experts and gave the sources credit. The writer worked to explain how the reasons and evidence she gave supported her claim(s) and strengthened her argument. To do this the writer referred to earlier parts of her text, summarized background information, raised questions, or highlighted possible implications.	Mid-level	The writer included varied kinds of evidence such as facts, quotations, examples, and definitions. He analyzed or explained the reasons and evidence, showing how they fit with his claim(s) and built his argument. The writer consistently incorporated and cited trustworthy sources. The writer wrote about another possible position or positions—a different claim or claims about this subject—and explained why the evidence for his position outweighed the counterclaim(s). The writer worked to make his argument compelling as well as understandable. He brought out why it mattered and why the audience should care about it.	

*Elaboration and Craft are double-weighted categories: Whatever score a student would get in these categories is worth double the amount of points. For example, if a student exceeds expectations in Elaboration, then that student would receive 8 points instead of 4 points. If a student meets standards in Elaboration, then that student would receive 6 points instead of 3 points.

May be photocopied for classroom use. © 2014 by Lucy Calkins and Colleagues from the Teachers College Reading and Writing Project from *Units of Study in Argument, Information, and Narrative Writing* (firsthand: Portsmouth, NH).

ARGUMENT: TEACHING RUBRIC—SIXTH GRADE (continued)

	Grade 4 (1 POINT)	1.5 PTS	Grade 5 (2 POINTS)	2.5 PTS	Grade 6 (3 POINTS)	3.5 PTS	Grade 7 (4 POINTS)	SCORE
DEVELOPMENT (cont.)								
Craft*	The writer made deliberate word choices to convince his readers, perhaps by emphasizing or repeating words that would make his readers feel emotions. If it felt right to do so, the writer chose precise details and facts to help make his points and used figurative language to draw the readers into his line of thought. The writer made choices about which evidence was best to include or not include to support his points. The writer used a convincing tone.	Mid-level	The writer made deliberate word choices to have an effect on her readers. The writer reached for the precise phrase, metaphor, or image that would convey her ideas. The writer made choices about how to angle her evidence to support her points. When it seemed right to do so, the writer tried to use a scholarly voice and varied her sentences to create the pace and tone of the different sections of her piece.	Mid-level	The writer chose his words carefully to support his argument and to have an effect on his reader. The writer worked to include concrete details, comparisons, and/or images to convey his ideas, build his argument, and keep his reader engaged. When necessary, the writer explained terms to readers, providing definitions, context clues or parenthetical explanations. The writer made his piece sound serious.	Mid-level	The writer used words purposefully to affect meaning and tone. The writer chose precise words and used metaphors, images, or comparisons to explain what she meant. The writer included domain-specific, technical vocabulary relevant to her argument and audience and defined these when appropriate. The writer used a formal tone, but varied it appropriately to engage the reader.	
CONVENTIONS								
Spelling	The writer used what she knew about word families and spelling rules to help her spell and edit. She used the word wall and dictionaries to help her when needed.	Mid-level	The writer used what he knew about word patterns to spell correctly and he used references to help him spell words when needed. The writer made sure to correctly spell words that were important to his topic.	Mid-level	The writer used resources to be sure the words in her writing were spelled correctly, including returning to sources to check spelling.	Mid-level	The writer matched the spelling of technical vocabulary to that found in resources and text evidence. He spelled material in citations correctly.	
							TOTAL:	

*Elaboration and Craft are double-weighted categories: Whatever score a student would get in these categories is worth double the amount of points. For example, if a student exceeds expectations in Elaboration, then that student would receive 8 points instead of 4 points. If a student meets standards in Elaboration, then that student would receive 6 points instead of 3 points.

ARGUMENT: TEACHING RUBRIC—SIXTH GRADE (continued)

	Grade 4 (1 POINT)	1.5 PTS	Grade 5 (2 POINTS)	2.5 PTS	Grade 6 (3 POINTS)	3.5 PTS	Grade 7 (4 POINTS)	SCORE
CONVENTIONS (cont.)								
Punctuation and Sentence Structure	When writing long, complex sentences, the writer used commas to make them clear and correct. The writer used periods to fix his run-on sentences.	Mid-level	The writer used commas to set off introductory parts of sentences (*At this time in history, . . .*). The writer used a variety of punctuation to fix any run-on sentences. The writer used punctuation to cite her sources.	Mid-level	The writer used punctuation such as dashes, colons, parentheses, and semicolons to help him include or connect information in some of his sentences. The writer punctuated quotes and citations accurately.	Mid-level	The writer varied her sentence structure, sometimes using simple and sometimes using complex sentence structure. The writer used internal punctuation appropriately within sentences and when citing sources, including commas, dashes, parentheses, colons, and semicolons.	
								TOTAL:

Total score: _____

If you want to translate this score into a grade, you can use the provided table to score each student on a scale of 0–4.

Number of Points	Scaled Score
1–11	1
11.5–16.5	1.5
17–22	2
22.5–27.5	2.5
28–33	3
33.5–38.5	3.5
39–44	4

Teachers, we created these rubrics so you will have your own place to pull together scores of student work. You can use these assessments immediately after giving the on-demands and also for self-assessment and setting goals.

Scoring Guide

In each row, circle the descriptor in the column that matches the student work. Scores in the categories of Elaboration and Craft are worth double the point value (2, 3, 4, 5, 6, 7, or 8 instead of 1. 1.5, 2, 2.5, 3, 3.5, or 4).

Total the number of points and then track students' progress by seeing when the total points increase.

Name: _____ Date: _____

Rubric for Argument Writing—Seventh Grade

STRUCTURE

	Grade 5 (1 POINT)		Grade 6 (2 POINTS)		Grade 7 (3 POINTS)		Grade 8 (4 POINTS)	SCORE
		1.5 PTS		2.5 PTS		3.5 PTS		
Overall	The writer made a claim or thesis on a topic or text, supported it with reasons, and provided a variety of evidence for each reason.	Mid-level	The writer explained the topic/text and staked out a position that can be supported by a variety of trustworthy sources. Each part of the text built her argument, and led to a conclusion.	Mid-level	The writer laid out a well-supported argument and made it clear that this argument is part of a bigger conversation about a topic/text. He acknowledged positions on the topic or text that might disagree with his own position, but still showed why his position makes sense.	Mid-level	The writer laid out an argument about a topic/text and made it clear why her particular argument is important and valid. She stayed fair to those who might disagree with her by describing how her position is one of several and making it clear where her position stands in relation to others.	
Lead	The writer wrote an introduction that led to a claim or thesis and got his readers to care about his opinion. He got readers to care by not only including a cool fact or jazzy question, but also figuring out what was significant in or around the topic and giving readers information about what was significant about the topic. The writer worked to find the precise words to state his claim; he let readers know the reasons he would develop later.	Mid-level	The writer wrote an introduction to interest readers and help them understand and care about a topic or text. She thought backward between the piece and the introduction to make sure that the introduction would fit with the whole. Not only did the writer clearly state her claim, she also told her readers how her text would unfold.	Mid-level	The writer interested readers in his argument and helped them to understand the backstory behind it. He gave the backstory in a way that got readers ready to see his point. The writer made it clear to readers what his piece would argue and forecasted the parts of his argument.	Mid-level	After hooking her readers, the writer provided specific context for her own as well as another's position(s), introduced her position, and oriented readers to the overall line of argument she would develop.	

ARGUMENT: TEACHING RUBRIC—SEVENTH GRADE (continued)

STRUCTURE (cont.)

	Grade 5 (1 POINT)	1.5 PTS	Grade 6 (2 POINTS)	2.5 PTS	Grade 7 (3 POINTS)	3.5 PTS	Grade 8 (4 POINTS)	SCORE
Transitions	The writer used transition words and phrases to connect evidence back to her reasons using phrases such as *this shows that.* . . . The writer helped readers follow her thinking with phrases such as *another reason* and *the most important reason.* She used phrases such as *consequently* and *because of* to show what happened. The writer used words such as *specifically* and *in particular* to be more precise.	Mid-level	The writer used transitions to help readers understand how the different parts of his piece fit together to explain and support his argument. The writer used transitions to help connect claim(s), reasons, and evidence and to imply relationships, such as when material exemplifies, adds to, is similar to, explains, is a result of, or contrasts. The writer used transitions such as *for instance, in addition, one reason, furthermore, according to, this evidence suggests,* and *thus we can say that.*	Mid-level	The writer used transitions to link the parts of her argument. The transitions help readers follow from part to part and make it clear when she is stating a claim or counterclaim, giving a reason, or offering or analyzing evidence. These transitions include terms such as *the text states, as, this means, another reason, some people may say, but, nevertheless,* and *on the other hand.*	Mid-level	The writer used transitions to lead readers across parts of the text and to help them note how parts of the text relate back to earlier parts. He used phrases such as *now some argue, while this may be true, it is also the case that, despite this, as stated earlier, taken as a whole, this is significant because, the evidence points to,* and *by doing so.*	
Ending	The writer worked on a conclusion in which he connected back to and highlighted what the text was mainly about, not just the preceding paragraph.	Mid-level	In the conclusion, the writer restated the important points and offered a final insight or implication for readers to consider. The ending strengthened the overall argument.	Mid-level	In his conclusion, the writer reinforced and built on the main point(s) in a way that made the entire text a cohesive whole. The conclusion reiterated how the support for his claim outweighed the counterclaim(s), restated the main points, responded to them, or highlighted their significance.	Mid-level	In the conclusion, the writer described the significance of her argument for stakeholders or offered additional insights, implications, questions, or challenges.	

May be photocopied for classroom use. © 2014 by Lucy Calkins and Colleagues from the Teachers College Reading and Writing Project from *Units of Study in Argument, Information, and Narrative Writing (firsthand:* Portsmouth, NH).

ARGUMENT: TEACHING RUBRIC—SEVENTH GRADE (continued)

STRUCTURE (cont.)

	Grade 5 (1 POINT)	1.5 PTS	Grade 6 (2 POINTS)	2.5 PTS	Grade 7 (3 POINT)	3.5 PTS	Grade 8 (4 POINTS)	SCORE
Organization	The writer grouped information and related ideas into paragraphs. She put the parts of her writing in the order that most suited her purpose and helped her prove her reasons and claim.	Mid-level	The writer organized his argument into sections: he arranged reasons and evidence purposefully, leading readers from one claim or reason to another. The order of the sections and the internal structure of each section made sense.	Mid-level	The writer purposely arranged parts of her piece to suit her purpose and lead readers from one claim, counterclaim, reason, or piece of evidence to another. The writer used topic sentences, transitions, and formatting (where appropriate) to clarify the structure of the piece and to highlight her main points.	Mid-level	The writer organized claims, counterclaims, reasons, and evidence into sections and clarified how sections are connected. The writer created an organizational structure that supports a reader's growing understanding across the whole of his argument, arranging the sections to build on each other in a logical, compelling fashion.	

DEVELOPMENT

Elaboration*	The writer gave reasons to support his opinion that were parallel and did not overlap. He put them in an order that he thought would be most convincing. The writer included evidence such as facts, examples, quotations, micro-stories, and information to support his claim. The writer discussed and unpacked the way that the evidence went with the claim.	Mid-level	The writer included and arranged a variety of evidence such as facts, quotations, examples, and definitions. The writer used trusted sources and information from experts and gave the sources credit. The writer worked to explain how the reasons and evidence she gave supported her claim(s) and strengthened her argument. To do this the writer referred to earlier parts of her text, summarized background information, raised questions, or highlighted possible implications.	Mid-level	The writer included varied kinds of evidence such as facts, quotations, examples, and definitions. He analyzed or explained the reasons and evidence, showing how they fit with his claim(s) and build his argument. The writer consistently incorporated and cited trustworthy sources. The writer wrote about another possible position or positions—a different claim or claims about this subject—and explained why the evidence for his position outweighed the counterclaim(s). The writer worked to make his argument compelling as well as understandable. He brought out why it mattered and why the audience should care about it.	Mid-level	The writer brought out the aspects of the argument that were most significant to her audience and to her overall purpose(s). The writer incorporated trustworthy and significant sources and explained if sources seemed problematic. The writer analyzed the relevance of the reasons and evidence for her claims as well as for the counterclaim(s) and helped readers understand each position. The writer made sure all of her analysis led readers to follow her line of argument.	TOTAL:

*Elaboration and Craft are double-weighted categories: Whatever score a student would get in these categories is worth double the amount of points. For example, if a student exceeds expectations in Elaboration, then that student would receive 8 points instead of 4 points. If a student meets standards in Elaboration, then that student would receive 6 points instead of 3 points.

	Grade 5 (1 POINT)	1.5 PTS	Grade 6 (2 POINTS)	2.5 PTS	Grade 7 (3 POINTS)	3.5 PTS	Grade 8 (4 POINTS)	SCORE
			DEVELOPMENT (cont.)					
Craft*	The writer made deliberate word choices to have an effect on her readers. The writer reached for the precise phrase, metaphor, or image that would convey her ideas. The writer made choices about how to angle her evidence to support her points. When it seemed right to do so, the writer tried to use a scholarly voice and varied her sentences to create the pace and tone of the different sections of her piece.	Mid-level	The writer chose his words carefully to support his argument and to have an effect on his reader. The writer worked to include concrete details, comparisons, and/or images to convey his ideas, build his argument, and keep his reader engaged. When necessary, the writer explained terms to readers, providing definitions, context clues or parenthetical explanations. The writer made his piece sound serious.	Mid-level	The writer used words purposefully to affect meaning and tone. The writer chose precise words and used metaphors, images, or comparisons to explain what she meant. The writer included domain-specific, technical vocabulary relevant to her argument and audience and defined these when appropriate. The writer used a formal tone, but varied it appropriately to engage the reader.	Mid-level	The writer intended to affect his reader in particular ways—to make the reader think, realize or feel a particular way—and he chose language to do that. The writer consistently used comparisons, analogies, vivid examples, anecdotes, or other rhetorical devices to help readers follow his thinking and grasp the meaning and significance of a point or a piece of evidence. The writer varied his tone to match the different purposes of different sections of his argument.	
			CONVENTIONS					
Spelling	The writer used what he knew about word patterns to spell correctly and he used reference to help him spell words when needed. He made sure to correctly spell words that were important to his topic.	Mid-level	The writer used resources to be sure the words in her writing were spelled correctly, including returning to sources to check spelling.	Mid-level	The writer matched the spelling of technical vocabulary to that found in resources and text evidence. He spelled material in citations correctly.	Mid-level	The writer spelled technical vocabulary and literary vocabulary accurately. She spelled material in citations according to sources, and spelled citations accurately.	
							TOTAL:	

*Elaboration and Craft are double-weighted categories: Whatever score a student would get in these categories is worth double the amount of points. For example, if a student exceeds expectations in Elaboration, then that student would receive 8 points instead of 4 points. If a student meets standards in Elaboration, then that student would receive 6 points instead of 3 points.

May be photocopied for classroom use. © 2014 by Lucy Calkins and Colleagues from the Teachers College Reading and Writing Project from *Units of Study in Argument, Information, and Narrative Writing (firsthand:* Portsmouth, NH).

ARGUMENT: TEACHING RUBRIC—SEVENTH GRADE (continued)

CONVENTIONS (cont.)

	Grade 5 (1 POINT)	1.5 PTS	Grade 6 (2 POINTS)	2.5 PTS	Grade 7 (3 POINT)	3.5 PTS	Grade 8 (4 POINTS)	SCORE
Punctuation and Sentence Structure	The writer used commas to set off introductory parts of sentences, for example, *At this time in history,* and *it was common to. . . .* The writer used a variety of punctuation to fix any run-on sentences. The writer used punctuation to cite her sources.	Mid-level	The writer used punctuation such as dashes, colons, parentheses, and semicolons to help him include or connect information in some of his sentences. The writer punctuated quotes and citations accurately.	Mid-level	The writer varied her sentence structure, sometimes using simple and sometimes using complex sentence structure. The writer used internal punctuation appropriately within sentences and when citing sources, including commas, dashes, parentheses, colons, and semicolons.	Mid-level	The writer used different sentence structures to achieve different purposes throughout his argument. The writer used verb tenses that shift when needed (as in when moving from a citation back to his own writing), deciding between active and passive voice where appropriate. The writer used internal punctuation effectively, including the use of ellipses to accurately insert excerpts from sources.	
							TOTAL:	

Teachers, we created these rubrics so you will have your own place to pull together scores of student work. You can use these assessments immediately after giving the on-demands and also for self-assessment and setting goals.

Scoring Guide

In each row, circle the descriptor in the column that matches the student work. Scores in the categories of Elaboration and Craft are worth double the point value (2, 3, 4, 5, 6, 7, or 8 instead of 1, 1.5, 2, 2.5, 3, 3.5, or 4).

Total the number of points and then track students' progress by seeing when the total points increase.

Total score: _____

If you want to translate this score into a grade, you can use the provided table to score each student on a scale of 0–4.

Number of Points	Scaled Score
1–11	1
11.5–16.5	1.5
17–22	2
22.5–27.5	2.5
28–33	3
33.5–38.5	3.5
39–44	4

Name: _____   Date: _____

Rubric for Argument Writing—Eighth Grade

STRUCTURE

	Grade 6 (1 POINT)	1.5 PTS	Grade 7 (2 POINTS)	2.5 PTS	Grade 8 (3 POINTS)	3.5 PTS	Grade 9 (4 POINTS)	SCORE
Overall	The writer explained the topic/text and staked out a position that could be supported by a variety of trustworthy sources. Each part of the writer's text helped build her argument, and led to a conclusion.	Mid-level	The writer laid out a well-supported argument and made it clear that this argument is part of a bigger conversation about a topic/text. He acknowledged positions on the topic or text that might disagree with his own position, but still showed why his position makes sense.	Mid-level	The writer laid out an argument about a topic/text and made it clear why her particular argument is important and valid. She stayed fair to those who might disagree with her by describing how her position is one of several and making it clear where her position stands in relation to others.	Mid-level	The writer presented an argument, offering context, honoring other points of view, and indicating the conditions under which the position holds true. The writer developed the argument with logical reasoning and convincing evidence, acknowledging the limitations of the position and citing—and critiquing—sources.	
Lead	The writer wrote an introduction to interest readers and help them understand and care about a topic or text. She thought backward between the piece and the introduction to make sure that the introduction fit with the whole. Not only did the writer clearly state her claim, she also told her readers how her text would unfold.	Mid-level	The writer interested readers in his argument and helped them to understand the backstory behind it. He gave the backstory in a way that got readers ready to see his point. The writer made it clear to readers what his piece would argue and forecasted the parts of his argument.	Mid-level	After hooking her readers, the writer provided specific context for her own as well as another's position(s), introduced her position, and oriented readers to the overall line of argument she would develop.	Mid-level	The writer demonstrated the significance of the argument and may have offered hints of upcoming parts of the essay. The writer presented needed background information to show the complexity of the issue. In addition to introducing the overall line of development the argument will take, the writer distinguished that argument from others.	

May be photocopied for classroom use. © 2014 by Lucy Calkins and Colleagues from the Teachers College Reading and Writing Project from *Units of Study in Argument, Information, and Narrative Writing* (firsthand: Portsmouth, NH).

ARGUMENT: TEACHING RUBRIC—EIGHTH GRADE (continued)

STRUCTURE (cont.)

	Grade 6 (1 POINT)	1.5 PTS	Grade 7 (2 POINTS)	2.5 PTS	Grade 8 (3 POINTS)	3.5 PTS	Grade 9 (4 POINTS)	SCORE
Transitions	The writer used transitions to help readers understand how the different parts of her piece fit together to explain and support her argument. The writer used transitions to help connect claim(s), reasons, and evidence, and to imply relationships such as when material exemplifies, adds on to, is similar to, explains, is a result of, or contrasts. She used transitions such as *for instance, in addition, one reason, furthermore, according to, this evidence suggests,* and *thus we can say that.*	Mid-level	The writer used transitions to link the parts of her argument. The transitions help readers follow from part to part and make it clear when she is stating a claim or counterclaim, giving a reason, or offering or analyzing evidence. These transitions include terms such as *the text states, as, this means, another reason, some people may say, but, nevertheless,* and *on the other hand.*	Mid-level	The writer used transitions to lead readers across parts of the text and to help them note how parts of the text relate back to earlier parts. He used phrases such as *now some argue, while this may be true, it is also the case that, despite this, as stated earlier, taken as a whole, this is significant because, the evidence points to,* and *by doing so.*	Mid-level	The writer used transitions to clarify the relationship between claims, reasons, and evidence, and help the reader follow the logic in the argument. The writer also used transitions to make clear the relationship of sources to each other and to the claim, such as *while it may be true that, nevertheless, there are times when/certain circumstances when,* and *others echo this idea.*	
Ending	In her conclusion, the writer restated the important points and offered a final insight or implication for readers to consider. The ending strengthened the overall argument.	Mid-level	In his conclusion, the writer reinforced and built on the main point(s) in a way that made the entire text a cohesive whole. The conclusion reiterated how the support for his claim outweighed the counterclaim(s), restated the main points, responded to them, or highlighted their significance.	Mid-level	In the conclusion, the writer described the significance of her argument for stakeholders or offered additional insights, implications, questions, or challenges.	Mid-level	In the concluding section, the writer may have clarified the conditions under which the position holds true, discussed possible applications or consequences, and/or offered possible solutions.	

ARGUMENT: TEACHING RUBRIC—EIGHTH GRADE *(continued)*

	Grade 6 (1 POINT)	1.5 PTS	Grade 7 (2 POINTS)	2.5 PTS	Grade 8 (3 POINTS)	3.5 PTS	Grade 9 (4 POINTS)	SCORE
STRUCTURE (cont.)								
Organization	The writer organized her argument into sections: She arranged reasons and evidence purposefully, leading readers from one claim or reason to another. The order of the sections and the internal structure of each section the writer used made sense.	Mid-level	The writer purposely arranged parts of her piece to suit her purpose and to lead readers from one claim, counterclaim, reason, or piece of evidence to another. The writer used topic sentences, transitions, and formatting (where appropriate) to clarify the structure of the piece and to highlight her main points.	Mid-level	The writer organized claims, counterclaims, reasons, and evidence into sections and clarified how sections are connected. The writer created an organizational structure that supports a reader's growing understanding across the whole of his argument, arranging the sections to build on each other in a logical, compelling fashion.	Mid-level	The writer created a logical and compelling structure for the argument so that each part builds on a prior section, and the whole moves the reader toward understandings.	
								TOTAL:
DEVELOPMENT								
Elaboration*	The writer included and arranged a variety of evidence such as facts, quotations, examples, and definitions. The writer used trusted sources and information from experts and gave the sources credit. The writer worked to explain how the reasons and evidence she gave supported her claim(s) and strengthened her argument. To do this, she may have referred to earlier parts of her text, summarized background information, raised questions, or highlighted possible implications.	Mid-level	The writer included varied kinds of evidence such as facts, quotations, examples, and definitions. He analyzed or explained the reasons and evidence, showing how they fit with his claim(s) and built his argument. The writer consistently incorporated and cited trustworthy sources. The writer wrote about another possible position or positions—a different claim or claims about this subject—and explained why the evidence for his position outweighed the counterclaim(s). The writer worked to make his argument compelling as well as understandable. He brought out why it mattered and why the audience should care about it.	Mid-level	The writer brought out the aspects of the argument that were most significant to her audience and to her overall purpose(s). The writer incorporated trustworthy and significant sources and explained if and when a source seemed problematic. The writer analyzed the relevance of the reasons and evidence for her claims as well as for the counterclaim(s) and helped readers understand each position. The writer made sure all of her analysis led readers to follow her line of argument.	Mid-level	The writer brought out the aspects of the argument that were most significant to the audience and to the purposes. When appropriate, the writer acknowledged limitations or critiques of sources—perhaps evaluating sources' reasoning or suspect motivations. The writer angled and/or framed evidence to clearly and fairly represent various perspectives, while also maintaining a clear position.	

*Elaboration and Craft are double-weighted categories: Whatever score a student would get in these categories is worth double the amount of points. For example, if a student exceeds expectations in Elaboration, then that student would receive 8 points instead of 4 points. If a student meets standards in Elaboration, then that student would receive 6 points instead of 3 points.

May be photocopied for classroom use. © 2014 by Lucy Calkins and Colleagues from the Teachers College Reading and Writing Project from *Units of Study in Argument, Information, and Narrative Writing* (firsthand: Portsmouth, NH).

ARGUMENT: TEACHING RUBRIC—EIGHTH GRADE (continued)

DEVELOPMENT (cont.)

	Grade 6 (1 POINT)	1.5 PTS	Grade 7 (2 POINTS)	2.5 PTS	Grade 8 (3 POINTS)	3.5 PTS	Grade 9 (4 POINTS)	SCORE
Craft*	The writer chose her words carefully to support her argument and to have an effect on her reader. The writer worked to include concrete details, comparisons, and/or images to convey her ideas, build her argument, and keep her reader engaged. When necessary, the writer explained terms to readers, providing definitions, context clues, or parenthetical explanations. The write made her piece sound serious.	Mid-level	The writer used words purposefully to affect meaning and tone. The writer chose precise words and used metaphors, images, or comparisons to explain what she meant. The writer included domain-specific, technical vocabulary relevant to her argument and audience and defined these when appropriate. The writer used a formal tone, but varied it appropriately to engage the reader.	Mid-level	The writer intended to affect his reader in particular ways—to make the reader think, realize, or feel a particular way—and he chose language to do that. The writer consistently used comparisons, analogies, vivid examples, anecdotes, or other rhetorical devices to help readers follow his thinking and grasp the meaning and significance of a point or a piece of evidence. The writer varied his tone to match the different purposes of different sections of his argument.	Mid-level	The writer intended to make the reader think, realize, or feel a particular way—and chose language to do that. In addition to using other literary devices, the writer may have used allusions. The writer varied the tone to match the purposes of different sections of the argument, as well as to develop an overall impact.	

CONVENTIONS

	Grade 6	1.5 PTS	Grade 7	2.5 PTS	Grade 8	3.5 PTS	Grade 9	SCORE
Spelling	The writer used resources to be sure the words in her writing were spelled correctly, including returning to sources to check spelling.	Mid-level	The writer matched the spelling of technical vocabulary to that found in resources and text evidence. He spelled material in citations correctly.	Mid-level	The writer spelled technical vocabulary accurately. She spelled material in citations according to sources, and spelled citations accurately.	Mid-level	The writer used accurate spelling, including cited text and citations.	TOTAL:

*Elaboration and Craft are double-weighted categories: Whatever score a student would get in these categories is worth double the amount of points. For example, if a student exceeds expectations in Elaboration, then that student would receive 8 points instead of 4 points. If a student meets standards in Elaboration, then that student would receive 6 points instead of 3 points.

ARGUMENT: TEACHING RUBRIC—EIGHTH GRADE *(continued)*

	Grade 6 (1 POINT)	1.5 PTS	Grade 7 (2 POINTS)	2.5 PTS	Grade 8 (3 POINTS)	3.5 PTS	Grade 9 (4 POINTS)	SCORE
CONVENTIONS (cont.)								
Punctuation and Sentence Structure	The writer used punctuation such as dashes, colons, parentheses, and semicolons to help her include or connect information in some of her sentences. The writer punctuated quotes and citations accurately.	Mid-level	The writer varied her sentence structure, sometimes using simple and sometimes using complex sentence structure. The writer used internal punctuation appropriately within sentences and when citing sources, including commas, dashes, parentheses, colons, and semicolons.	Mid-level	The writer used different sentence structures to achieve different purposes throughout his argument. The writer used verb tenses that shift when needed (as in when moving from a citation back to his own writing), deciding between active and passive voice where appropriate. The writer used internal punctuation effectively, including the use of ellipses to accurately insert excerpts from sources.	Mid-level	The writer used sentence structure and verb tense purposefully (i.e., using fragments to emphasize key points, using present tense to create immediacy). The writer used punctuation to emphasize connections, to strengthen tone, to clarify, and to add complexity.	
							TOTAL:	

Total score: _____

If you want to translate this score into a grade, you can use the provided table to score each student on a scale of 0–4.

Number of Points	Scaled Score
1–11	1
11.5–16.5	1.5
17–22	2
22.5–27.5	2.5
28–33	3
33.5–38.5	3.5
39–44	4

Teachers, we created these rubrics so you will have your own place to pull together scores of student work. You can use these assessments immediately after giving the on-demands and also for self-assessment and setting goals.

Scoring Guide

In each row, circle the descriptor in the column that matches the student work. Scores in the categories of Elaboration and Craft are worth double the point value (2, 3, 4, 5, 6, 7, or 8 instead of 1, 1.5, 2, 2.5, 3, 3.5, or 4).

Total the number of points and then track students' progress by seeing when the total points increase.

Name: _____ Date: _____

Argument Writing Checklist

	Grade 6	NOT YET	STARTING TO	YES!
Structure				
Overall	I explained the topic/text and staked out a position that can be supported by a variety of trustworthy sources. Each part of my text helped build my argument, and led to a conclusion.	☐	☐	☐
Lead	I wrote an introduction to interest readers and help them understand and care about a topic or text. I thought backwards between the piece and the introduction to make sure that the introduction fit with the whole.	☐	☐	☐
	Not only did I clearly state my claim, I also told my readers how my text would unfold.	☐	☐	☐
Transitions	I used transitions to help readers understand how the different parts of my piece fit together to explain and support my argument.	☐	☐	☐
	I used transitions to help connect claim(s), reasons, and evidence, and to imply relationships such as when material exemplifies, adds on to, is similar to, explains, is a result of, or contrasts. I use transitions such as *for instance, in addition, one reason, furthermore, according to, this evidence suggests,* and *thus we can say that.*	☐	☐	☐
Ending	In my conclusion, I restated the important points and offered a final insight or implication for readers to consider. The ending strengthened the overall argument.	☐	☐	☐
Organization	I organized my argument into sections: I arranged reasons and evidence purposefully, leading readers from one claim or reason to another.	☐	☐	☐
	The order of the sections and the internal structure of each section made sense.	☐	☐	☐
Development				
Elaboration	I included and arranged a variety of evidence such as facts, quotations, examples, and definitions.	☐	☐	☐
	I used trusted sources and information from experts and gave the sources credit.	☐	☐	☐
	I worked to explain how the reasons and evidence I gave supported my claim(s) and strengthened my argument. To do this I may have referred to earlier parts of my text, summarized background information, raised questions, or highlighted possible implications.	☐	☐	☐

Grade 6	NOT YET	STARTING TO	YES!
Craft I chose my words carefully to support my argument and to have an effect on my reader.	☐	☐	☐
I worked to include concrete details, comparisons, and/or images to convey my ideas, build my argument, and keep my reader engaged.	☐	☐	☐
When necessary, I explained terms to readers, providing definitions, context clues, or parenthetical explanations.	☐	☐	☐
I made my piece sound serious.	☐	☐	☐
Conventions			
Spelling I used resources to be sure the words in my writing were spelled correctly, including returning to sources to check spelling.	☐	☐	☐
Punctuation and Sentence Structure I used punctuation such as dashes, colons, parentheses, and semicolons to help me include or connect information in some of my sentences.	☐	☐	☐
I punctuated quotes and citations accurately.	☐	☐	☐

ARGUMENT Student Checklists

Name: _____   Date: _____

Argument Writing Checklist

	Grade 7	NOT YET	STARTING TO	YES!
	Structure			
Overall	I laid out a well-supported argument and made it clear that this argument is part of a bigger conversation about a topic/text. I acknowledged positions on the topic or text that might disagree with my own position, but I still showed why my position makes sense.	☐	☐	☐
Lead	I interested the reader in my argument and helped them to understand the backstory behind it. I gave the backstory in a way that got the reader ready to see my point.	☐	☐	☐
	I made it clear to readers what my piece will argue and forecasted the parts of my argument.	☐	☐	☐
Transitions	I used transitions to link the parts of my argument. The transitions help the reader follow from part to part and make it clear when I am stating a claim or counterclaim, giving a reason, or offering or analyzing evidence. These transitions include terms such as *as the text states, this means, another reason, some people may say, but, nevertheless,* and *on the other hand.*	☐	☐	☐
Ending	In my conclusion, I reinforced and built on the main point(s) in a way that makes the entire text a cohesive whole. The conclusion may reiterate how the support for my claim outweighed the counterclaim(s), restate the main points, respond to them, or highlight their significance.	☐	☐	☐
Organization	The parts of my piece are arranged purposefully to suit my purpose and to lead readers from one claim or counterclaim, reason, or piece of evidence to another.	☐	☐	☐
	I used topic sentences, transitions, and formatting (where appropriate) to clarify the structure of the piece and to highlight my main points.	☐	☐	☐
	Development			
Elaboration	I included varied kinds of evidence such as facts, quotations, examples, and definitions. I analyzed or explained the reasons and evidence, showing how they fit with my claim(s) and built my argument.	☐	☐	☐
	I consistently incorporated and cited trustworthy sources.	☐	☐	☐
	I wrote about another possible position or positions—a different claim or claims about this subject—and explained why the evidence for my position outweighed the counterclaim(s).	☐	☐	☐
	I worked to make my argument compelling as well as understandable. I brought out why it mattered and why the audience should care about it.	☐	☐	☐

Grade 7	NOT YET	STARTING TO	YES!
Craft I used words purposefully to affect meaning and tone.	☐	☐	☐
I chose precise words and used metaphors, images, or comparisons to explain what I meant.	☐	☐	☐
I included domain-specific, technical vocabulary relevant to my argument and audience and defined these terms when appropriate.	☐	☐	☐
I used a formal tone, but varied it appropriately to engage the reader.	☐	☐	☐
Conventions			
Spelling I matched the spelling of technical vocabulary to that found in resources and text evidence. I spelled material in citations correctly.	☐	☐	☐
Punctuation and Sentence Structure I varied my sentence structure, sometimes using simple and sometimes using complex sentence structure.	☐	☐	☐
I used internal punctuation appropriately within sentences and when citing sources, including commas, dashes, parentheses, colons, and semicolons.	☐	☐	☐

Name: _____   **Date:** _____

Argument Writing Checklist

	Grade 8	NOT YET	STARTING TO	YES!
	Structure			
Overall	I laid out an argument about a topic/text and made it clear why my particular argument is important and valid. I stayed fair to those who might disagree with me by describing how my position is one of several and making it clear where my position stands in relation to others.	☐	☐	☐
Lead	After hooking the reader, I provided specific context for my own as well as another position(s), introduced my position, and oriented readers to the overall line of argument I planned to develop.	☐	☐	☐
Transitions	I used transitions to lead the reader across parts of the text and to help the reader note how parts of the text relate back to earlier parts. I used phrases such as *now some argue, while this may be true, it is also the case that, despite this, as stated earlier, taken as a whole, this is significant because, the evidence points to,* and *and by doing so.*	☐	☐	☐
Ending	In the conclusion, I described the significance of my argument for stakeholders, or offered additional insights, implications, questions, or challenges.	☐	☐	☐
Organization	I organized claims, counterclaims, reasons, and evidence into sections and clarified how sections are connected.	☐	☐	☐
	I created an organizational structure that supports a reader's growing understanding across the whole of my argument, arranging the sections to build on each other in a logical, compelling fashion.	☐	☐	☐
	Development			
Elaboration	I brought out the aspects of the argument that were most significant to my audience and to my overall purpose(s).	☐	☐	☐
	I incorporated trustworthy and significant sources and explained if and when a source seemed problematic.	☐	☐	☐
	I analyzed the relevance of the reasons and evidence for my claims as well as for the counterclaim(s) and helped the reader understand what each position is saying. I made sure all of my analysis led my readers to follow my line of argument.	☐	☐	☐
Craft	I intended to affect my reader in particular ways—to make the reader think, realize, or feel a particular way—and I chose language to do that.	☐	☐	☐
	I consistently used comparisons, analogies, vivid examples, anecdotes, or other rhetorical devices to help readers follow my thinking and grasp the meaning and significance of a point or a piece of evidence.	☐	☐	☐
	I varied my tone to match the different purposes of different sections of my argument.	☐	☐	☐

Grade 8		NOT YET	STARTING TO	YES!
Conventions				
Spelling	I spelled technical vocabulary and literary vocabulary accurately. I spelled materials in citations according to sources, and spelled citations accurately.	☐	☐	☐
Punctuation and Sentence Structure	I used different sentence structures to achieve different purposes throughout my argument.	☐	☐	☐
	I used verb tenses that shift when needed (as in when moving from a citation back to my own writing), deciding between active and passive voice where appropriate.	☐	☐	☐
	I used internal punctuation effectively, including the use of ellipses to accurately insert excerpts from sources.	☐	☐	☐

Sample 1, page 1

Asmita

Egyptians Created Advanced Civilization!

Did Egyptians start a great civilization? Well they didn't use technology to built pyramids. Another reason is that they were the first to mummify people. They were also first to start great education.

My first reason is that they built enormous pyramids without technology. It is shown in research that "Workers used t-shaped tools to make sure the ground was leveled." To make the ground was leveled, they started by making the center of the crossing and hanging a weight cord from the top t. The builders would determine if it was perfectly leveled. After each lock was leveled and cut workers saved it to a wooden sled. They then put it to a flat bottomed wooden boat. They used wooden mallet, stoned hammer with wooden handles.

Another reason is that they mummify people. They were very skilled at preserving the bodies of dead. They developed the art of making mummies of the loved ones.

Sample 1, page 2

can stay after life. They removed all their internal organs. The lungs, liver and stomach with stored in a jar. The Egyptians spent seventy days preserving bodies. They took the brain out of their head. Scientist have proven that "They kept the heart in the human body, because they believed it stored intelligence and emotion." Egyptians myth had said "The dead took the heart to the final test to see if it. They passed or failed. The Gun that stored the internal organs were stored with the mummy's bodies in a tomb."

First reason is that they started a good education. They were the first people to learn about math, 3,500 years ago. It is believed that "Chinese, the moon all wrote the book." How to obtain information about all things mysterious and stuff." He explained how to add, subtract, multiply and divide fractions, how to calculate the area of circles, squares and triangles. People believe "They used millimeter stone gauges with lines to measure how much the Nile river rose. They could determine whether it was a good harvest or bad. They hoped a good harvest or bad.

it would be 7.6 m. which meant it would
be just enough water. The Egyptians were
also first to drink Castor berries oil to
cure upset stomach. They also chewed
it for the same ointment.
For obvious reasons, Egyptians
started a great civilization. They also
made big pyramids without technology.
They were first to make mummy.
Last reason is that they had great
education.

Sample 1, page 3

Sample 2, page 1

Vindy

In this essay, I will discuss my opinions about global warming. Global warming is a very serious issue. Global warming is changing the earth in ways like never before. The actions of humans led to the melting of once frozen glaciers, dividing seas, and change in climate. Us, the humans, must change our ways in order to survive.

One reason global warming is serious is because glaciers are melting. The destruction of glaciers will lead to the loss of many civilizations. For example if glaciers melt, their water will rise up sea-levels and cause floods. As Al Gore has said in his movie, "The Inconvenient Truth," if the seas rise, many cities, near bodies of water will be completely under water, including Manhattan.

We need to change our impact on the earth. Another reason humans need to change is because they pollute a lot. Business men, greedy animals, harm Mother Nature for their profit. For example, the toxic wastes are rising in numbers and wanna room in the landfill. Business men dump it into the sea, harming/poisoning the sea creatures in the seas. As it one happened in history, when farmers began using DDT's to kill pests, it resulted in a near loss of species. The insects were poisoned and since they are the beginning of a food chain the eagles eat the fish that eat the insects that were poisoned. The eagle race couldn't reproduce because when the females layed eggs. The shell was too soft and the hatching died before it came out

Sample 2, page 2

of its shell. This shows that another species might become extinct and this time the damage is too great.

The final reason global warming is serious is because it has the disastrous ability to change the climate. Climate is another form of mother nature; whoever controls it controls nature. For example, the hurricanes are getting stranger and the heat is melting Antarctica. Al Gore also said that "For the first time since 1980, the heat level is very much over normal and is bigger than 1920."

Stop global warming now!

In this essay, I have supported my claim and provided realistic information. What I am trying to say is, this planet is ours! We ourselves are destroying it. Help mother earth!

Too Small?

A lot of amusement parks have
a height limit, meaning a kid has to
be over a certain height to go on the
ride. I think that it shouldn't be the
amusement parks decision that the
kid has to be a certain height to go on
those rides alone. The parents should be able
to let their kid go on the ride. Some
people think that the equipment is too
big for the kid, and and that theres no
way to fix that problem, but there is. If
the parent gives permission to the child,
then its not any one's problem whether the
child goes on or not, just the parents.
Kids love to have fun at amusement
parks. When little kids go to the amusement
parks and start waiting on line
just to find out they're too small to
go on the ride. Thats not fun. The parents
should be the ones to allow their kid
to go on the ride they want to go on.
Having the parents be the judge and
allow their kid to go on the ride
is important because instead of
waiting on ridiculous lines to find
out you are too small, you can
create memories.

Sample 1, page 1

Another reason parents should
be allowed to choose whether
their kid can go alone a ride or not
is because some parents don't
want to go on rides kids end
up being forced to go on kiddy rides
because their parent doesn't want
to go with them on the ride. If
amusement parks would let the
parents decide, the parents don't
have to go on the ride, the
parents and the kids are happy.
Some people think that the
equipment is too big for the kids or
that theres no way to fix that
problem. the child might slip out
of the gear and fall off, A child
might not be mature enough and
they'll cry and want to get off.
I disagree because it amusement
parks just make their equipment
adjustable, anyone can go on.
If a parent who lives with their
child every day and knows their
behavior and knows that the child
is independent and responsible
enough to go a certain ride, they
should go. A kid shouldn't be held
back from having fun just because
the equipment is too big.

Sample 1, page 2

As you can see there are many reasons why a kid should be able to go alone on rides at an amvesment park. Under their parents permission. If amvesment parks just made their equipment ajustable everyone could go and have a great time. This is important because everyone deserves to have a great time, not only the kids but the parents. Amvesment parks are made for people to have fun, so let them!

Sample 1, page 3

"Vampires [Bats] could hold the key to a problem we want to solve, like Aids or cancer. But if you distroy them, they are lost for eternity." Says Francisco Oliva. Animals should never be killed.

They can benefit humans by helping maintain other animal populations, being loyal companions, and by allowing scientific research to commence.

To begin, different kind of animals can actually help keep humans safe by eliminating harsh populations. Such as the vampire bat does with the insect population. Vampire bats are many insects' natural predators, meaning that the bats in actuality, control the insect population. The insects can be harmful and carry diseases that could hurt humans. Vampire bats aren't the only helpful creatures that do this. Raccoons do too. Without the natural doing of raccoons eating reptile eggs "We would be knee-deep in turtles in 20 years." says herpetologist Michael Dorcas. If we killed these animals, it would only cause problems for us in this way.

Another reason why we should not kill animals is that they make absolutely wonderful companions. Even the most unlikely of species can make good friends. For example, a worker at the North American bear center says, "I have learned to trust Cedar bears and bear families to the extent that they mostly ignore me as I walk and sleep with them at up to 24 hrs at a time." The chances of being murdered are 60,000 times greater than being killed by a black bear. There is very little to be afraid of even of a bear. And that they can actually grow on humans as great companions. It would be preposterous to kill a dear friend.

Animals can also be the future of scientific discoveries and research, for example, Vampire Bats can also be of use to science and could give scientists what they need to potentially find the cure to Cancer or even AIDS. "Who would have thought reef sponges could lead to anti-cancer drugs, that the scales of butterfly wings could help bring about better kinds of paint?" Knows a German Zoologist said. This shows that animals can actually benefit humans in matters of life or death. If we kill these creatures we are only hurting ourselves in the future.

Many may say that the black bear is dangerous, having killed 61 people in North America since 1900. But in reality, it is more likely to be killed by lightning, or even a swarm of bees. Black bears are very rarely ever aggressive at first glance, the only circumstance where a Black bear would be aggressive is when they are defending themselves; meaning that the human would have also initiate negative contact first. Killing animals can also slow down the progression of medical research, which could only allow more people to die of insidious diseases. If we are the cause of animal species being harmed we are also the cause of our own species being harmed.

As these examples show us as human beings should not kill animals. They can provide scientists with needed research, they can be life-long friends, and they can even naturally get rid of harmful infections caused by their prey. Animals are important to this earth, and the ecosystem that surrounds us. It would be morally, scientifically and utterly wrong to disturb such natural treasures, creatures that help us in the present, and in the future.

Sample 2, page 2

Sample 2, page 1

Do celebrities deserve their high salaries?

Celebrities shouldn't get paid so much. They sometimes act incredibly spoiled. Especially younger generations, like Justin Bieber, who jump into fame so quickly that they don't realize what they have that others would kill for. And all of the reality tv stars, who participate in shows that are not real but scripted and do terrible, pointless things. And don't forget all the annoying celebrities selling products after products. Because really, who's going to pay that much for tube socks. And don't forget the false advertisements that's endorsed by celebrities that don't even use the product they endorse. Even some celebs like to act as though they are "bigger" than others because of their fame and fortune. Celebrities get overpaid for garbage. Garbage fights, products, you name it, they have it. In all, celebrities get paid for being diseases to society.

Justin Bieber. Of course he is most likely to come to minds of people when they are thinking about teenage celebrities that nag and whine. Apparently, we are supposed to "Believe" that he truly appreciates all he has. At first he had been that guy that twelve year old girls would die for, and he still is. But those girls that are able to see past all the good things and stop being blinded actually parted away from the pack. Even guys are still swooning over him, as surprising as it may sound. Even as he becomes more prone to drug abuse and breaking countless laws, crazy adults become attracted to him. Last Thursday he was arrested for drunk driving, resisting arrest, and driving without a valid license. On Wednesday he had even turned himself in for abusing a limo driver. If that wasn't bad enough, there was a petition to revoke his green card! Why you ask? Because Bieber abuses his power. He does whatever he wants and doesn't expect any consequences. Guess what? There are. And they're finally catching up with him.

You think reality shows are a reality? Guess again. Some of your favorite shows might be scripted. Many are, but others are just rumors. Tia and Tamera's show wasn't getting many views due to the fact that they had happy lives. After they had been directed to start fights over nothing, the show bombed and got canceled. A lot of people think that these shows are simply annoying, but they tend to watch them anyways to make fun of them. What they don't realize is the fact that they are feeding the show. One of the main reasons that the show is still on air is because of the people who actually hate it. They watch and watch and tell everyone what garbage it is, but they continue to watch anyways. Sometimes there are pointless episodes. Once there had been a trailer for an episode of a show where they had been driving in a car and someone had to pee. Seriously, this is what people watch. Viewers complain about the countless money they get for not doing work, but they are just donating to them! In the next episode of *The Real Housewives Of Orange County*: Watch everyone swim around on piles of money!

Watch out world, because here comes Rob Kardashian's new line of socks! The Neiman Marcus website (www.neimanmarcus.com) says that for only $100.00+tax, they can be yours! Yes, These socks cost up to a hundred dollars, but who cares, because a Kardashian is selling them! Reality TV isn't enough? Why don't you invest your money in some pair of socks that are eventually going to get holes in them and become a thrift shop owners new best selling item. Oh, and by the way! While, you're at it, might as well buy some

Sketchers Shape Ups endorsed by Kim Kardashian! Plus a major bonus, some false advertising! She doesn't even wear them. And you don't even want to know how much money she got for falsely claiming that she does. Gooo Kardashian's!

Wait a minute, looks like there are some major publicity stunts going on as well. In a *Shane And Friends* podcast, actress Tara Reid spoke about old friend Paris Hilton and her encounter with her at a restaurant. Paris had said to Tara, "You think your big, I am so much bigger than you. I am the most photographed person in the world right now." Tara now responding said, "How could you say that? I was always honestly nice to you." Of course that wasn't quite major, but there are much worse.

As you can see, celebrities do not deserve the money they make. People should stop supporting their terrible behavior.

Sources:

http://www.neimanmarcus.com/Arthur-George-by-Robert-Kardashian/Designers/cat45940749/c.cat

https://itunes.apple.com/us/podcast/shane-and-friends/id658136421?mt=2&ign-mpt=uo%3D4 (#13 Starts at 38:14)

Fracking Essay

Hydralic

Miyu

I believe that fracking should not be allowed in the New York City. It causes a bunch of health problems and causes toxic pollution into neighboring areas. Hydraulic Fracking may be beneficial, but many die or get sick because of the problems it causes. In 2013, New York temporarily banned Hydraulic Fracking because of health concerns. But Hydraulic Fracking isn't all bad, it helps with the economy, the debate of whether it remains or does not remain continues.

The first reason why I believe that fracking should be banned in NYC is because of health issues developing. More and more health concerns are issued as fracking continues. For example in an Upfront Magazine article from January 28, 2013 Frances Beinecke said that researchers from Colorado School of Public Health tested the air near fracking sites and found a bunch of chemicals known to cause headaches, breathing problems, childhood leukemia and other types of cancer. In a NY Times article from November 2011 Eliza Griswold wrote about the Haney family who lives next to a fracking factory. All of the family pets have died and she lives in fear knowing what could come next. "They've ruined our lives. I have to worry everyday if my kids will have cancer," she said. Mrs. Haney lives in fear and panic. Fracking companies might help the economy grow but they are ruining families. Fracking can be dangerous and if we use it as a method for getting electricity, it can cause lots of problems for families.

Another reason why fracking should be completely banned from New York is because it causes a pollution. For example in The Upfront Magazine article it said that fracking happens right next to us and they are pumping toxic fluid into the ground, and that releases toxic pollution into the air we breath. Although fracking causes less pollution than oil or coal, it still does pollute and contaminate water and the air. And what makes it worse is that there is toxic pollution going up into the air. With contaminated water and polluted air, it can cause ^dangerous health problems, as I said before. That is why we should not allow fracking in NY.

Some may say that fracking should be allowed because it produces less green house gases and carbon dioxide (pollution). And yes, I agree with that. Coal and oil emit a ton of carbon dioxide that can lead to Global warming, which is something we have to prevent from getting worse. In the Daily News article by Ed Rendell, published in March 2013, he stated that during transportation natural gas produces 30% less carbon dioxide than petroleum. BUT just because fracking causes less pollution, it doesn't mean it's all good. gum drops. The toxic fluids do cause major health problems to people living near it. There are better options like windmills, solar panels, and other clean ways to get energy without anyone being in danger.

In conclusion, hydraulic fracking should not be allowed (and should be dismissed) because it causes nasty health problems to citizens nearby and contaminates water and pollutes the air. We should be thinking of better, cleaner alternatives without killing lives and ruining the air. The United States wants to make money off of fracking but it is at the cost of lives.

Grade 6

The writer's introduction helps the reader understand and care about the topic. The writer clearly thought through his *entire* argument, ensuring the points made in the opening fit the whole of the piece.

The writer used transitional phrases to help the reader understand how each part fits with the next.

The writer included and arranged a variety of evidence to support his claim. He used trusted sources and information from authorities on the topic, citing those sources as needed.

The writer explained why and how various pieces of evidence support his points, explaining which evidence supports which point.

The writer's conclusion restates the main points of the essay and may offer a lingering thought or a new insight for the reader. The ending adds to and strengthens the argument as a whole.

Until two weeks ago, sixth graders could be found tossing footballs, running for touchdowns, and working through sports-related conflicts. Recess was a time to play, learn, and exercise. Then, football was banned for being "too dangerous." Now you'll find us lounging on the grass and wishing for something to fill our time with. What the adults at M.S. 293 need to understand is that football is not dangerous. In fact, it is great for kids. Football is a good source of exercise, is a game that everyone can participate in, and helps you learn important life lessons.

The first reason football should not be banned from recess is because it is great exercise. The *TIME for Kids* article, "First Lady Fights Fat in Kids," talks about the different ways that Mrs. Obama is fighting obesity in America. One of the reasons kids get obese is because they don't get enough exercise. This shows how important sports like football are. Also, Sam Rapoport, a senior manager for USA Football says "Football is great exercise." Teachers and kids could play together and everyone would be more active. We need football so we don't grow up to be unhealthy and get diseases like diabetes or heart disease.

Another reason we should be able to play football during recess is because everyone can play. You don't need to spend money on fancy equipment or uniforms. Football will not cost the school any money. Football has big teams so it doesn't leave anyone out like other games. Just picture it: Every child in sixth grade invited to play together! Whether you are a great player or a beginner, there is always a place for you on the team! Some people think football is only for boys, but that's not true. Out of 25 kids, all 25 said they wanted football. Even my mom and sister love to play. This proves that football is a valuable part of recess and should not be banned.

The final and most important reason why we should have football is because it will help us learn important things. For example, we can learn to solve problems. For instance, sometimes a play is made and both teams argue because they think they should get the point. This gives kids a chance to work out their problems on their own and make a solution. In "Flag Football: It's the Girls' Turn to Play," Christine McAndrews, a parent, argues that football is good for kids. She says that "It's great for their social skills and they resolve things on their own. It's good for them." As a parent, she should know. This proves that football can teach us a lot.

Please allow football again at recess. We will be healthier, stronger kids if you do. We will get more exercise, we will build community, and we will learn important skills. These are lessons we need, and as long as we are careful, we can be safe. Please take the football ban away and let us play again.

Sources:
- "First Lady Fights Fat in Kids." *TIME for Kids* (2010)
- "Flag Football: It's the Girls' Turn to Play." *Washington Post* (2011)

The writer stated his claim clearly and forecasted the reasons he will provide to support it.

The writer arranged paragraphs, reasons, and evidence purposefully. That is, there is evidence that the writer has thought about a logical progression for his argument.

The writer used powerful, precise words that have an effect on the reader. He also reached for phrases, metaphors, analogies, or images that will help strengthen and convey his argument.

The writer used a serious, scholarly tone when writing.

The writer may have acknowledged different sides of the argument.

The writer used punctuation such as dashes, colons, parentheses, and semicolons to help include or connect extra information in some sentences.

Grade 7

The writer made it clear that this argument is a part of a bigger conversation about a topic/text.

The writer interested the reader in the argument and helped the reader to understand the backstory behind it. The writer gave the backstory in a way that got the reader ready to understand the point being made.

Dear Administration and Members of the PTA,

Imagine that you were told that you could no longer do what you loved to do because someone thought it might be too dangerous. How would you feel? Recently, the students at our school were told that we could no longer play football on the school grounds. Every day we gather before school and after to play football but now we are told that this is no longer allowed. This is an unfair decision for many reasons. Football is an important source of physical fitness and it teaches us important life lessons. In addition, it's an inexpensive and inclusive game that many of us are passionate about. Denying us the chance to play it is taking away an important part of our interests. I am writing this letter to ask you to please remove the ban and allow us to play football on the school grounds again.

The writer made it clear to readers what the piece will argue and forecasted the parts of the upcoming argument.

First, you should consider that by taking away the chance to play football before and after school, you are taking away an opportunity for us to be healthier. America is facing a big problem—its youth are unhealthy. In the article "Couch Culture: Only a Quarter of U.S. Youth Get Recommended Exercise" by Alexandra Sifferlin it says that one out of every three children in the U.S. is overweight or obese (2014). The article refers to scientific studies done by the National Center for Health Statistics in which researchers found that only about 24.8% of youth surveyed in the National Health and Nutrition Examination Survey (NHANES)'s National Youth Fitness Survey gets the amount of physical fitness that the U.S. government has recommended. That means that most kids in America are not getting enough physical fitness and they are in danger of growing up to become adults who are sick with diseases like cancer, diabetes, and heart trouble. Playing football is one way that we could stay much more active. Football offers lots of exercise for many muscle groups. Kimberly Nunley (2013) wrote a blog for Livestrong.com about the main muscles used to play football and she claims, "Football is a sport that requires strength and power in nearly every muscle throughout the body." That means every single muscle is getting used and getting exercise when you play football! Plus, there are other physical benefits, too. According to another article "5 Mental and Physical Benefits of Playing Football," Schienbaum (2013) says that football teaches agility, hand-eye coordination, builds muscle, and requires strategy. He also argues that these benefits of football will help players to do better when they play other sports and off the field. Football is not like games like baseball or kickball where players spend a lot of time waiting around for it to be your turn. Stopping us from playing on the grounds is cutting off a major form of exercise and physical fitness for lots of students.

The writer arranged the parts of the piece purposefully and led readers from one claim or counterclaim or reason or piece of evidence to another.

The writer incorporated and cited trustworthy sources.

The writer included varied kinds of evidence such as facts, quotations, examples, and definitions.

(continues)

Grade 7 (*continued*)

The writer used topic sentences and transitions to clarify the structure of the piece and to highlight main points.

The writer included domain-specific, technical vocabulary relevant to the argument.

The writer's argument is compelling as well as understandable. It is clear why this argument matters and why the audience should care about it.

The writer wrote about another possible position and explained why the evidence for his/her position outweighed the counterclaims.

Another reason why you should take away the ban on playing football in the school grounds is that football teaches important life lessons. According to the article "3 Ways Your Child Will Benefit from Playing Football," by Steve Alic (2013), "by playing this sport, young athletes learn football's timeless qualities of leadership, responsibility, perseverance and teamwork." This means that playing football teaches lessons about leadership and dedication and pushing yourself to do more than you thought you could. As the quarterback of our team, I have personal experience with gaining leadership skills through playing football. When I pulled the team into a huddle a few weeks ago and ran through our plays, I really felt like a leader. Everyone on the team was looking at me and nodding and then when we ran the play and scored a touchdown, they all ran up to me and slapped me five. "Great job leading," they said. Without these kinds of experiences, how do you learn to be a leader? Playing football is not just about exercise. What happens inside your mind—thinking about the strategies you need to use to get the ball and to take it down the yard and how you are going to work as a team—that's important, too. These are lessons that we could carry with us our whole lives. Taking away football means you are taking away those lessons.

You should consider how inexpensive and inclusive football is. You don't need fancy equipment. Just grab the pigskin and your friends and you are set. No one is excluded. If someone else wants to join in the game, then we take turns rotating who is on the field. Football is not like sports like tennis where people get left out and you have to pay lots of money for fancy rackets. Football is just a bunch of people running around having a great time. And it's part of our community. Students have been playing football before and after school for years. When I was a little kid in elementary school I would watch kids in middle school running around in all kinds of weather because they loved playing football so much. It was like I was watching a joyful future and now that is gone. Many of us want to play football in high school and college. We are losing out on a chance to practice and get better. When tryouts come in high school, we'll be unprepared and likely will not make the team.

Some people say football is too dangerous. They say that kids shouldn't play football because they will get injured and get concussions. This is not the whole story. Saying that football causes injuries overlooks all the good that comes out of playing football like the exercise and the mental good. Football is an important game for youth to play. In his article, Steve Alic (2013) argues "to the kids, though, the game is about fun, friendships and camaraderie. It's about achieving success or learning from failure then lining right back up to try again." In addition, I surveyed all of the kids I know who played football and out of 36 kids, 7 have gotten hurt and only 3 have been hurt badly enough to have to go to the doctor or

The writer used transitions to link different parts of the argument and to make it clear when the writer is stating a claim or counterclaim, giving a reason or offering or analyzing evidence. The transitions help the reader follow from part to part.

The writer analyzed or explained the reasons and evidence given, showing how they fit with the claim and support the argument.

The writer varied sentence structure.

The writer used words purposefully to affect meaning and tone.

The writer used metaphors to explain concepts.

(continues)

Grade 7 (*continued*)

the hospital. Sure, you could get hurt playing football (you could get hurt playing ANY sport) but on the other hand, there are ways we could make football safer. In the article, "The Problem with Football: How to Make it Safer" by Sean Gregory (2010), it says that NFL Competition Committee is thinking of ways to make football safer and they have suggestions for youth football too. They say that players should be more careful not to head butt or to not keep pushing themselves if they think they are injured. We, the students who want to play, could write up a list of rules and make sure that everyone signs them. That way we could make sure that our game is safer. That would be a fair compromise. To take football away completely is unfair.

> The writer acknowledged alternate positions but refuted them.

In conclusion I would like to say that we have nowhere else to go play. You do need a lot of space to play football and there aren't a ton of football fields or yards around everywhere. If we have to go play in football leagues, our parents will have to pay money for us to join and that is not fair. We need the space on the school grounds. Schools should support students' passions and interests. Football is a fun game which is full of invigorating exercise both physical and mental. It is a passion for many of us and we are all asking you to reconsider your ban. Please let us continue to play football on the school grounds. We promise you we will make sure we play safely. That way everyone will be happy.

> The writer used a formal tone, but varied it appropriately to engage the reader.

Sincerely,

A concerned student who misses football

> The writer used internal punctuation appropriately within sentences and when citing sources, including commas, dashes, parentheses, colons, and semicolons.

> In the conclusion, the writer reinforced and built on the main points in a way that makes the text a cohesive whole. The writer restated main points and highlighted their significance.

P.S. I listed my sources below in case you want to check them:

Alic, S. (2013). *3 Ways Your Child Will Benefit from Playing Youth Football.* [Web Log Entry] Retrieved from http://usafootball.com/blogs/americas-game/post/7269

Gregory, S. (2010). The Problem with Football: How to Make it Safer. *Time Magazine.* Retrieved from http://content.time.com/time/magazine/article/0,9171,1957459,00.html

Nunley, K. (2013). *Main Muscles Used in Football.* Retrieved from http://www.livestrong.com/article/461382-main-muscles-used-in-football/

> The writer spelled material in citations correctly.

(continues)

ARGUMENT Annotated Writing
Developed through the Progression

ARGUMENT Annotated Writing
Developed through the Progression

Grade 7 (*continued*)

Grade 8

Improve it, Don't Ban It: A Position Paper on Football

The writer used different sentence structures to achieve different purposes throughout his/her argument.

The writer used shifting verb tenses when needed and appropriate.

The writer hooked the reader and then provided specific context for his/her own as well as other positions.

The writer stayed fair to those who might disagree with the position taken by describing how this position is one of several and making it clear where it stands in relation to others.

The writer laid out an argument on a topic and made it clear why this particular argument is important and valid.

The writer analyzed the relevance of the reasons and evidence given (including those given for the counterclaims) and helped the reader understand what each position is saying.

It is a fall Friday night. The moon hangs low, the air is crisp. You are walking into our town. As soon as you enter the town, you see a warm glow from the edge of the high school and you hear a low wave of noise. Get a little closer. The glow becomes lights, bright and bold hanging over the field behind the high school. The wave of noise? If you walk toward the field, you'll hear that wave of noise separate and become hundreds of voices, all cheering and screaming their hearts out. For their team. For our team. For football.

For hundreds of years, American high schools have been hubs for communities to come together and hope and root for their teams on Friday nights. Football is a pastime as American as apple pie and fireworks. It brings communities together and once a year, on the night of the Super Bowl, it brings all of America together. Yet, recently in the media, football has come under attack for being a sport that is dangerous. Critics of football and even former team players have come forward to claim that football causes concussions and that its players suffer shorter life spans. And seeing that football may be damaging for adult players has trickled down to people now fearing what happens when children play. Even President Obama has weighed in on the dangers of football for youth (see Downes, 2013). Articles aimed at people of every age from adults to children have appeared in news outlets, all urging people to take a stand against football for youth and see that it is not worth the injuries it causes. Their point—a game that causes injury is not one we want for our children. Yet, this argument overlooks the positives around football. The negative media storm has been drowning out anyone who might say that football is fun or good. Reporters paint football players as modern day gladiators fighting thoughtlessly for the entertainment of the crowd. However, this is not the full story. Football is an important form of physical exercise, a game which offers many mental benefits and a community tradition which brings joy to many. This paper will argue that rather than seeing football as entirely negative, people should be finding ways to make football safer and improve the game so that it can continue to remain a key, enjoyable pastime.

There seems to be no end to the anecdotal and scientific evidence about the injuries football causes. In "The Problem with Football: How to Make it Safer" Sean Gregory (2010) begins by describing a high school player walking into a researcher's office to see the brains of dead football players and looking at how these brains are damaged. The effect of that anecdote is shocking. The reader clearly sees that injuries, particularly head injuries caused over time do have long-term consequences. Gregory states that high school players alone suffer 43,000 to 67,000 concussions a year (although this number could be higher since these are only the number of reported concussions). In 2013, five former Kansas City

The writer used techniques from other genres (in this case, narrative writing) to hook the reader and set the stage for the argument.

The writer intended to affect the reader in particular ways—to make the reader think, realize, or feel a particular way—and chose language to do that.

The writer used comparisons, analogies, vivid examples, and other rhetorical devices to clarify the writer's thinking and help readers grasp the meaning and significance of a point.

The writer introduced the position and oriented readers to the way in which the argument would unfold across the position paper.

(continues)

ARGUMENT Annotated Writing
Developed through the Progression

May be photocopied for classroom use. © 2014 by Lucy Calkins and Colleagues from the Teachers College Reading and Writing Project from *Units of Study in Argument, Information, and Narrative Writing* (firsthand: Portsmouth, NH).

Grade 8 (*continued*)

> The writer incorporated trustworthy and significant sources.

> The writer organized claims, counterclaims, reasons, and evidence into sections and clarified how sections are connected.

> The writer worked to ensure that readers are able to follow the logical progression of the argument.

Chief players sued the Chiefs for not warning them about the long-term dangers of concussions and in August of that month, the NFL agreed to pay $765 million to settle those cases (Belson, 2013). So no one is arguing that football is totally safe. And no one is saying that football is safer than other sports, although it is the case that that there may be sports as dangerous or more dangerous than football—like, for example, cheerleading as Rick Reilly (1999) would assert. Instead, one might argue that steps need to be taken to make football safer. Just outright banning youth football is not the answer. That's like throwing the baby out with the bathwater as my grandma says. And the baby may want to grow up and play football.

There are many reasons to find ways to improve football for youth rather than just ban it outright. Think of the positives about football. Like the physical exercise. Football requires strength and speed and endurance. In her article for Livestrong.com, Nunely (2013) argues that you use almost every muscle when you play football. As she claims, upper and lower body muscles are used when players are "running, jumping, blocking, catching and throwing" and core muscles have to keep working to keep your "spine stable and perform twisting movements when throwing or going up to catch a ball." Silverman (2014), another writer for Livestrong.com would agree with Nunely, as he argues, "Despite the dangers, football players enjoy greater strength and cardiovascular health, not only during the regular playing season, but during the off-season when in training." This means that football does offer health benefits that should not be overlooked. Football doesn't just improve your cardiovascular health and your muscle tone but it also strengthens your hand-eye coordination, agility, speed, and more (Scheinbaum, 2013). Now, yes, these are blogs written for organizations that have a vested interest in sports but the truth is that youth do need to be healthier and sports, including football, are key. In a time when American youth have never been unhealthier and the National Center for Health Statistics is reporting that only about 24.8% of youth surveyed in the National Health and Nutrition Examination Survey (NHANES)'s National Youth Fitness Survey gets the amount of physical fitness that the US government has recommended (Sifferlin, 2014), is getting rid of a form of important exercise really the way to go? Do we really want youth sitting around playing video games? Isn't it important to find some way, any way, to get them active and moving? As a pop culture writer Daniel Flynn (2013) said when he was interviewed by the NFL Evolution, "there are always risks to every human endeavor but on the whole people who play football are going to walk away from playing the game healthier than people who sit in the stands and watch it."

> The writer brought out aspects of the argument that were significant to the audience and to the overall purpose of the piece.

> The writer explained when a source seemed problematic.

> The writer used internal punctuation appropriately within sentences and when citing sources, including commas, dashes, parentheses, colons, and semicolons.

(continues)

Grade 8 (*continued*)

Another key reason for finding ways to improve football rather than ban it for youth are the mental benefits of football. Scheinbaum (2013) assert that playing football requires more strategy than any other sport. As he explains, football is a game "made up of dozens of individual plays, each with its own complicated patterns of movement and logic." According to Scheinbaum, this game requires a player to be constantly evaluating what is working and what is not. The strategy involved means that youth who play are learning to be more strategic, considering which plays will work and in what situations. In addition, playing on a football team can teach important leadership skills. According to the article "3 Ways Your Child Will Benefit from Playing Football," by Steve Alic (2013), "by playing this sport, young athletes learn football's timeless qualities of leadership, responsibility, perseverance and teamwork." This is significant because students who play football are learning lessons that will matter off the field. Research also shows that students in middle school who play sports are healthier and more satisfied with their lives than those who do not (2010). So students who are playing football no matter what are gaining things they would not be gaining otherwise. If football is banned, those gains will be lost.

Perhaps the most important reason to consider how to make football safer than just banning it outright is the fact that it is a passion and a tradition that is important for many. When three million children ages 6-14 take to football fields every year (Alic, 2013) we have to concede that there must be at least some enjoyment for the game. When towns gather to huddle around their teams, cheering them on, even in freezing cold weather, we have to acknowledge that this game is more than a game to some. It is part of a tradition. And sure, there are traditions that should not always be kept but it seems an indifferent, cold attitude to look at how many people have their hearts in this sport and say, "no get rid of it." Wouldn't it be better to study more carefully how it could be improved? And, I am arguing that there are ways to improve the game.

Rather than start banning youth leagues, more communities need to start putting policies in place that keep students safer. Like reading the research on which helmets are safest. Like making sure coaches go through tougher training programs so they are more aware of what plays are dangerous and should not be run and of how to make sure that youth do not overwork certain muscles. Like making it illegal for players to use certain head-butting moves. Like making it okay and even admirable to leave the field if you get hit rather than playing through pain. In "The Problem with Football: How to Make it Safer," Sean Gregory offers suggestions for how to make football safer and if more communities read this kind of work, then perhaps football would be a safer game and less people would be bad-mouthing it. There is some evidence that raising awareness of the dangers of football may be the best first step toward

> The writer used transitions such as "perhaps the most important reason," "this is significant because," "there is some evidence that" to lead the reader across parts of the text.

> The writer created an organizational structure that supports the reader's growing understanding across the whole of the argument, arranging the sections to build on each other in a logical, compelling fashion.

(continues)

Grade 8 (*continued*)

| The writer spelled technical and literacy vocabulary accurately. |

improvement. A recent New York Times article by Belson (2014) stated that the NFL had reported a 13% decline in concussions this year. The NFL credited "improved medical diagnoses, stiffer penalties for striking with a helmet, and fewer practices" for this decline although officials did say that this number is based on a small sample size and there may still be unreported concussions. Still though, this decline may point to a positive sign—that an increased awareness of the dangers and a more vigilant understanding of how to be safer may lead to greater safety.

| The writer used transitions to lead the reader across parts of the text and to help the reader note how parts of the text relate back to earlier parts. |

So, there you are, in our town on a Friday night in autumn, watching football. You see families in the stands huddled together under blankets, their breaths blowing frosty in the night. You see the players giving it their all, pumping each other up and keeping each other going under the warm glow of the lights. And as you watch, you'll see lots of problems, sure, but you'll see something to cheer about, too, of that I'm sure. Football has a ways to go but banning it is not the answer. More needs to be done to make youth football safer and then that will be something we can all cheer about.

| The writer varied the tone to match the different purposes of different sections of the argument. |

| In the conclusion, the writer described the significance of the argument for stakeholders and offered additional insights and implications. |

References

Alic, S. (2013). 3 Ways Your Child Will Benefit from Playing Youth Football. [Web Log Entry] Retrieved from http://usafootball.com/blogs/americas-game/post/7269

Belson, K. (2014, January 30). Concussions Show Decline of 13%, N.F.L. Says. The New York Times. Retrieved from http://www.nytimes.com/2014/01/31/sports/football/nfl-reports-concussions-dropped-13-percent-in-2013.html

Belson, K (2013, December 3). Five Former N.F.L. Players Sue the Chiefs Over Head Injuries. The New York Times. Retrieved from http://www.nytimes.com/2013/12/04/sports/football/five-former-nfl-players-sue-the-kansas-city-chiefs-over-head-injuries.html

Downes, L. (2013). The Dangerous Game. Taking Note: The Editorial Page Editor's Blog [web log entry]. Retrieved from http://takingnote.blogs.nytimes.com/2013/01/30/the-dangerous-game

Flynn, D. (2013). Author's 'War on Football' sees positive aspects at all levels. Retrieved from http://www.nfl.com/news/story/0ap1000000243729/article/authors-war-on-football-sees-positive-aspects-at-all-levels

Gregory, S. (2010). The Problem with Football: How to Make it Safer. Time Magazine. Retrieved from http://content.time.com/time/magazine/article/0,9171,1957459,00.html

Nunley, K. (2013). Main Muscles Used in Football. Retrieved from http://www.livestrong.com/article/461382-main-muscles-used-in-football/

(continues)

Grade 8 (*continued*)

The writer spelled material in citations accurately.

Reilly, R. (1999, October). Sis! Boom! Bah! Humbug! Sports Illustrated, vol. 91 (issue 15). Retrieved from http://sportsillustrated. cnn.com/vault/article/magazine/MAG1017375/

Scheinbaum, C. (2013). 5 Mental and Physical Benefits of Playing Football. [Web Log Entry] Retrieved from http://www.theadrenalist. com/sports/5-mental-and-physical-benefits-of-playing-football/

Sifferlin, A. (2014). Couch Culture: Only a Quarter of U.S. Youth Get Recommended Exercise. Retrieved from http://healthland.time. com/2014/01/08/couch-culture-only-a-quarter-of-u-s-youth-get-recommended-exercise/

Study Shows Physical and Mental Health Benefits of Sports Participation in Adolescents. (2010, September 22). Retrieved from http://www.news-medical.net/news/20100922/Study-shows-physical-and-mental-health-benefits-of-sports-participation-in-adolescents.aspx

Learning Progression for Information Writing

	Grade 3	Grade 4	Grade 5
STRUCTURE			
Overall	The writer taught readers information about a subject. He put in ideas, observations, and questions.	The writer taught readers different things about a subject. He put facts, details, quotes, and ideas into each part of his writing.	The writer used different kinds of information to teach about the subject. Sometimes she included little essays, stories, or how-to sections in her writing.
Lead	The writer wrote a beginning in which she got readers ready to learn a lot of information about the subject.	The writer hooked her readers by explaining why the subject mattered, telling a surprising fact, or giving a big picture. She let readers know that she would teach them different things about a subject.	The writer wrote an introduction in which he helped readers get interested in and understand the subject. He let readers know the subtopics that he would later develop, as well as the sequence.
Transitions	The writer used words to show sequence such as *before, after, then,* and *later.* He also used words to show what did not fit such as *however* and *but.*	The writer used words in each section that helped readers understand how one piece of information connected with others. If he wrote the section in sequence, he used words and phrases such as *before, later, next, then,* and *after.* If he organized the section in kinds or parts, he used words such as *another, also,* and *for example.*	When the writer wrote about results, she used words and phrases like *consequently, as a result,* and *because of this.* When she compared information, she used words and phrases such as *in contrast, by comparison,* and *especially.* In narrative parts, she used phrases that go with stories such as *a little later* and *three hours later.* In the sections that stated an opinion, she used words such as *but the most important reason, for example,* and *consequently.*
Ending	The writer wrote an ending that drew conclusions, asked questions, or suggested ways readers might respond.	The writer wrote an ending in which she reminded readers of her subject and may either have suggested a follow-up action or left readers with a final insight. She added her thoughts, feelings, and questions about the subject at the end.	The writer wrote a conclusion in which he restated the main points and may have offered a final thought or question for readers to consider.

Learning Progression for Information Writing

STRUCTURE

Grade 6	Grade 7	Grade 8	Grade 9
The writer conveyed ideas and information about a subject in a well-structured text. Sometimes she incorporated arguments, explanations, stories, or procedural passages.	The writer brought together ideas and information about a subject in a text that develops a subtopic and/or an idea. He incorporated a variety of text structures as needed, including argument, explanation, narrative, and procedural passages.	The writer discussed key concepts within a topic and made it clear why these concepts are important. She provided examples with relevant information, using a variety of text structures and formatting, as needed, to make concepts and information compelling and accessible.	The writer discussed complex concepts, presenting facts and information in an engaging manner, teaching the reader significant concepts and information. The writer conveyed the sources of the information and analyzed them when relevant.
The writer wrote an introduction in which she interested readers, perhaps with a quote or significant fact. She let readers know the subtopics that she would develop later and how her text would unfold.	The writer interested the reader in the topic by explaining its significance or providing a compelling fact, statistic, or anecdote. He made it clear what parts of this topic his text would tackle, and how the ideas and information in the text would unfold.	After hooking the reader, the writer provided context, introduced a focus/main idea, and oriented readers to the overall structure of the text (compare/contrast, cause and effect, claims and support, classification, etc.).	The writer wrote an engaging lead that explained the topic's significance, contextualized it with background information, and mentioned key points of view or issues that would be discussed.
The writer used transitions to help readers understand how different bits of information and different parts of his writing fit together. He used transitions to help connect ideas, information, and examples, and to imply relationships such as when material *exemplifies, adds to, is similar to, explains, is a result of, or contrasts*. He used transitions such as *for instance, such as, similarly, therefore, as a result, in contrast to,* and *on the other hand*.	The writer used transitions to link concepts with related information. The transitions help the reader follow from part to part and make it clear when information is an example of a bigger idea, follows from an earlier point, introduces a new idea, or suggests a contrast. The writer used such transitions as *specifically, for instance, related to, just as, turning to, on the other hand,* and *however*.	The writer used transitions to lead the reader across parts of the text and to help the reader note how parts of the text relate back to earlier parts, using phrases such as *just as, returning to, as we saw earlier, similarly to, unlike,* and *yet*.	The writer used transitional phrases to show the relationship between parts of the text, including references to prior sections and previewing future sections. The writer may have used transitions to show the source of cited information. These transitions might include *adapted from, excerpted from, according to, building from, revealed in, suggested by, illustrated by,* and *demonstrated in*.
The writer wrote a conclusion in which she restated the important ideas and offered a final insight or implication for the reader to consider.	In his conclusion, the writer reinforced and built on the main point(s) in a way that made the entire piece a cohesive whole. The conclusion may have restated the main points, responded to them, or highlighted their significance.	In her conclusion, the writer suggested implications, built up the significance of her main points, and/or alluded to potential challenges.	In his conclusion, the writer strengthens implication, suggested action to take, and/or mentioned multiple perspective or potential challenges.

INFORMATION Learning Progression, 3–9

	Grade 3	Grade 4	Grade 5
STRUCTURE (cont.)			
Organization	The writer grouped his information into parts. Each part was mostly about one thing that connected to his big topic.	The writer grouped information into sections and used paragraphs and sometimes chapters to separate those sections. Each section had information that was mostly about the same thing. He may have used headings and subheadings.	The writer organized her writing into a sequence of separate sections. She may have used headings and subheadings to highlight the separate sections. The writer wrote each section according to an organizational plan shaped partly by the genre of the section.
DEVELOPMENT			
Elaboration	The writer wrote facts, definitions, details, and observations about her topic and explained some of them.	The writer taught her readers different things about the subject. She chose those subtopics because they were important and interesting. The writer included different kinds of facts and details such as numbers, names, and examples. The writer got her information from talking to people, reading books, and from her own knowledge and observations. The writer made choices about organization, perhaps using compare/contrast, cause/effect, or pro/con. She may have used diagrams, charts, headings, bold words, and definition boxes to help teach her readers.	The writer explained different aspects of a subject. She included a variety of information such as examples, details, dates, and quotes. The writer used trusted sources and gave credit when appropriate. She made sure to research any details that would add to her writing. The writer worked to make her information understandable to readers. To do this, she referred to earlier parts of her text or summarized background information. The writer let readers know when she was discussing facts and when she was offering her own thinking.

Grade 6	Grade 7	Grade 8	Grade 9
STRUCTURE (cont.)			
The writer chose a focused subject. The writer used subheadings and/or clear introductory transitions to separate sections. The writer made deliberate choices about how to order sections and about the sequence of information and ideas within sections. He chose structures such as compare and contrast, categories, or claim and support to organize information and ideas. Some sections are written as argument, explanation, stories, or procedural passages.	The writer focused her writing on a subtopic or a particular point or two. The writer organized her piece into parts and used structures (claims and supports, problem/solution, sequence, etc.) to organize those parts (and perhaps the whole). The writer used introductions, topic sentences, transitions, formatting, and graphics, where appropriate, to clarify the structure of the piece and to highlight main points.	The writer focused on key concepts within the topic. The writer organized information and ideas into broader categories and clarified how sections are ordered and connected. The writer used his organizational structure to help the reader's comprehension, perhaps holding back details until first conveying broader points, or only offering a second perspective after the first was established. The sections and information built on each other throughout the piece: concepts and examples were introduced in a logical fashion.	The writer's organizational structure introduced and layered key concepts and information. The writer layered information to maintain tension, engage the reader's interest, and/or build complexity. The writer built the sections upon each other logically, allowing the reader to build knowledge and deeper understandings.
DEVELOPMENT			
The writer included varied kinds of information such as facts, quotations, examples, and definitions. The writer used trusted sources and information from authorities on the topic and gave the sources credit. The writer worked to make his information understandable and interesting. To do this, he referred to earlier parts of his text, summarized background information, raised questions, or considered possible implications.	The writer included varied kinds of information such as facts, quotations, examples, and definitions. She analyzed or explained the information, showing how the information fits with her key points or subtopics, including graphics where appropriate. The writer consistently incorporated and cited sources. The writer worked to make her topic compelling as well as understandable. She brought out why it mattered and why the audience should care about it.	The writer brought out the parts of the topic that were most significant to his audience and to his point(s). The writer analyzed the relevance of his information and made sure the information supported the major concepts. The writer incorporated trustworthy and significant sources, and explained if and when a source seemed problematic.	The writer developed key concepts, giving some context and background. The writer used examples to clarify, explain, and interest. The writer analyzed the facts and information, explaining the relevance of cited source material. The writer included trustworthy and significant sources of information, analyzing and critiquing these sources when relevant.

	Grade 3	Grade 4	Grade 5
		DEVELOPMENT (cont.)	
Craft	The writer chose expert words to teach readers a lot about the subject. He taught information in a way to interest readers. He may have used drawings, captions, or diagrams.	The writer made deliberate word choices to teach his readers. He may have done this by using and repeating key words about his topic. When it felt right to do so, the writer chose interesting comparisons and used figurative language to clarify his points. The writer made choices about which information was best to include or not include. The writer used a teaching tone. To do so, he may have used phrases such as *that means, what that really means is,* and *let me explain.*	The writer made deliberate word choices to have an effect on his readers. He used the vocabulary of experts and explained the key terms. The writer worked to include the exact phrase, comparison, or image to explain information and concepts. The writer not only made choices about which details and facts to include but also made choices about how to convey his information so it would make sense to readers. The writer blended storytelling, summary, and other genres as needed and used text features. The writer used a consistent, inviting, teaching tone and varied his sentences to help readers take in and understand the information.
		CONVENTIONS	
Spelling	The writer used what she knew about spelling patterns to help her spell and edit before she wrote her final draft. The writer got help from others to check her spelling and punctuation before she wrote her final draft.	The writer used what she knew about word families and spelling rules to help her spell and edit. She used the word wall and dictionaries to help her when needed.	The writer used what she knew about word families and spelling rules to help her spell and edit. She used the word wall and dictionaries to help her when needed.
Punctuation and Sentence Structure	The writer punctuated dialogue correctly, with commas and quotation marks. The writer put punctuation at the end of every sentence while writing. The writer wrote in ways that helped readers read with expression, reading some parts quickly, some slowly, some parts in one sort of voice and others in another.	When writing long, complex sentences, the writer used commas to make them clear and correct.	The writer used commas to set off introductory parts of sentences (*for example, as you might know*). The writer used a variety of punctuation to fix any run-on sentences. He used punctuation to cite his sources.

Grade 6	Grade 7	Grade 8	Grade 9
DEVELOPMENT (cont.)			
The writer chose her words carefully to explain her information and ideas and to have an effect on the reader. The writer worked to include concrete details, comparisons, and/or images to explain information and concepts and to keep her reader engaged. The writer incorporated domain-specific vocabulary and, when necessary, she explained terms to readers, providing context clues, parenthetical explanations, text boxes, or similar support. The writer supported readers' learning by using a teaching tone and a formal style, as appropriate.	The writer used words purposefully to affect meaning and tone. The writer chose precise words and used metaphors, anecdotes, images, or comparisons to explain what he meant. The writer included domain-specific, technical vocabulary, and defined these when appropriate. The writer used a formal tone, but varied it appropriately to engage the reader.	The writer intended to affect her reader in particular ways—to make the reader think, realize, or feel a particular way—and she chose language to do that. The writer consistently used comparisons, analogies, vivid examples, and/or anecdotes to help readers grasp the meaning of concepts and the significance of information. The writer varied her tone to match the different purposes of different sections of her piece.	The writer intended to affect the reader in particular ways—to make the reader think, realize, or feel a particular way—and chose particular language to do that. In addition to using other literary devices, the writer may have used allusions. The writer varied the tone to match the different purposes of different sections of the argument, as well as to develop its overall impact. The writer made choices about formatting, considering the form to best convey the content.
CONVENTIONS			
The writer used resources to be sure the words in his writing were spelled correctly, including technical vocabulary.	The writer checked spelling of technical, domain-specific words and was careful with the spelling of citations.	The writer checked spelling of technical, domain-specific words and was careful with the spelling and details of citations, excerpts, quotations, and statistics.	The writer spelled accurately throughout, including cited text and citations.
The writer used punctuation such as dashes, parentheses, colons, and semicolons to help her include extra information and explanation in some of her sentences. The writer accurately cited her references, using appropriate punctuation.	The writer varied his sentence structure, sometimes using simple and sometimes using complex sentence structure. The writer used internal punctuation appropriately within sentences and when citing sources, including commas, dashes, parentheses, colons, and semicolons.	The writer used different sentence structures to achieve different purposes throughout her piece. The writer used verb tenses that shift when needed (as in when moving from a citation back to her own writing), deciding between active and passive voice where appropriate. The writer used internal punctuation effectively, including the use of ellipses to accurately insert excerpts from sources.	The writer used sentence structure and verb tense purposefully (i.e., using fragments to emphasize key points; using present tense to create immediacy). The writer used punctuation to emphasize connections, to strengthen tone, to clarify, and to add complexity.

May be photocopied for classroom use. © 2014 by Lucy Calkins and Colleagues from the Teachers College Reading and Writing Project from *Units of Study in Argument, Information, and Narrative Writing* (firsthand: Portsmouth, NH).

ON-DEMAND PERFORMANCE ASSESSMENT PROMPT

Information Writing

Say to students:

"Think of a topic that you've studied or that you know a lot about. Tomorrow, you will have forty-five minutes to write an informational (or all-about) text that teaches others interesting and important information and ideas about that topic. If you want to find and use information from a book or another outside source to help you with this writing, you may bring that with you tomorrow. Please keep in mind that you'll have only forty-five minutes to complete this. You will only have this one period, so you'll need to plan, draft, revise, and edit in one sitting. Write in a way that shows all that you know about information writing.

"In your writing, make sure you:

- Write an introduction.

- Elaborate with a variety of information.

- Organize your writing.

- Use transition words.

- Write a conclusion."

Use the teaching rubrics to assess and score these pieces of on-demand writing.

Name: _____ Date: _____

Rubric for Information Writing—Sixth Grade

STRUCTURE

	Grade 4 (1 POINT)	1.5 PTS	Grade 5 (2 POINTS)	2.5 PTS	Grade 6 (3 POINTS)	3.5 PTS	Grade 7 (4 POINTS)	SCORE
Overall	The writer taught readers different things about a subject. He put facts, details, quotes, and ideas into each part of his writing.	Mid-level	The writer used different kinds of information to teach about the subject. Sometimes she included little essays, stories, or how-to sections in her writing.	Mid-level	The writer conveyed ideas and information about a subject in a well-structured text. Sometimes she incorporated arguments, explanations, stories, or procedural passages.	Mid-level	The writer brought together ideas and information about a subject in a text that develops a subtopic and/or an idea. He incorporated a variety of text structures as needed, including argument, explanation, narrative, and procedural passages.	
Lead	The writer hooked her readers by explaining why the subject mattered, telling a surprising fact, or giving a big picture. She let readers know that she would teach them different things about a subject.	Mid-level	The writer wrote an introduction in which he helped readers get interested in and understand the subject. He let readers know the subtopics that she would develop later, as well as the sequence.	Mid-level	The writer wrote an introduction in which she interested readers, perhaps with a quote or significant fact. She let readers know the subtopics that she would develop later and how her text would unfold.	Mid-level	The writer interested the reader in the topic by explaining its significance or providing a compelling fact, statistic, or anecdote. He made it clear what parts of this topic his text would tackle, and how the ideas and information in the text would unfold.	
Transitions	The writer used words in each section that helped readers understand how one piece of information connected with others. If he wrote the section in sequence, he used words and phrases such as *before, later, next, then,* and *after.* If he organized the section in kinds or parts, he used words such as *another, also,* and *for example.*	Mid-level	When the writer wrote about results, she used words and phrases like *consequently, as a result,* and *because of this.* When she compared information, she used words and phrases such as *in contrast, by comparison,* and *especially.* In narrative parts, she used phrases that go with stories such as *a little later* and *three hours later.* In the sections that stated an opinion, she used words such as *but the most important reason, for example,* and *consequently.*	Mid-level	The writer used transitions to help readers understand how different bits of information and different parts of his writing fit together. He used transitions to help connect ideas, information, and examples, and to imply relationships such as when material exemplifies, adds to, is similar to, explains, is a result of, or contrasts. He used transitions such as *for instance, as a result, in contrast to, and on the other hand.*	Mid-level	The writer used transitions to link concepts with related information. The transitions help the reader follow from part to part and make it clear when information is an example of a bigger idea, follows from an earlier point, introduces a new idea, or suggests a contrast. The writer used such transitions as *specifically, for instance, related to, just as, turning to, on the other hand, and however.*	

INFORMATION: TEACHING RUBRIC—SIXTH GRADE (continued)

STRUCTURE (cont.)

	Grade 4 (1 POINT)	1.5 PTS	Grade 5 (2 POINTS)	2.5 PTS	Grade 6 (3 POINTS)	3.5 PTS	Grade 7 (4 POINTS)	SCORE
Ending	The writer wrote an ending in which she reminded readers of her subject and may either have suggested a follow-up action or left readers with a final insight. She added her thoughts, feelings, and questions about the subject at the end.	Mid-level	The writer wrote a conclusion in which he restated the main points and may have offered a final thought or question for readers to consider.	Mid-level	The writer wrote a conclusion in which she restated the important ideas and offered a final insight or implication for the reader to consider.	Mid-level	In his conclusion, the writer reinforced and built on the main point(s) in a way that made the entire piece a cohesive whole. The conclusion may have restated the main points, responded to them, or highlighted their significance.	
Organization	The writer grouped information into sections and used paragraphs and sometimes chapters to separate those sections. Each section had information that was mostly about the same thing. He may have used headings and subheadings.	Mid-level	The writer organized her writing into a sequence of separate sections. She may have used headings and subheadings to highlight the separate sections. The writer wrote each section according to an organizational plan shaped partly by the genre of the section.	Mid-level	The writer chose a focused subject. The writer used subheadings and/or clear introductory transitions to separate sections. The writer made deliberate choices about how to order sections and about the sequence of information and ideas within sections. He chose structures such as compare and contrast, categories, or claim and support to organize information and ideas. Some sections are written as argument, explanation, stories, or procedural passages.	Mid-level	The writer focused her writing on a subtopic or a particular point or two. The writer organized her piece into parts and used structures (claims and supports, problem/solution, sequence, etc.) to organize those parts (and perhaps the whole). The writer used introductions, topic sentences, transitions, formatting, and graphics, where appropriate, to clarify the structure of the piece and to highlight main points.	
							TOTAL:	

INFORMATION: TEACHING RUBRIC—SIXTH GRADE (continued)

	Grade 4 (1 POINT)	1.5 PTS	Grade 5 (2 POINTS)	2.5 PTS	Grade 6 (3 POINTS)	3.5 PTS	Grade 7 (4 POINTS)	SCORE
				DEVELOPMENT				
Elaboration*	The writer taught her readers different things about the subject. She chose those subtopics because they were important and interesting. The writer included different kinds of facts and details such as numbers, names, and examples. The writer got her information from talking to people, reading books, and from her own knowledge and observations. The writer made choices about organization, perhaps using compare/contrast, cause/effect, or pro/con. She may have used diagrams, charts, headings, bold words, and definition boxes to help teach her readers.	Mid-level	The writer explained different aspects of a subject. She included a variety of information such as examples, details, dates, and quotes. The writer used trusted sources and gave credit when appropriate. She made sure to research any details that would add to her writing. The writer worked to make her information understandable to readers. To do this, she referred to earlier parts of her text or summarized background information. The writer let readers know when she was discussing facts and when she was offering her own thinking.	Mid-level	The writer included varied kinds of information such as facts, quotations, examples, and definitions. The writer used trusted sources and information from authorities on the topic and gave the sources credit. The writer worked to make his information understandable and interesting. To do this, he referred to earlier parts of his text, summarized background information, raised questions, or considered possible implications.	Mid-level	The writer included varied kinds of information such as facts, quotations, examples, and definitions. She analyzed or explained the information, showing how the information fits with her key points or subtopics, including graphics where appropriate. The writer consistently incorporated and cited sources. The writer worked to make her topic compelling as well as understandable. She brought out why it mattered and why the audience should care about it.	

*Elaboration and Craft are double-weighted categories: Whatever score a student would get in these categories is worth double the amount of points. For example, if a student exceeds expectations in Elaboration, then that student would receive 8 points instead of 4 points. If a student meets standards in Elaboration, then that student would receive 6 points instead of 3 points.

INFORMATION: TEACHING RUBRIC—SIXTH GRADE (continued)

	Grade 4 (1 POINT)		Grade 5 (2 POINTS)		Grade 6 (3 POINTS)		Grade 7 (4 POINTS)	SCORE
		1.5 PTS	2.5 PTS		3.5 PTS			

DEVELOPMENT (cont.)

	Grade 4	Mid-level	Grade 5	Mid-level	Grade 6	Mid-level	Grade 7	SCORE
Craft*	The reader made deliberate word choices to teach his readers. He may have done this by using and repeating key words about his topic. When it felt right to do so, the writer chose interesting comparisons and used figurative language to clarify his points. The write made choices about which information was best to include or not include. The writer used a teaching tone. To do so, he may have used phrases such as *that means, what that really means is,* and *let me explain.*		The writer made deliberate word choices to have an effect on his readers. He used the vocabulary of experts and explained the key terms. The writer worked to include the exact phrase, comparison, or image to explain information and concepts. The writer not only made choices about which details and facts to include but also made choices about how to convey his information so it would make sense to readers. The writer blended other genres as needed and used text features. The writer used a consistent, inviting, teaching tone and varied his sentences to help readers take in and understand the information.		The writer chose her words carefully to explain her information and ideas and to have an effect on the reader. The writer worked to include concrete details, comparisons, and/or images to explain information and concepts and to keep her reader engaged. The writer incorporated domain-specific vocabulary and, when necessary, she explained terms to readers, providing context clues, parenthetical explanations, text boxes, or similar support. The writer supported readers' learning by using a teaching tone and a formal style, as appropriate.		The writer used words purposefully to affect meaning and tone. The writer chose precise words and used metaphors, anecdotes, images, or comparisons to explain what he meant. The writer included domain-specific, technical vocabulary, and defined these when appropriate. The writer used a formal tone, but varied it appropriately to engage the reader.	

CONVENTIONS

	Grade 4	Mid-level	Grade 5	Mid-level	Grade 6	Mid-level	Grade 7	SCORE
Spelling	The writer used what she knew about word families and spelling rules to help her spell and edit. She used the word wall and dictionaries to help her when needed.		The writer used what she knew about word families and spelling rules to help her spell and edit. She used the word wall and dictionaries to help her when needed.		The writer used resources to be sure the words in his writing were spelled correctly, including technical vocabulary.		The writer checked spelling of technical, domain-specific words and was careful with the spelling of citations.	

TOTAL:

*Elaboration and Craft are double-weighted categories: Whatever score a student would get in these categories is worth double the amount of points. For example, if a student exceeds expectations in Elaboration, then that student would receive 8 points instead of 4 points. If a student meets standards in Elaboration, then that student would receive 6 points instead of 3 points.

INFORMATION: TEACHING RUBRIC—SIXTH GRADE (continued)

	Grade 4 (1 POINT)	1.5 PTS	Grade 5 (2 POINTS)	2.5 PTS	Grade 6 (3 POINTS)	3.5 PTS	Grade 7 (4 POINTS)	SCORE
CONVENTIONS (cont.)								
Punctuation and Sentence Structure	When writing long, complex sentences, the writer used commas to make them clear and correct.	Mid-level	The writer used commas to set off introductory parts of sentences (for example, as you might know,). The writer used a variety of punctuation to fix any run-on sentences. He used punctuation to cite his sources.		The writer used punctuation such as dashes, parentheses, colons, and semicolons to help her include extra information and explanation in some of her sentences. The writer accurately cited her references, using appropriate punctuation.		The writer varied his sentence structure, sometimes using simple and sometimes using complex sentence structure. The writer used internal punctuation appropriately within sentences and when citing sources, including commas, dashes, parentheses, colons, and semicolons.	
							TOTAL:	

Teachers, we created these rubrics so you will have your own place to pull together scores of student work. You can use these assessments immediately after giving the on-demands and also for self-assessment and setting goals.

Scoring Guide

In each row, circle the descriptor in the column that matches the student work. Scores in the categories of Elaboration and Craft are worth double the point value (2, 3, 4, 5, 6, 7, or 8 instead of 1, 1.5, 2, 2.5, 3, 3.5, or 4).

Total the number of points and then track students' progress by seeing when the total points increase.

Total score: _____

If you want to translate this score into a grade, you can use the provided table to score each student on a scale of 0–4.

Number of Points	Scaled Score
1–11	1
11.5–16.5	1.5
17–22	2
22.5–27.5	2.5
28–33	3
33.5–38.5	3.5
39–44	4

Rubric for Information Writing—Seventh Grade

	Grade 5 (1 POINT)	1.5 PTS	**Grade 6** (2 POINTS)	2.5 PTS	**Grade 7** (3 POINTS)	3.5 PTS	**Grade 8** (4 POINTS)	SCORE
STRUCTURE								
Overall	The writer used different kinds of information to teach about the subject. Sometimes she included little essays, stories, or how-to sections in her writing.	Mid-level	The writer conveyed ideas and information about a subject in a well-structured text. Sometimes she incorporated arguments, explanations, stories, or procedural passages.	Mid-level	The writer brought together ideas and information about a subject in a text that develops a subtopic and/or an idea. He incorporated a variety of text structures as needed, including argument, explanation, narrative, and procedural passages.	Mid-level	The writer discussed key concepts within a topic and made it clear why these concepts are important. She provided examples with relevant information, using a variety of text structures and formatting, as needed, to make concepts and information compelling and accessible.	
Lead	The writer wrote an introduction in which he helped readers get interested in and understand the subject. He let readers know the subtopics that he would develop later as well as the sequence.	Mid-level	The writer wrote an introduction in which she interested readers, perhaps with a quote or significant fact. She let readers know the subtopics that she would develop later and how her text would unfold.	Mid-level	The writer interested the reader in the topic by explaining its significance or providing a compelling fact, statistic, or anecdote. He made it clear what parts of this topic his text would tackle, and how the ideas and information in the text would unfold.	Mid-level	After hooking the reader, the writer provided context, introduced a focus/main idea, and oriented readers to the overall structure of the text (compare/contrast, cause and effect, claims and support, classification, etc.).	

INFORMATION: TEACHING RUBRIC—SEVENTH GRADE (continued)

STRUCTURE (cont.)

	Grade 5 (1 POINT)	1.5 PTS	Grade 6 (2 POINTS)	2.5 PTS	Grade 7 (3 POINTS)	3.5 PTS	Grade 8 (4 POINTS)	SCORE
Transitions	When the writer wrote about results, she used words and phrases such as *consequently, as a result,* and *because of this.* When she compared information, she used phrases such as *in contrast, by comparison,* and *especially.* In narrative parts, she used phrases that go with stories such as *a little later* and *three hours later.* If she wrote sections that stated an opinion, she used words such as *but the most important reason, for example,* and *consequently.*	Mid-level	The writer used transitions to help readers understand how different bits of information and different parts of his writing fit together. He used transitions to help connect ideas, information, and examples, and to imply relationships such as when material exemplifies, adds to, is similar to, explains, is a result of, or contrasts. He used transitions such as *for instance, such as, similarly, therefore, as a result, in contrast to,* and *on the other hand.*	Mid-level	The writer used transitions to link concepts with related information. The transitions help the reader follow from part to part and make it clear when information is an example of a bigger idea, follows from an earlier point, introduces a new idea, or suggests a contrast. The writer used such transitions as *specifically, for instance, related to, just as, turning to, on the other hand,* and *however.*	Mid-level	The writer used transitions to lead the reader across parts of the text and to help the reader note how parts of the text relate back to earlier parts, using phrases such as *just as, returning to, as we saw earlier, similarly to, unlike,* and *yet.*	
Ending	The writer wrote a conclusion in which he restated the main points and may have offered a final thought or question for readers to consider.	Mid-level	The writer wrote a conclusion in which she restated the important ideas and offered a final insight or implication for the reader to consider.	Mid-level	In his conclusion, the writer reinforced and built on the main point(s) in a way that made the entire piece a cohesive whole. The conclusion may have restated the main points, responded to them, or highlighted their significance.	Mid-level	In her conclusion, the writer suggested implications, built up the significance of her main points, and/or alluded to potential challenges.	

INFORMATION: TEACHING RUBRIC—SEVENTH GRADE (continued)

	Grade 5 (1 POINT)	1.5 PTS	Grade 6 (2 POINTS)	2.5 PTS	Grade 7 (3 POINTS)	3.5 PTS	Grade 8 (4 POINTS)	SCORE
STRUCTURE (cont.)								
Organization	The writer organized her writing into a sequence of separate sections. She may have used headings and subheadings to highlight the separate sections. The writer wrote each section according to an organizational plan shaped partly by the genre of the section.	Mid-level	The writer chose a focused subject. The writer used subheadings and/or clear introductory transitions to separate sections. The writer made deliberate choices about how to order sections and about the sequence of information and ideas within sections. He chose structures such as compare and contrast, categories, or claim and support to organize information and ideas. Some sections are written as argument, explanation, stories, or procedural passages.	Mid-level	The writer focused her writing on a subtopic or a particular point or two. The writer organized her piece into parts and used structures (claims and supports, problem/solution, sequence, etc.) to organize those parts (and perhaps the whole). The writer used introductions, topic sentences, transitions, formatting, and graphics, where appropriate, to clarify the structure of the piece and to highlight main points.	Mid-level	The writer focused on key concepts within the topic. The writer organized information and ideas into broader categories and clarified how sections are ordered and connected. The writer used his organizational structure to help the reader's comprehension, perhaps holding back details until first conveying broader points, or only offering a second perspective after the first was established. The sections and information built on each other throughout the piece: concepts and examples were introduced in a logical fashion.	
DEVELOPMENT								
Elaboration*	The writer explained different aspects of a subject. He included a variety of information such as examples, details, dates, and quotes. The writer used trusted sources and gave credit when appropriate. He made sure to research any details that would add to his writing.	Mid-level	The writer included varied kinds of information such as facts, quotations, examples, and definitions. The writer used trusted sources and information from authorities on the topic and gave the sources credit.	Mid-level	The writer included varied kinds of information such as facts, quotations, examples, and definitions. She analyzed or explained the information, showing how the information fits with her key points or subtopics, including graphics where appropriate.	Mid-level	The writer brought out the parts of the topic that were most significant to his audience and to his point(s). The writer analyzed the relevance of his information and made sure the information supported the major concepts.	TOTAL:

*Elaboration and Craft are double-weighted categories: Whatever score a student would get in these categories is worth double the amount of points. For example, if a student exceeds expectations in Elaboration, then that student would receive 8 points instead of 4 points. If a student meets standards in Elaboration, then that student would receive 6 points instead of 3 points.

INFORMATION: TEACHING RUBRIC—SEVENTH GRADE (continued)

	Grade 5 (1 POINT)	1.5 PTS	Grade 6 (2 POINTS)	2.5 PTS	Grade 7 (3 POINTS)	3.5 PTS	Grade 8 (4 POINTS)	SCORE
			DEVELOPMENT (cont.)					
Elaboration (cont.)	The writer worked to make his information understandable to readers. To do this, he may have referred to earlier parts of his text and summarized background information. He let readers know when he was discussing facts and when he was offering his own opinion.	Mid-level	The writer worked to make his information understandable and interesting. To do this, he referred to earlier parts of his text, summarized background information, raised questions, or considered possible implications.	Mid-level	The writer consistently incorporated and cited sources. The writer worked to make her topic compelling as well as understandable. She brought out why it mattered and why the audience should care about it.	Mid-level	The writer incorporated trustworthy and significant sources, and explained if and when a source seemed problematic.	
Craft*	The writer made deliberate word choices to have an effect on her readers. She used the vocabulary of experts and explained key terms. The writer not only made choices about which details and facts to include but also made choices about how to convey her information so it would make sense to readers. She blended storytelling, summary, and other genres as needed and used text features. The writer used a consistent, inviting teaching tone and varied her sentences to help readers take in and understand the information.	Mid-level	The writer chose her words carefully to explain her information and ideas and to have an effect on the reader. The writer worked to include concrete details, comparisons, and/or images to explain information and concepts and to keep her reader engaged. The writer incorporated domain-specific vocabulary and, when necessary, she explained terms to readers, providing context clues, parenthetical explanations, text boxes, or similar support. The writer supported readers' learning by using a teaching tone and a formal style, as appropriate.	Mid-level	The writer used words purposefully to affect meaning and tone. The writer chose precise words and used metaphors, anecdotes, images, or comparisons to explain what she meant. The writer included domain-specific, technical vocabulary, and defined these when appropriate. The writer used a formal tone, but varied it appropriately to engage the reader.	Mid-level	The writer intended to affect her reader in particular ways—to make the reader think, realize, or feel a particular way—and she chose language to do that. The writer consistently used comparisons, analogies, vivid examples, and/ or anecdotes to help readers grasp the meaning of concepts and the significance of information. The writer varied her tone to match the different purposes of different sections of her piece.	
								TOTAL:

*Elaboration and Craft are double-weighted categories: Whatever score a student would get in these categories is worth double the amount of points. For example, if a student exceeds expectations in Elaboration, then that student would receive 8 points instead of 4 points. If a student meets standards in Elaboration, then that student would receive 6 points instead of 3 points.

May be photocopied for classroom use. © 2014 by Lucy Calkins and Colleagues from the Teachers College Reading and Writing Project from *Units of Study in Argument, Information, and Narrative Writing* (firsthand: Portsmouth, NH).

INFORMATION: TEACHING RUBRIC—SEVENTH GRADE (continued)

	Grade 5 (1 POINT)	1.5 PTS	Grade 6 (2 POINTS)	2.5 PTS	Grade 7 (3 POINTS)	3.5 PTS	Grade 8 (4 POINTS)	SCORE
				CONVENTIONS				
Spelling	The writer used what he knew about word families and spelling rules to help him spell and edit. He used the word wall and dictionaries to help him when needed.	Mid-level	The writer used resources to be sure the words in his writing are spelled correctly, including technical vocabulary.	Mid-level	The writer checked spelling of technical, domain-specific words and was careful with the spelling of citations.	Mid-level	The writer checked spelling of technical, domain-specific words and was careful with the spelling and details of citations, excerpts, quotations, and statistics.	
Punctuation and Sentence Structure	The writer used commas to set off introductory parts of sentences (for example, As you might know,). The writer used a variety of punctuation to fix any run-on sentences. She used punctuation to cite her sources.	Mid-level	The writer used punctuation such as dashes, parentheses, colons, and semicolons to help her include extra information and explanation in some of her sentences. The writer accurately cited her references, using appropriate punctuation.	Mid-level	The writer varied his sentence structure, sometimes using simple and sometimes using complex sentence structure. The writer used internal punctuation appropriately within sentences and when citing sources, including commas, dashes, parentheses, colons, and semicolons.	Mid-level	The writer used different sentence structures to achieve different purposes throughout her piece. The writer used verb tenses that shift when needed (as in when moving from a citation back to her own writing), deciding between active and passive voice where appropriate. The writer used internal punctuation effectively, including the use of ellipses to accurately insert excerpts from sources.	
								TOTAL:

Teachers, we created these rubrics so you will have your own place to pull together scores of student work. You can use these assessments immediately after giving the on-demands and also for self-assessment and setting goals.

Scoring Guide

In each row, circle the descriptor in the column that matches the student work. Scores in the categories of Elaboration and Craft are worth double the point value (2, 3, 4, 5, 6, 7, or 8 instead of 1, 1.5, 2, 2.5, 3, 3.5, or 4).

Total the number of points and then track students' progress by seeing when the total points increase.

Total score: _____

If you want to translate this score into a grade, you can use the provided table to score each student on a scale of 0–4.

Number of Points	Scaled Score
1–11	1
11.5–16.5	1.5
17–22	2
22.5–27.5	2.5
28–33	3
33.5–38.5	3.5
39–44	4

Name: _____   Date: _____

Rubric for Information Writing—Eighth Grade

STRUCTURE

	Grade 6 (1 POINT)	1.5 PTS	Grade 7 (2 POINTS)	2.5 PTS	Grade 8 (3 POINTS)	3.5 PTS	Grade 9 (4 POINTS)	SCORE
Overall	The writer conveyed ideas and information about a subject in a well-structured text. Sometimes she incorporated arguments, explanations, stories, or procedural passages.	Mid-level	The writer brought together ideas and information about a subject in a text that develops a subtopic and/or an idea. He incorporated a variety of text structures as needed, including argument, explanation, narrative, and procedural passages.	Mid-level	The writer discussed key concepts within a topic and made it clear why these concepts are important. She provided examples with relevant information, using a variety of text structures and formatting, as needed, to make concepts and information compelling and accessible.	Mid-level	The writer discussed complex concepts, presenting facts and information in an engaging manner, teaching the reader significant concepts and information. The writer conveyed the sources of the information and analyzed them when relevant.	
Lead	The writer wrote an introduction in which she interested readers, perhaps with a quote or significant fact. The writer let readers know the subtopics she would develop later and how her text would unfold.	Mid-level	The writer interested the reader in the topic by explaining its significance or providing a compelling fact, statistic, or anecdote. He made it clear what parts of this topic his text would tackle, and how the ideas and information in the text would unfold.	Mid-level	After hooking the reader, the writer provided context, introduced a focus/main idea, and oriented readers to the overall structure of the text (compare/contrast, cause and effect, claims and support, classification, etc.).	Mid-level	The writer wrote an engaging lead that explained the topic's significance, contextualized it with background information, and mentioned key points of view or issues that would be discussed.	

INFORMATION: TEACHING RUBRIC—EIGHTH GRADE (continued)

STRUCTURE (cont.)

	Grade 6 (1 POINT)	1.5 PTS	Grade 7 (2 POINTS)	Mid-level	2.5 PTS	Grade 8 (3 POINTS)	Mid-level	3.5 PTS	Grade 9 (4 POINTS)	Mid-level	SCORE
Transitions	The writer used transitions to help readers understand how different bits of information and different parts of her writing fit together. The writer used transitions to help connect ideas, information, and examples, and to imply relationships such as when material exemplifies, adds on to, is similar to, explains, is a result of, or contrasts. The writer used transitions such as, *similarly, therefore, as a result, in contrast to,* and *on the other hand.*	Mid-level	The writer used transitions to link concepts with related information. The transitions help the reader follow from part to part and make it clear when information is an example of a bigger idea, follows from an earlier point, introduces a new idea, or suggests a contrast. The writer used such transitions as *specifically, for instance, related to, just as, turning to, on the other hand,* and *however.*	Mid-level		The writer used transitions to lead the reader across parts of the text and to help the reader note how parts of the text relate back to earlier parts, using phrases such as *just as, returning to, as we saw earlier, similarly to, unlike,* and *yet.*	Mid-level		The writer used transitional phrases to show the relationship between parts of the text, including references to prior sections, and previewing future sections. The writer may have used transitions to show the source of cited information. These transitions might include *adapted from, excerpted from, according to, building from, revealed in, suggested by, illustrated by,* and *demonstrated in.*	Mid-level	
Ending	The writer wrote a conclusion in which she restated the important ideas and offered a final insight or implication for the reader to consider.	Mid-level	In his conclusion, the writer reinforced and built on the main point(s) in a way that made the entire piece a cohesive whole. The conclusion may have restated the main points, responded to them, or highlighted their significance.	Mid-level		In her conclusion, the writer suggested implications, built up the significance of her main points, and/or alluded to potential challenges.	Mid-level		In the conclusion, the writer strengthened implications, suggested implications, suggested action to take, and/or mentioned multiple perspectives or potential challenges.	Mid-level	
Organization	The writer chose a focused subject. The writer used subheadings and/or clear introductory transitions to separate sections.	Mid-level	The writer focused her writing on a subtopic or a particular point or two. The writer organized her piece into parts and used structures (claims and supports, problem/solution, sequence, etc.) to organize those parts (and perhaps the whole).	Mid-level		The writer focused on key concepts within the topic. The writer organized information and ideas into broader categories and clarified how sections are ordered and connected.	Mid-level		The writer's organizational structure introduced and layered key concepts and information. The writer layered information to maintain tension, engage the reader's interest, and/or build complexity.	Mid-level	

INFORMATION: TEACHING RUBRIC—EIGHTH GRADE *(continued)*

STRUCTURE (cont.)

	Grade 6 (1 POINT)	1.5 PTS	Grade 7 (2 POINTS)	2.5 PTS	Grade 8 (3 POINTS)	3.5 PTS	Grade 9 (4 POINTS)	SCORE
Organization (cont.)	The writer made deliberate choices about how to order sections and about the sequence of information and ideas within sections. The writer chose structures such as compare-and-contrast, categories, and claim-and-support to organize information and ideas. The writer wrote some sections as argument, explanation, stories, or procedural passages.	Mid-level	The writer used introductions, topic sentences, transitions, formatting, and graphics, where appropriate, to clarify the structure of the piece and to highlight main points.	Mid-level	The writer used his organizational structure to help the reader's comprehension, perhaps holding back details until first conveying broader points, or only offering a second perspective after the first was established. The sections and information built on each other throughout the piece: concepts and examples were introduced in a logical fashion.	Mid-level	The writer build the sections upon each other logically, allowing the reader to build knowledge and deeper understandings.	
							TOTAL:	

DEVELOPMENT

	Grade 6 (1 POINT)	1.5 PTS	Grade 7 (2 POINTS)	2.5 PTS	Grade 8 (3 POINTS)	3.5 PTS	Grade 9 (4 POINTS)	SCORE
Elaboration*	The writer included varied kinds of information such as facts, quotations, examples, and definitions. The writer used trusted sources and information from authorities on the topic and gave the sources credit. The writer worked to make her information understandable and interesting. To do this, she may have referred to earlier parts of her text, summarized background information, raised questions, and considered possible implications.	Mid-level	The writer included varied kinds of information such as facts, quotations, examples, and definitions. She analyzed or explained the information, showing how the information fits with her key points or subtopics, including graphics where appropriate. The writer consistently incorporated and cited sources. The writer worked to make her topic compelling as well as understandable. She brought out why it mattered and why the audience should care about it.	Mid-level	The writer brought out the parts of the topic that were most significant to his audience and to his point(s). The writer analyzed the relevance of his information and made sure the information supported the major concepts. The writer incorporated trustworthy and significant sources, and explained if and when a source seemed problematic.	Mid-level	The writer developed key concepts, giving some context and background. The writer used examples to clarify, explain, and interest. The writer analyzed the facts and information, explaining the relevance of cited source material. The writer included trustworthy and significant sources of information, analyzing and critiquing these sources when relevant.	

*Elaboration and Craft are double-weighted categories: Whatever score a student would get in these categories is worth double the amount of points. For example, if a student exceeds expectations in Elaboration, then that student would receive 8 points instead of 4 points. If a student meets standards in Elaboration, then that student would receive 6 points instead of 3 points.

May be photocopied for classroom use. © 2014 by Lucy Calkins and Colleagues from the Teachers College Reading and Writing Project from *Units of Study in Argument, Information, and Narrative Writing* (firsthand: Portsmouth, NH).

INFORMATION: TEACHING RUBRIC—EIGHTH GRADE (continued)

DEVELOPMENT (cont.)

	Grade 6 (1 POINT)	1.5 PTS	Grade 7 (2 POINTS)	2.5 PTS	Grade 8 (3 POINTS)	3.5 PTS	Grade 9 (4 POINTS)	SCORE
Craft*	The writer chose her words carefully to explain her information and ideas to have an effect on her reader. The writer worked to include concrete details, comparisons, and/or images to explain information and concepts, and to keep her reader engaged. The writer incorporated domain-specific vocabulary and when necessary explained terms to readers, providing context clues, parenthetical explanations, text boxes, or similar support. The writer supported readers' learning by using a teaching tone and a formal style, as appropriate.	Mid-level	The writer used words purposefully to affect meaning and tone. The writer chose precise words and used metaphors, anecdotes, images, or comparisons to explain what he meant. The writer included domain-specific, technical vocabulary, and defined these when appropriate. The writer used a formal tone, but varied it appropriately to engage the reader.	Mid-level	The writer intended to affect her reader in particular ways—to make the reader think, realize, or feel a particular way—and she chose language to do that. The writer consistently used comparisons, analogies, vivid examples, and/or anecdotes to help readers grasp the meaning of concepts and the significance of information. The writer varied her tone to match the different purposes of different sections of her piece.	Mid-level	The writer intended to affect the reader in particular ways—to make the reader think, realize, or feel a particular way—and chose particular language to do that. In addition to using other literary devices, the writer may have used allusions. The writer varied the tone to match the different purposes of different sections of the argument, as well as to develop its overall impact. The writer made choices about formatting, considering the best form to best convey the content.	

CONVENTIONS

	Grade 6	1.5 PTS	Grade 7	2.5 PTS	Grade 8	3.5 PTS	Grade 9	SCORE
Spelling	The writer used resources to be sure the words in her writing were spelled correctly, including technical vocabulary.	Mid-level	The writer checked spelling of technical, domain-specific words and was careful with the spelling of citations.	Mid-level	The writer checked spelling of technical, domain-specific words and was careful with the spelling and details of citations, excerpts, quotations, and statistics.	Mid-level	The writer spelled accurately throughout, including cited text and citations.	
							TOTAL:	

*Elaboration and Craft are double-weighted categories: Whatever score a student would get in these categories is worth double the amount of points. For example, if a student exceeds expectations in Elaboration, then that student would receive 8 points instead of 4 points. If a student meets standards in Elaboration, then that student would receive 6 points instead of 3 points.

INFORMATION: TEACHING RUBRIC—EIGHTH GRADE *(continued)*

	Grade 6 (1 POINT)	1.5 PTS	Grade 7 (2 POINTS)	2.5 PTS	Grade 8 (3 POINTS)	3.5 PTS	Grade 9 (4 POINTS)	SCORE
CONVENTIONS (cont.)								
Punctuation and Sentence Structure	The writer used punctuation such as dashes, parentheses, colons, or semicolons to help her include extra information and explanation in some of her sentences. The writer accurately cited her references, using appropriate punctuation.	Mid-level	The writer varied his sentence structure, sometimes using simple and sometimes using complex sentence structure. The writer used internal punctuation appropriately within sentences and when citing sources, including commas, dashes, parentheses, colons, and semicolons.	Mid-level	The writer used different sentence structures to achieve different purposes throughout her piece. The writer used verb tenses that shift when needed (as in when moving from a citation back to her own writing), deciding between active and passive voice where appropriate. The writer used internal punctuation effectively, including the use of ellipses to accurately insert excerpts from sources.	Mid-level	The writer used sentence structure and verb tense purposefully (i.e., using fragments to emphasize key points; using present tense to create immediacy). The writer used punctuation to emphasize connections, to strengthen tone, to clarify, and to add complexity.	
							TOTAL:	

Total score: _____

If you want to translate this score into a grade, you can use the provided table to score each student on a scale of 0–4.

Number of Points	Scaled Score
1–11	1
11.5–16.5	1.5
17–22	2
22.5–27.5	2.5
28–33	3
33.5–38.5	3.5
39–44	4

Teachers, we created these rubrics so you will have your own place to pull together scores of student work. You can use these assessments immediately after giving the on-demands and also for self-assessment and setting goals.

Scoring Guide

In each row, circle the descriptor in the column that matches the student work. Scores in the categories of Elaboration and Craft are worth double the point value (2, 3, 4, 5, 6, 7, or 8 instead of 1, 1.5, 2, 2.5, 3, 3.5, or 4).

Total the number of points and then track students' progress by seeing when the total points increase.

PART II: THE ASSESSMENT TOOLS—INFORMATION WRITING

Name: _____ Date: _____

Information Writing Checklist

	Grade 6	NOT YET	STARTING TO	YES!
Structure				
Overall	I conveyed ideas and information about a subject in a well-structured text. Sometimes I incorporated arguments, explanations, stories, or procedural passages.	☐	☐	☐
Lead	I wrote an introduction in which I interested readers, perhaps with a quote or significant fact. I let readers know the subtopics that I would develop later and how my text would unfold.	☐	☐	☐
Transitions	I used transitions to help readers understand how different bits of information and different parts of my writing fit together. I used transitions to help connect ideas, information, and examples, and to imply relationships such as when material exemplifies, adds on to, is similar to, explains, is a result of, or contrasts. I used transitions such as *for instance, such as, similarly, therefore, as a result, in contrast to,* and *on the other hand.*	☐	☐	☐
Ending	I wrote a conclusion in which I restated the important ideas and offered a final insight or implication for the reader to consider.	☐	☐	☐
Organization	I chose a focused subject.	☐	☐	☐
	I used subheadings and/or clear introductory transitions to separate sections.	☐	☐	☐
	I made deliberate choices about how to order sections and about the sequence of information and ideas within sections. I chose structures such as compare-and-contrast, categories, and claim-and-support to organize information and ideas. Some sections are written as argument, explanation, stories, or procedural passages.	☐	☐	☐
Development				
Elaboration	I included varied kinds of information such as facts, quotations, examples, and definitions.	☐	☐	☐
	I used trusted sources and information from authorities on the topic and gave the sources credit.	☐	☐	☐
	I worked to make my information understandable and interesting. To do this, I may have referred to earlier parts of my text, summarized background information, raised questions, and considered possible implications.	☐	☐	☐

	Grade 6	NOT YET	STARTING TO	YES!
Craft	I chose my words carefully to explain my information and ideas and to have an effect on my reader.	☐	☐	☐
	I worked to include concrete details, comparisons, and/or images to explain information and concepts, and to keep my reader engaged.	☐	☐	☐
	I incorporated domain-specific vocabulary and when necessary I explained terms to readers, providing context clues, parenthetical explanations, text boxes, or similar support.	☐	☐	☐
	I supported readers' learning by using a teaching tone and a formal style, as appropriate.	☐	☐	☐
Conventions				
Spelling	I used resources to be sure the words in my writing are spelled correctly, including technical vocabulary.	☐	☐	☐
Punctuation and Sentence Structure	I used punctuation such as dashes, parentheses, colons, and semicolons to help me include extra information and explanation in some of my sentences.	☐	☐	☐
	I accurately cited my references, using appropriate punctuation.	☐	☐	☐

Name: _____ **Date:** _____

Information Writing Checklist

	Grade 7	NOT YET	STARTING TO	YES!
Structure				
Overall	I brought together ideas and information about a subject in a text that develops a subtopic and/or an idea. I incorporated a variety of text structures as needed, including argument, explanation, narrative, and procedural passages.	☐	☐	☐
Lead	I interested the reader in the topic by explaining its significance, or providing a compelling fact, statistic, or anecdote. I made it clear what parts of the topic this text would tackle, and how the ideas and information in the text would unfold.	☐	☐	☐
Transitions	I used transitions to link concepts with related information. The transitions help the reader follow from part to part and make it clear when information is an example of a bigger idea, follows from an earlier point, introduces a new idea, or suggests a contrast. I used such transitions as *specifically*, *for instance*, *related to*, *just as*, *turning to*, *on the other hand*, and *however*.	☐	☐	☐
Ending	In my conclusion, I reinforced and built on the main point(s) in a way that made the entire piece a cohesive whole. The conclusion may have restated the main points, responded to them, or highlighted their significance.	☐	☐	☐
Organization	I focused my writing on a subtopic or a particular point or two.	☐	☐	☐
	I organized my piece into parts and used structures (claims and supports, problem/solution, sequence, etc.) to organize those parts (and perhaps the whole).	☐	☐	☐
	I used introductions, topic sentences, transitions, formatting and graphics, where appropriate, to clarify the structure of the piece and to highlight main points.	☐	☐	☐
Development				
Elaboration	I included varied kinds of information such as facts, quotations, examples, and definitions. I analyzed or explained the information, showing how the information fit with my key points or subtopics, including graphics where appropriate.	☐	☐	☐
	I consistently incorporated and cited sources.	☐	☐	☐
	I worked to make my topic compelling as well as understandable. I brought out why it mattered and why the audience should care about it.	☐	☐	☐
Craft	I used words purposefully to affect meaning and tone.	☐	☐	☐
	I chose precise words and used metaphors, anecdotes, images, or comparisons to explain what I mean.	☐	☐	☐
	I included domain-specific, technical vocabulary, and defined these terms when appropriate.	☐	☐	☐
	I used a formal tone, but varied it appropriately to engage the reader.	☐	☐	☐

Grade 7		NOT YET	STARTING TO	YES!
Conventions				
Spelling	I checked spelling of technical, domain-specific words and was careful with the spelling of citations.	☐	☐	☐
Punctuation and Sentence Structure	I varied my sentence structure, sometimes using simple and sometimes using complex sentence structure.	☐	☐	☐
	I used internal punctuation appropriately within sentences and when citing sources, including commas, dashes, parentheses, colons and semicolons.	☐	☐	☐

INFORMATION Student Checklists

Name: _____ **Date:** _____

Information Writing Checklist

	Grade 8	NOT YET	STARTING TO	YES!
	Structure			
Overall	I discussed key concepts within a topic and made it clear why these concepts are important. I provided examples with relevant information, using a variety of text structures and formatting as needed to make concepts and information compelling and accessible.	☐	☐	☐
Lead	After hooking the reader, I provided context, introduced a focus/main idea, and oriented readers to the overall structure of the text (compare/contrast, cause and effect, claims and support, classification, etc.)	☐	☐	☐
Transitions	I used transitions to lead the reader across parts of the text and to help the reader note how parts of the text relate back to earlier parts, using phrases such as *just as*, *returning to*, *as we saw earlier*, *similarly to*, *unlike*, and *and yet*.	☐	☐	☐
Ending	In the conclusion, I suggested implications, built up the significance of the main points, and/or alluded to potential challenges.	☐	☐	☐
Organization	I focused on key concepts within the topic.	☐	☐	☐
	I organized information and ideas into broader categories and clarified how sections are ordered and connected.	☐	☐	☐
	I used the organizational structure to help the reader's comprehension, perhaps holding back details until first conveying broader points, or only offering a second perspective after the first was established.	☐	☐	☐
	The sections and information built on each other throughout the piece: concepts and examples were introduced in a logical fashion.	☐	☐	☐
	Development			
Elaboration	I brought out the parts of the topic that were most significant to my audience and to my point(s).	☐	☐	☐
	I analyzed the relevance of my information and made sure the information supported the major concepts.	☐	☐	☐
	I incorporated trustworthy and significant sources, and explained if and when a source seemed problematic.	☐	☐	☐
Craft	I intended to affect my reader—to make the reader think, realize, or feel—a particular way, and I chose language to do that.	☐	☐	☐
	I consistently used comparisons, analogies, vivid examples, and/or anecdotes to help readers grasp the meaning of concepts and the significance of information.	☐	☐	☐
	I varied my tone to match the different purposes of different sections of my piece.	☐	☐	☐

	Grade 8	NOT YET	STARTING TO	YES!
	Conventions			
Spelling	I checked spelling of technical, domain-specific words and was careful with the spelling and details of citations, excerpts, quotations, and statistics.	☐	☐	☐
Punctuation and Sentence Structure	I used different sentence structures to achieve different purposes throughout my piece.	☐	☐	☐
	I used verb tenses that shift when needed (as in when moving from a citation back to my own writing), deciding between active and passive voice where appropriate.	☐	☐	☐
	I used internal punctuation effectively, including the use of ellipses to accurately put in excerpts from sources.	☐	☐	☐

INFORMATION: LEVELED STUDENT WRITING SAMPLES

Sample 1, page 1

Space is vast. It may be brim-
ming with life. Or it may be desolate,
dangerous, and lonely. We may never know,
but as Carl Sagan once said, "Extraordinary
claims require extraordinary evidence." Evidence
suggests that life would be difficult due
to many dangerous objects in space. Despite
this evidence there is huge argument over
the possibility of extraterrestrial life in the
universe. But we may resolve this argument
soon, because scientists are researching new
technology to find these hidden E.T.s.

Space is full of dangerous objects. Black
holes are incredibly dense objects. They are formed
when a large star explodes. If you were able to
arrive the crash of a black hole, you would
start to experience time slowing down. The area in
which this happens is called an "event horizon." But
if you couldn't survive you would die an incredibly
painful and gruesome death.

There is an everlasting argument because of
this question "Are we alone in the universe?" Less
than half of the United States' population says
yes. According to the Drake Equation we
have galactic company. But two ways to think about
this are (a) The universe is so vast, there
are definately other life forms out there, or
(b) life is a mistake.

Scientists use different tools to search
for extraterrestrial life. One tool is the
radio telescope. It can receive and transmit
messages. When you watch T.V., some of the signals

Sample 1, page 2

go off into space. You can send messages with
your T.V.

And those are just the basics. But we need to
I know Space is a mind boggling thing.
be prepared. For if a war-like race comes,
we must fight back, not stare in disbelief as
they destroy everything.

May be photocopied for classroom use. © 2014 by Lucy Calkins and Colleagues from the Teachers College Reading and Writing Project from *Units of Study in Argument, Information, and Narrative Writing* (firsthand: Portsmouth, NH).

WRITING PATHWAYS: PERFORMANCE ASSESSMENTS AND LEARNING PROGRESSIONS, 6–8

must expand.

Does this mean that democracy cannot survive, could the unthinkable happen, and turn the bastions of liberty into an Empire? Throughout history many civilizations have proclaimed Democracy of Republic, In almost everyone of these states they became an Empire. I draw one conclusion from this analysis; The Empire will come again.

Sample 2, page 2

THE FUTURE OF GOVERMENT

The Empire. Throughout history the Empire has overwhelmed its opponents At times of great threats, and devestating civil disorder their has been the Empire. In Rome 450 years of role under a Republic it turned to the Empire. In Greece the Athenians who prided themselves on their democracy turned to the Empire. Even though much of the 1900's are Empires were nations of power.

Three greats threats to modern democracy came from the Empires of Japan, Russia, and Germany. The the 1000 year period known as the Middle Ages the most powerful nations were Empires like the Holy Roman Empire, England, and Spain. Even in the legendary age of rebirth, the Renaissance the nations that spaned the world were the colonial Empires of Spain, Portugal, France, and England.

Throughout history the key to expansion has always been, a will continue to be, the Empire, And to survive, one

Sample 2, page 1

Sample 3, page 1

America's Pastime   By: Carson

Baseball has been around a long time. Baseball is a part of America's heritage. For many of us America's pastime. According to Mlb.com "baseball was a development from an older game that was made popular in Great Britain and Ireland." It became a popular sport during the American civil war." Baseball will always be America's favorite sports Abner Doubleday Created baseball, and some people think it is the best sport ever invented. There are many famous baseball players, such as; Jackie Robinson, Honus Wagner, and of course Babe Ruth. Like Ruth always said, "Baseball was, is and always will be to me the best game in the world." (The Babe Ruth story written by George Callahan.)

How To Play The Game.

Baseball is a similar sport to Basketball, Rugby, and Soccer. They may seem different, and not related. They all have things in common to make up the sport. They involve running, strength, endurance, and most important team work. Baseball is a 9 on 9 sport. There are three outfielders a Right Fielder, a Center Fielder, and a Right Fielder. Six people make up the infield A Pitcher, Catcher, First Baseman, Second Baseman, A batter steps a Shortstop, and a Third Baseman, A batter steps

Sample 3, page 2

up to the plate. The pitcher has to throw the ball in the strike zone. According to strike zone Mlb "the strike zone is from midpoint, meaning chest to beneath the kneecap. If the pitcher throws the ball in the strike zone and the batter swings it is a strike. You get three strikes before your out. If the pitcher throws and the ball is not in the strike zone, it is a ball. You get four balls You advance to first base. If there is a player already on first the player advances to second. If the pitcher throws the ball outside of the strike zone, but the batter swings, it counts as a strike. However if the batter hits the ball he has to get to first base without the ball getting to second they have to get the ball and tag him However, if the batter runs there before him However this for every base except hit/hit is like this for every base except first. If the batter hits the ball and the infield of outfield catch it, it is considered an out. The object of the game is to get the runner to home plate, by getting hits and driving the runner in to score. The infielders and outfielders make it harder to score, whoever has the most runs by the end of 9 innings wins. There are foul bases in order for a player to score he must touch all foul bases.

Equipment

The Equipment plays a big role in
the game of baseball. Without equipment
there could be a lot of injuries. You
need a helmet, a bat, cleats, mouth guards, and
a jersy. These things are small, but play
a big role in the game. According to
Baseball safety tips "some pitchers at high
school level throw fastballs that reach
up to 80 mph." "Most injuries occur from
wild pitching to running in the wrong way."
These things can hurt players careers.
In the MLB pitchers can pitch
90 mph and above. If it hits you in
the head who knows what could
happen.

Conclusion

Baseball is a great sport, some
say the best ever invented. People
live to play the game.
Baseball is a lot of things
but it is certainly America's pastime.

Sample 3, page 3

On demand: Transfering

September 12th,

Brianna ,

Have you ever transfered from
one school to another? If you
have, Today I am going to teach
you how to cope with being
at an all new school.

If you feel shy, like everyone is
looking down on you, that is completely normal. One way to feel
less uncomfortable is to pick and
stick. What I mean by "Pick and Stick"
is that you find one person and
Stick to them. The first time
that you walk into a classroom,
look at all of the students. See
who reminds you of the people
that you used to hang out
with at your old school. Once
you find someone, ask them to
lunch, or sit next to them. If
you're the shy type of person,
who wants to make friends
but can't find the courage
to just be subtle, but friendly.
try to remember peoples name,
too. That will show them that
you care about others, and

Sample 1, page 1

May be photocopied for classroom use. © 2014 by Lucy Calkins and Colleagues from the Teachers College Reading and Writing Project from *Units of Study in Argument, Information, and Narrative Writing* (firsthand: Portsmouth, NH).

Hey will want to be your
friend.

Another struggle that lots of
people go through is getting
used to the teachers. There
are many types of teachers
at school, and in order to
get used to them, you have
to know how to deal with
them

The Hardie

The hardie is the type of
teacher who is really strict
with his/her students. Just
do whatever this teacher
says. Stay out of their way
and NEVER try to joke with
this teacher, because you never
know if you joke is really
bad (No offense) or its offensive
to this teacher. Usually
they aren't bad people. They are
there to help you, and that's
all. Some of the strictest,
teachers are my favorites.

Sample 1, page 2

The Cool One

This teacher is real easy-going, and chances are, it's a Male Science teacher. These know how to get through to their students, with humor. They like to joke around, but they teach you at the same time. These people are really cool, but that doesn't mean that they don't have a bad side. Stay safe and do as you're told.

The Sweetest

You're always going to have that one teacher who's really sweet, no matter what. They usually care a lot for their job, so don't give them a hard time.

There are lots of teachers at school, but they all are dedicated to being a teacher. You should always try to be a good student.

If anyone is being mean to you, or bullying you, don't stand for it. Tell them that they can't bully you, and that no one deserves to be bullied. If they keep on bothering you, tell their teacher, or their parents. You can't controll their actions, but their parents can.

Don't know where your classes are? ask the teacher for a map of the school, and highlight where your classes are, you'll get used to it after a while.

Whether you like it or not, school is something you have to do, and if you need some help, get it.

Sample 1, page 3

Sample 1, page 4

Sample 2, page 1

Deep Dark Pit, or Gravity's Ultimate Triumph

Do you know what black holes are? A lot of people don't even think they exist. But they do. Do you know why black holes are important? A lot of people think they are things floating in space with no significance or importance. But are they really? Black holes are fascinating objects that are important to learn about. They hold the answers to many mysteries and puzzles of the universe.

What are they?

Black holes are stars after they have ended their lives in an explosion called a supernova. Black holes are extremely dense massive objects that will suck up anything that passes within their event horizon.

An event horizon is an imaginary sphere around the black hole. If anything goes inside the event horizon it will get sucked into the black hole no matter what. Even light will get sucked into the black hole if it passes within the event horizon.

Black holes form from massive super dense stars that have blown themselves apart in a ▮ supernova. A supernova is when a star explodes, ending its life. After the star blows up the tremendous gravitational force of the explosion together and packs it so tight, that it becomes a black hole, with an even bigger gravitational force than before.

Sample 2, page 2

why should we care?

Black holes are important to know about because if scientists learn enough about them we may get a much better ▮ understanding of our universe.

Some things about black holes suggest that our present day theories in physics may not be correct, says Paneswa▮an Nair, professor of physics. "We will continue to observe and study black holes so we can correct our errors and get a better understanding about the universe we live in."

Black holes also shape our universe. With their tremendous gravitational forces, they are believed to hold galaxies together. By being in the center of most galaxies, black holes are also believed to have led to the formation of galaxies billions of years ago by "pulling" ▮ stars together to form galaxies.

"No one knows precisely how and why there is gravity," says Panaswaran Nair, "But that is one of the many puzzles of the universe that we hope to answer by studying black holes."

Pictures and other data from the Hubble Space Telescope (A telescope orbiting the Earth in space which takes pictures and other data of celestial objects.) suggest that black holes could be the seeds of galaxies. If scientists can come up with a consistent theory for black holes we will get a much better understanding of the universe we live in.

Vegetarianism: The Protein Problem

by Madeline, Grade 8

page 1

"Are you getting enough protein?" "How can your body function without meat?" "You need to eat meat! You're growing and you need protein!" These are some of the endless questions from concerned friends and family members of a vegetarian. It seems as though the world has been brainwashed into believing that meat is the only source for the protein a human body has to get protein. This, however, is most definitely not the case. Thousands of vegetarians across the globe are able to consume the needed amount of protein without eating a bite of meat. Through the wonderful sources of nuts, ancient grains and eggs, vegetarians are more than able to live a healthy, protein-filled lifestyle.

By consuming nuts - cashews, walnuts, pistachios almonds and more - a vegetarian is filling himself with a nutritious and delicious supply of protein. Nuts are a tasty and quick alternative to a large beef steak. They can be eaten straight from the can or

---

page 2   Madeline, Grade 8

sprinkled on top of a vegetarian salad. They have a salty, delicious satisfying taste that either a vegetarian or an unrestricted eater can savor. Instead of feeling guilty about consuming the maliciously chopped off wings of a chicken, one can feel great about him or herself while snacking on nature's high in protein delicacies- nuts.

Vegetarians can not simply rely on nuts and nuts alone for their daily protein needs, however. Although high in protein, another food that can supply a vegetarian with protein is ancient grains. Ancient grains are the forgotten jems of the earth that are rich in protein and flavor. Some ancient grains include quinoa, farro, amaranth, and buckwheat. These can be cooked and boiled in water or vegetable both and be eaten alone, or they can be added to dishes to amp up the protein. For example, Examples include a meal of beans and quinoa, which together form a complete protein, is a hearty dinner

page 3   Madeline, Grade 8

perfect for the protein-needing vegetarian. Ancient grains can be found at most healthfood stores and are a simple way to get the protein that one needs.

One more food that is rich in protein is eggs. Just like nuts and ancient grains, eggs are a meatless form of way to stay healthy while alternative to munching on dead animal carcasses. *NOTE: Although eggs do not have meat in them and are okay to eat for vegetarians, they come from animals, thus making them not vegan. *

Eggs have a high amount of protein packed inside their thin white shells. They can be prepared in various ways. Many vegetarians protein-filled Many non-vegetarians eat eggs as well, making it a bit easier to find vegetarian food while out and about. They are just one more form of a protein packed food that vegetarian can consume.

"Yes, Grandpa, I am getting enough protein." "Mom, Quinoa is on my plate every day, and I'm living very healthfully!" "Don't worry! I'm getting tons of protein from eggs, nuts, and ancient grains!"

page 4   Madeline, Grade 8

These are some of the endless responses from educated vegetarians, to concerned friends and family members. Although from the outside, living without meat can seem impossible, there are many other foods both filled with protein and flavor that one can eat, meat free! This is why thousands of vegetarians across the globe are able to consume enough protein without eating a bite of meat. Thanks to the many meatless, protein packed alternatives to meat such as nuts, ancient grains, and eggs, vegetarians worldwide are more than able to live a healthy, protein-filled lifestyle.

Kevin

Information Piece

The Magna Carta

The people who wrote the Magna Carta were English barons. This document of charter was written in England on June 15, 1215, on a field at Runnymede. The English barons wrote this important charter because they believed that the king (King John) had to much power over them and thought his laws and decisions he made were very unjust. In other words, they didn't like the way they were being treated by the higher class people or the government because they were lower class citizens.

As a result of the Magna Carta being made and sent to the King he had to give up a lot of things according to the document. However, he's plan was intentionally to break the peace treaty sent by the barons, which he eventually did. It was said that the charter lasted only "10 weeks." Also it was ruled to be unsuccessful because of the information as forementioned. However, as a result of the King breaking the peace treaty it totally destroyed what the barons had tried to achieve; equality in England and balanced power. Finally, this resulted in the Magna Carta to have a gigantic impact on England because it resulted into a brief Civil War (1215 -1217). This shows that the more the

Sample 2, page 1

King rebuked the charter, the angrier the barons got and resulted in a civil war. However, even with the Civil war it ended up not resolving the conflict at hand.

One of the first choices the authors of the Magna Carta made was to explain the rights the people of England were entitled to. They wrote "Earls and Barons shall be fined only by their equals, and in proportion to the gravity of their offense." This means that the people of England will be fined or taxed based on their social class and in proportion to the gravity of their offense. This means that the people of England will be fined or taxed based on their social class and in Court will be judged by the weight of their offense not by how much money they have of property they have. Everyone will be judged equally by their evil act. This helps to demonstrate that the people wanted rights rights that protected them and for all people, rich or poor, to be treated equally.

In the same way the barons and Earls wanted rights that protected them and treated all people equal. So did the author of the Magna Carta. To do this, they wanted to move sure the King of England knew they wanted equality and justice. They wrote "In future no offical shall place a man on trial upon own unsupported statement without producing credible witnesses." In other words, no one should put a person on trial or court without evidence or a witness to the crime. Along with

Sample 2, page 2

the quotations from the previous paragraph, this in-formation shows how determined the people of England were to established their rights and treat all people equal.

In Conclusion, the Magna Carta was written to balance and bring peace to the people of England. However, this attempt by the barons was unsuccessful because it resulted into a civil war that caused chaos in England. All in all, the Magna Carta was a brave attempt to balance power but failed.

Grade 6

English Bulldogs

Introduction

> The writer conveyed ideas and information about the topic. There are essays (being a bulldog owner section), explanations, stories (health and bulldog owner sections), and procedural passages (caring for a bulldog).

I curl up on my sofa, getting ready to read my favorite book. My best friend, Lanie, jumps on the sofa next to me. She snuggles in, curls herself up, and starts to snore. It's very loud. This might sound very rude, but Lanie isn't a person. She's a six-year-old English Bulldog. She has a tired, wrinkled face, that looks as if she is 100 years old. She shuffles around and makes lots of grunting sounds. Sometimes she refuses to budge when we are out walking. But she is loyal, kind, and never lets me down. Her breed is one that is very special and is a very popular pet with an interesting history. In this report, you will learn all about the appearance of bulldogs, how to care for them, what they are like as pets, and a bit about their history.

> The introduction hooked readers with a significant anecdote. The writer let the reader know how the passage would unfold.

Appearance

The English Bulldog is considered a compact dog, which means it has a short, smooth coat. A characteristic that all bulldogs share is a wide head and shoulders. They also have a big **prognathism**, which is where its jaw comes out from its head. Its eyebrows are like thick folds of skin, and it was small black eyes. These small eyes and eyebrows with folds make it seem like it's angry, but it's usually not. Some of them, like Lanie, have what is called an **underbite**, which means its bottom teeth stick out.

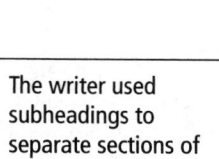

Bulldog underbite

There are several colors that bulldogs come in. Some of them are common names, like red and white. And some are special names, like **brindle** (mixed colors and stripes), **fawn** (a kind of light brown), and **piebald** (black and white spots).

> The writer used parentheses to define domain-specific vocabulary for readers.

> The writer used subheadings to separate sections of information.

Bulldogs are short but very heavy. The smallest are about 35 pounds, and the biggest males can be up to 55.

Caring for a Bulldog

All species require exercise to be healthy, and bulldogs are no different. If they aren't walked at least two times every day, they tend to become dangerously overweight. They don't usually move much on their own, consequently their owners have to make them move. According to Inforpedia.org, if they become too fat, they might start to get heart problems. In addition to walking bulldogs, owners can keep them sharp by practicing ball-handling skills with them. In my opinion, bulldogs are smarter than some often think and they can learn a few commands, even if they don't always want to chase a ball.

> The writer used transition words to show relationships between information and ideas (*in addition, despite*) and to help readers understand how different bits of information fit together.

Despite their short coats, bulldogs do shed. They should be brushed often so that they don't shed as much. Esther Gray's book, called *This Is a Bulldog*, explains how to properly **groom** a bulldog. To brush a bulldog, begin at the top of its head, called its **crown**,

(continues)

Grade 6 (*continued*)

and move in long strokes across its back. Then, brush its legs and underbelly. But be careful when brushing the underbelly because that part can hurt the dog. Additionally, you need to clean the folds of their skin every day. These can get infected if they are too dirty.

Balanced nutrition is essential for a bulldog. It has to have the right proportion of vitamins and water, just like people. Most experts, like James Thomas, who wrote *Bulldog Life*, agree that feeding bulldogs too often is not necessary. In fact, feeding them too often can lead to problems, and will train them to be hungry all the time. The book says, "A well-trained bulldog does not beg for food. If bulldogs are fed constantly, especially from the table, they will learn bad habits and will begin to beg. Also, they will be in danger of becoming overweight from eating too much." (p. 56)

Health Concerns

No dog owner wants to think about their dog getting sick, but unfortunately it can happen. Bulldogs don't live forever, only about 8–12 years. So owners should keep their dogs as healthy as possible to help them live as long as they can.

According to the Orthopedic Foundation for Animals, 73.9% of bulldogs have **hip dysplasia**. This is a problem where the hip gets out of joint. To add on, more bulldogs have this problem than any other dog breed.

Another common illness is cherry eye. This is caused by a swollen gland in a bulldog's eye. If this happens, most vets say to take the dog to be looked at right away. Once Lanie had Cherry eye, and her eye swelled up like a small balloon. We all felt awful for her. But when she got the medicine, she was much better.

Bulldogs can also get heart problems. One way this gets worse if they are out in the heat. Heat stroke is a serious health concern for bulldogs. If a bulldog starts **panting** heavily, it's best to get them to a cool place and give them water immediately.

Being a Bulldog Owner

Bulldogs are wonderful, loyal pets. Some say there are cons to owning a bulldog, such as that they don't live very long and that they must be cleaned often, and that they can be stubborn. As Mr. Thomas says in his book on page 75, they have the worst **flatulence** (gas) of any dog breed. But there are many more pros than cons. First of all, they are adorable. No one can resist their funny looking wrinkles and the way they waddle. Also, they are safe around kids, even babies. To illustrate this, my little sister was only a baby when we got my bulldog. Once, my sister Emmie was crawling across the living room. She went over to Lanie's food dish and started splashing around in her water. Lanie went over and gave her a look. She didn't like that Emmie was in her water. But she didn't even bark. She just stood there and watched Emmie. Some other dogs might have bitten the baby.

The writer used transitions and topic sentences to highlight main points. There are multiple paragraphs in each section.

The writer's subject was focused, and there was a variety of rich information.

The writer used outside sources and gives credit to these sources both in the text and in a bibliography.

The writer used comparisons, analogies, and images to make the writing interesting.

The writer made choices about how best to organize information, sequencing information within sections in a way that teaches and engages readers. She sometimes used text features to do this, as well.

The writer chose words carefully, including domain-specific vocabulary and explaining what these words mean.

She maintained a teaching tone throughout the piece.

(continues)

Grade 6 (*continued*)

History of English Bulldogs

Out of all the bulldog types, American, English, and French, in my opinion the English has the best history. In the early 1600s, they were bred to be strong, tough, and fierce. They were used in something called **bull-baiting**, which is to fight bulls (www. bulldoginfor.com). People would watch bulldogs chase bulls around for fun. They would bet on which dog would grab a bull by the nose and push the bull to the ground. Many dogs would die or become seriously hurt at these events because they were stomped on or trampled, or poked by the bulls. Consequently, this became illegal.

An older kind of bulldog used to fight bulls

A Chart: Characteristics of Bulldogs Created by Breeding
- Short legs so the bull couldn't get the dog's legs with its horns
- Large jaws, so the dog could grab the bull and hold on to its nose
- A larger and heavier body to fight big bulls
- A muzzle that curved up so the dog could breathe while it grabbed the bull's nose
- Wrinkles so blood from the bull wouldn't get into the dog's eyes

Conclusion

> In the conclusion, the writer offered final insights and implications for the reader to consider.

English Bulldogs are historical, beautiful, interesting animals. They need proper care and maintenance, but on the other hand they can be very loyal and gentle. It's always a good idea to see if you can adopt one from a rescue center. These are places where animals go if they are abandoned or treated badly by their owners. But if there isn't a bulldog there, you can visit your local pet shop. One day, maybe you will have a best friend like Lanie, curled up at your feet and snoring while you read a great book.

Bibliography

WWW.bulldoginfor.com
Gray, Esther. (1976) *This is a Bulldog*. (Schoolpub)
Thomas, James. (2009) *Bulldog Life*. (Schoolpub)

Grade 7

> The writer interested readers with a compelling anecdote and provided background information in the form of historical context.

> The writer developed not just information but also an idea about the information. The author made the claim, and made it clear how the ideas and information in the text would unfold.

> The writer attempted to vary the sentence structure, combining simple sentences with complex sentences.

The Bulldog: A Dog Like No Other

A small dog huddles in a corner, waiting to be released into a giant arena. Though it seems difficult to believe, there was a time when dogs were bred for sport, a brutal sport called bull-baiting. The dogs were trained to clamp on to a bull's nose and to not let go until either the bull killed the dog or the dog brought the bull to the ground (Gray, 1976). Not every kind of dog would have been up to this task. The dog bread for this sport is the dog that we know today as the bulldog. In fact, that's how this dog got its name. Maybe this is also why these dogs have a reputation for being fierce. However, bulldogs are one of the most special dogs out there, for many reasons. There are no other dogs that look like a bulldog, with its characteristic wrinkles. Bulldogs do require some unique care, as does any prized possession, so owning a bulldog isn't easy, but is very, very rewarding. Finally, Bulldogs have a fascinating history, unlike that of any other dog.

I. A Unique and Varied Appearance

The English Bulldog looks like no other. It is a compact dog with a short, smooth coat and a wide head and shoulders. Bulldogs typically have **prognathism,** essentially meaning its lower jaw sticks out beyond its upper jaw. This is also called an underbite. In contrast, dogs like golden retrievers rarely have an underbite. Their top teeth stick over their bottom teeth. Though this condition is not considered attractive in humans, many people find it to be quite adorable on a small dog.

> The writer used a transitional phrase to compare/contrast. Comparisons were used as a way to explain information and the explanation was further supported by text features.

Bulldog underbite

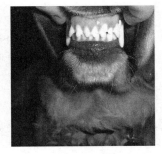

Golden retriever with no underbite

A bulldog's eyebrows are made of thick folds of skin, and it has small black eyes. These small eyes and eyebrows with folds give it the illusion of being angry, though that's typically not the case.

(continues)

Grade 7 (*continued*)

The writer used introductory sentences and phrases to clarify the structure of the piece.

Bulldogs' coats and even the names for them are as unique and varied as they are. For instance, some names for bulldog's coats are quite special, like **brindle** (mixed colors and stripes), **fawn** (a kind of light brown), and **piebald** (black and white spots). However, some of the coat colors have common names, like red and white.

The writer incorporated domain-specific vocabulary and defined these throughout the text.

Bulldogs weigh a surprising amount in relation to their size. According to James Thomas, bulldog expert and author of the text *Bulldog Life*, the smallest weigh about 35 pounds, with some of the biggest males reaching up to 55 (2009).

II. Special Care Requirements

The writer's formatting showed how the piece was structured and also highlighted the main points.

Though all species require exercise to be healthy, bulldogs require some unique considerations in order to be in top physical condition. To explain, if they aren't walked at least two times every day, they tend to become dangerously overweight. This problem is exacerbated because they don't usually move much on their own. According to Inforpedia.org, "When English Bulldogs are do not receive the prescribed amount of exercise, they can develop severe cardiac and pulmonary issues that may shorten their life span considerably" (2010, paragraph 3). Other ways that owners can help their bulldogs to maintain top physical condition is by practicing ball-handling skills and by teaching their pet a few simple commands.

The writer consistently incorporated and cited sources.

The writer used a variety of information to elaborate, including quotations, and also explained why the information was important to readers.

Like their exercise requirements, bulldogs have unique needs when it comes to grooming. A bulldog's trademark wrinkles, in particular, need special attention. Esther Gray, in her text *This is a Bulldog*, explains: "If the wrinkles around a bulldog's muzzle are not properly cleaned on a frequent basis, this can lead in infection" (1976). This means that if someone is considering getting a bulldog, they need to understand that they have to be responsible for cleaning its wrinkles so the dog does not sick. The best way to clean a bulldog's wrinkles is to carefully pull the skin tight, and gently scrub the skin with a soft brush and mild soap.

The writer incorporated a variety of text structures, here including a procedural passage.

The writer used transitions that helped readers follow from section to section and understand how parts are connected.

A final area of consideration when it comes to the special care that bulldogs require is balanced nutrition. Proper nutrition is essential for all dogs, and even more so for a bulldog. Most experts, like James Thomas, who wrote *Bulldog Life*, caution about the danger of feeding bulldogs too often. He writes, "A well-trained bulldog does not beg for food. If bulldogs are fed constantly, especially from the table, they will learn bad habits and will begin to beg. Also, they will be in danger of becoming overweight from eating too much" (p. 56). This information may be surprising, as bulldogs seem as if they could eat copious amounts of food. But in fact the opposite is true.

(continues)

INFORMATION Annotated Writing
Developed through the Progression

Grade 7 (*continued*)

> The writer not only organized the entire piece into parts, he/she also organized the chapters, or sections. Here, the writer forecasts the structure of this particular section.

III. Particular Health Concerns

Unfortunately, in addition to all of the characteristics that make bulldogs wonderful pets, they have a few unique characteristics that are not so wonderful. No dog owner wants to think about his or her dog getting sick, but unfortunately bulldogs have some unique health concerns. In order of seriousness, bulldogs can suffer from illnesses such as heart disease, hip dysplasia, and cherry eye.

Bulldogs can have grave heart problems. Owners should take special considerations when bulldogs are in hot weather. Heat stroke is a serious health concern for bulldogs. If a bulldog starts panting heavily, it's best to get them to a cool place and give them water immediately.

According to the Orthopedic Foundation for Animals, 73.9% of bulldogs have **hip dysplasia**. This is a problem where the hip gets out of joint. In fact, bulldogs have this problem more than any other dog breed, which further demonstrates their need for special care.

Another common illness is cherry eye. This is caused by a swollen gland in a bulldog's eye. If this happens, most veterinarians recommend taking the dog to be looked at right away.

Bulldogs don't live forever, some sources say as little as eight years on average, much less than many common dogs. Owners should keep their dogs as healthy as possible to help them live as long as they can and should appreciate each moment with this special dog.

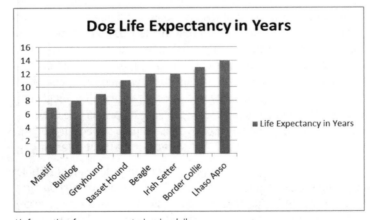

*information from www.veterinariandaily.com

> The writer used graphics to illustrate points.

(continues)

Grade 7 (*continued*)

> The writer incorporated a variety of text structures. This section has an argument structure, with a claim and supports, and it also includes a narrative to illustrate one of the reasons.

IV. Why You Should Consider Being a Bulldog Owner

There are three reasons why I recommend being a bulldog owner. First, bulldogs are wonderful, loyal pets. Next, they are particularly attractive. No one can resist their funny looking wrinkles and the way they waddle. Finally, they are safe around kids, even babies. To illustrate this, a family with a young baby had bulldog. Once, the baby went to the dog's food dish and splashed around in her water. The dog was not pleased, but she didn't even bark. She just stood there and watched the baby, whereas some other dogs might have bitten the baby. Some say there are cons to owning a bulldog, such as that they don't live very long and that they must be cleaned often, and that they can be stubborn. As Mr. Thomas says in his book on page 75, they have the worst **flatulence** (gas) of any dog breed. But there are many more pros than cons.

V. A Brutal, Unique History

Bulldogs come from a rather stunning history. As described earlier, they were bred for the sport **bull-baiting**. Though it is now difficult to imagine, in the 1600 and 1700s in England, people considered it great entertainment. They would bet on which dog would grab a bull by the nose and push the bull to the ground. Many dogs would die or become seriously hurt at these events because they were stomped on or trampled, or poked by the bulls. Finally, this sport became illegal in 1853 (Gray, 1976. p. 24). Very few other dog breeds have such brutality in their history.

> The writer attempted to maintain a formal tone throughout the text.

Dogs such as these were bred specifically to fight bulls. Hence the name: bulldog.

A Chart: Characteristics of Bulldogs Created by Breeding

- Short legs so the bull couldn't get the dog's legs with its horns
- Large jaws, so the dog could grab the bull and hold on to its nose
- A larger and heavier body to fight big bulls
- A muzzle that curved up so the dog could breathe while it grabbed the bull's nose
- Wrinkles so blood from the bull wouldn't get into the dog's eyes

Grade 7 (*continued*)

The writer reinforced the main points and highlighted their significance, encouraging readers to take action.

VI. Conclusion

Certainly, society has come a long way from the time that bulldogs were put in life-threatening danger for entertainment purposes. Many people are starting to realize that the bulldog is a dog unlike any other. Though it requires special care, its beauty and unique disposition make the extra care worth every minute. And even though it is no longer legal to throw bulldogs into an arena with a bull, some are mistreated. It's always a good idea to try to adopt a bulldog (or any pet) from a rescue center.

Bibliography

Bulldogs. (n.d.). In Inforpedia.org. Retrieved from www.inforpedia. org/bulldog

Gray, E. (1976) *This is a Bulldog*. New York, NY: Schoolpub

Hudson, T. (2013, October). *A Complete Guide to Bulldog Care*. Retrieved from www.bulldoginfor.com

Michael, J. (n.d.). *Typical Life Span of Common Dog Types*. Retrieved from www.veterinariandaily.com

Thomas, J. (2009) *Bulldog Life*. New York, NY: Schoolpub.

The writer used a standard format for citation and included a list of sources.

Grade 8

Reckless Breeding in Bulldogs

Bulldogs are one of the most beloved dog breeds in the country. According to inforpedia.org, bulldogs have risen to the sixth most popular dog breed, up from the twenty-first most popular in 2000. Bulldogs weren't always such sought-after pets. In the 1600 and 1700s in England, they were bread for a sport called bull-baiting, in which they were thrown into pens with bulls for a brutal fight to the death. They were bred for their powerful jaws and short, muscular bodies (Thomas, 2009, p. 24). Though bull-baiting became illegal in 1853, bulldogs continue to be bred specifically for certain characteristics. Owners and prospective owners cannot get enough of their adorable wrinkles; wide, square jaws; and short legs. However, it is these very features that make bulldogs so adorable that cause health problems for the breed. The way that bulldogs are bred is causing health crisis in the population. Unsafe breeding practices cause a plethora of problems for bulldogs, the three most notable being problems with their bodies, problems with disease, and problems with natural breeding.

> The writer discussed a key concept within the topic, creating a text that will take the form of an informational essay.

> The writer hooked readers and provided context with historical background about the topic.

> The writer introduced a focus and oriented readers to the overall structure of the text: claim and supports.

Image showing a bulldog 100 years ago and a bulldog today.

Physiological Concerns

According to current research by Tom Hudson, a bulldog expert, bulldogs have a higher rate of physical problems that almost any other dog (2013, parag 1). One particularly grave issue is that many bulldogs have hip dysplasia, a condition in which the hip joint becomes stressed because the dog's body is not aligned properly. Bulldogs have this condition at a rate much higher than any other dog, according to the Bone Science Foundation for Animals on their website (parag. 4). This condition is the result of the way that bulldogs have been bred. Their bodies are too stout for their legs, which places undue stress on their hip joints.

> The writer used transition phrases to show how parts of the text relate.

(continues)

Grade 8 (*continued*)

Another issue is the severe breathing problems that bulldogs often have as the result of breeding. Bulldogs are now breed to have very short muzzles, which makes them appear cuter, with a pushed-in face. However, this shorter muzzle makes it very difficult for bulldogs to breathe.

A final issue that is perhaps less severe but should be mentioned are the skin problems caused by bulldogs' wrinkles. Bulldogs are bred to have more and more wrinkles, in fact their faces are now 20% more wrinkled than they were 100 years ago, according to estimates by the Animal Research Foundation (2010, parag 7). The worst part of these physical problems is that dogs are suffering. Another concern is that the costs of giving bulldogs proper care can be quite high. Hip dysplasia surgery can be thousands of dollars, according to Hudson (2013), parag 6).

> The writer organized information into categories and clarified how those sections were connected and ordered.

Problems with Disease

Extreme breeding practices have also left bulldogs susceptible to disease. A common illness is cherry eye. This is caused by a swollen gland in a bulldog's eye. There isn't proof that this condition is exactly caused by breeding, but some people think breeding makes the problem worse because dogs with this condition are overbred. An example is long-time bulldog owner Mark David. Though Mr. David is not necessarily an expert on the subject, he says he has seen an increase in this illness now that bulldogs are bred to have shorter faces and larger eyes.

> The writer focused on a key concept within the topic and refered to this concept throughout the text.

> The writer incorporated trustworthy sources throughout the text, and made a note when a source was problematic or biased.

A more serious disease that affects overbred bulldogs is heart disease. This is explained in an article on vetrinariandaily.com posted by Joseph Michael, bulldogs tend toward heart problems because their hearts are not developed properly to work in conjunction with the way in which their large bodies have been bred (n.d., parag 5). Because of their weak hearts, bulldogs cannot tolerate extreme temperatures, particularly heat. If bulldogs overheat, they are at risk for heart attacks, a condition which could be avoided by outlawing unsafe breeding.

> Throughout the text, sections build on each other and are introduced in a logical fashion. The writer analyzed the relevance of information and explained how it supported the concepts throughout the text.

(continues)

Grade 8 (*continued*)

Problems with Natural Breeding

Because bulldogs are so overbred, they cannot breed and deliver puppies naturally themselves. Though breeders say that it isn't a problem because bulldogs can be bred in a lab, dog health advocates say that this is cruel and is a sign that bulldog breeders are creating dogs that go against nature (Michael, n.d.).

Another breeding problem is that bulldog puppies cannot be born naturally because their heads are too large to fit out of the birth canal. This means that unless a bulldog mother gets medical help, she would die if she tried to deliver her own babies. Breeding dogs that are so different from what they should be that they cannot even give birth to their own babies seems cruel, inhumane, and downright selfish. As Mr. Michael points out, "Imagine if we bred humans in such a way that women could no longer deliver babies. The thought is absurd. It seems just as absurd to allow bulldogs to suffer this fate" (n.d., parag. 9).

Solution

What is the solution? One person has an idea. Dr. Gerhard Oechtering, a vet and professor, has called for bulldogs to be banned. He believes that is the best way to stop the unethical breeding that has led to the health problems bulldogs face. In the documentary, *Pedigree Dogs Exposed* (February 2012), he also calls for flat-nosed breeds to be mated with long-nosed ones so that over time new generations do not suffer from blocked airways and other health problems they face now.

One reason why bulldogs continue to suffer so much is that many people fall in love with them because of the very characteristics that cause so many health problems. If people stopped buying bulldogs with extreme characteristics, like short faces and wide stocky bodies, and asked for dogs that were closer to their natural state, these breeding problems would be greatly decreased.

> The writer made word choices and used language to make readers feel a certain way about the topic.

> The writer used punctuation correctly to insert quotations and citations.

INFORMATION Annotated Writing
Developed through the Progression

(continues)

Grade 8 (*continued*)

> In the conclusion, the writer suggested implications and highlighted the significance of the main points, ending with a call to action.

> The writer used vivid examples and anecdotes to evoke certain feelings in readers.
>
> Additionally, the writer varied the tone to match different purposes.

> The writer used graphics to illustrate points.

Conclusion

The physiological problems, illness, and breeding problems caused by overbreeding have serious consequences. Mr. David tells one particularly heartbreaking story about a friend who purchased a bulldog puppy. The bulldog was healthy when he purchased the dog, but eventually the dog seemed to get nearly every bulldog illness possible. The dog suffered from cherry eye and seemed to be constantly wheezing. He had surgery for hip dysplasia, which was only partially successful. The dog eventually died from heart failure when he was only four years old. The owner spent thousands of dollars at the vet trying to save the dog. This could have been avoided if the dog had been bred more responsibly.

Proponents of bulldog breeding say that these problems are blown out of proportion and that bulldogs continue to be a healthy breed, even though they have changed so much physcially. Certainly statistics say otherwise. Life expectancy rates of bulldogs have declined over time (Michael, n.d.) and owners who have spent thousands of dollars like Mr. David would certainly disagree.

> The writer shifted verb tenses when needed and used different sentence structures to achieve different purposes throughout the text.

> The writer offered a second perspective once the first had been established.

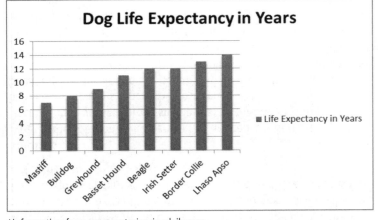

*information from www.veterinariandaily.com

(continues)

Grade 8 (*continued*)

> The writer used a standard format for citation and included a list of sources.

Bibliography

Animal Research Foundation (2010, February.) *Bulldog Facial Structures*. Retrieved from animalarf.org/bulldogs

Bone Science Foundation for Animals (n.d.) *Bulldogs and Bone Health*. Retrieved from www.bsfa.org/bulldogs

Bulldogs. (n.d.). In Inforpedia.org. Retrieved from www.inforpedia.org/bulldog

Gray, E. (1976) *This is a Bulldog*. New York, NY: Schoolpub

Hudson, T. (2013, October). *A Complete Guide to Bulldog Care*. Retrieved from www.bulldoginfor.com

Michael, J. (n.d.). *Typical Life Span of Common Dog Types*. Retrieved from www.veterinariandaily.com

Thomas, J. (2009) *Bulldog Life*. New York, NY: Schoolpub.

[Note: All of these sources and those used in other levels are fictionalized.]

Learning Progression for Narrative Writing

STRUCTURE

	Grade 3	Grade 4	Grade 5
Overall	The writer told the story bit by bit.	The writer wrote the important part of an event bit by bit and took out unimportant parts.	The writer wrote a story of an important moment. It reads like a story, even though it might be a true account.
Lead	The writer wrote a beginning in which he helped readers know who the characters were and what the setting was in his story.	The writer wrote a beginning in which she showed what was happening and where, getting readers into the world of the story.	The writer wrote a beginning in which she not only showed what was happening and where, but also gave some clues to what would later become a problem for the main character.
Transitions	The writer told her story in order by using phrases such as *a little later* and *after that.*	The writer showed how much time went by with words and phrases that mark time such as *just then* and *suddenly* (to show when things happened quickly) or *after a while* and *a little later* (to show when a little time passed).	The writer used transitional phrases to show the passage of time in complicated ways, perhaps by showing things happening at the same time (*meanwhile, at the same time*) or flashback and flash-forward (*early that morning, three hours later*).
Ending	The writer chose the action, talk, or feeling that would make a good ending and worked to write it well.	The writer wrote an ending that connected to the beginning or the middle of the story. The writer used action, dialogue, or feeling to bring her story to a close.	The writer wrote an ending that connected to the main part of the story. The character said, did, or realized something at the end that came from what happened previously in the story. The writer gave readers a sense of closure.
Organization	The writer used paragraphs and skipped lines to separate what happened first from what happened later (and finally) in her story.	The writer used paragraphs to separate the different parts or times of the story or to show when a new character was speaking.	The writer used paragraphs to separate different parts or times in the story and to show when a new character was speaking. Some parts of the story are longer and more developed than others.

Learning Progression for Narrative Writing

Grade 6	Grade 7	Grade 8	Grade 9
		STRUCTURE	
The writer wrote a story that has tension, resolution, and realistic characters, and also conveys an idea, lesson, or theme.	The writer created a narrative that has realistic characters, tension, and change, and that not only conveys, but also develops an idea, lesson, or theme.	The writer not only created a narrative with well-developed characters who change, he used the story to comment on a social issue, teach a lesson, and/or develop a point of view.	The writer created a narrative with well-developed characters whose interactions build tension and change over time. The writer used that story to comment on a social issue, teach a lesson, and/or develop a particular point of view.
The writer wrote a beginning that not only set the plot/story in motion, but also hinted at the larger meaning the story would convey. It introduced the problem, set the stage for the lesson that would be learned, or showed how the character relates to the setting in a way that matters in the story.	The writer wrote a beginning that not only sets the story in motion, it also grounds it in a place or situation. It includes details to the story. These details might point to the central issue or conflict, show how story elements connect, or hint at key character traits.	The writer wrote a beginning that establishes the situation and place, hinting at a bigger context for the story (revealing issues that have been brewing, showing how the setting affects the character, contextualizing a time in history, developing one out of many points of view).	The writer wrote a beginning establishing a situation, place, and/or atmosphere; foreshadowing the problem(s); and hinting at questions, issues, ideas, or themes. The writer introduced a particular narrative voice and point of view.
The writer not only used transitional phrases and clauses to signal complicated changes in time, she also used them to alert her readers to changes in the setting, tone, mood, point of view, or time in the story (such as *suddenly, unlike before, if only she had known*).	The writer used transitional phrases and clauses to connect what happened to why it happened (*If he hadn't . . . he might not have, because of, although, little did she know that*).	The writer used transitional phrases and clauses, grammatical structures (paragraphing, descriptive phrases, and clauses), and text structures (chapter divisions, extended italics) to alert his reader to changes in the setting, the mood, the point of view, or the time in the story.	The writer used transitional phrases and clauses, grammatical structures to demonstrate the passage of time, to connect parts of the story, to imply cause and effect, to raise questions, and/or to make allusions (*long before, as when, just as, without realizing, ever afterward*).
The writer wrote an ending that connected to what the story is really about. She gave the reader a sense of closure by showing a new realization or insight or a change in the character/narrator. The writer showed this through dialogue, action, inner thinking, or small actions the character takes.	The writer gave the reader a sense of closure by showing clearly how the character or place changed or the problem was resolved. If there was no resolution, he gave details to leave the reader thinking about a central idea or theme.	The writer gave the reader a sense of closure by revealing character change(s) that followed from events in the story, or a resolution. If there was no resolution, she wrote to convey how the events of the story affected the characters, and to circle back to a central idea, issue, or theme.	The writer gave the reader a sense of closure by returning to a theme, and/or revealing how characters changes or make a change. If there wasn't resolution, the writer made a connection to a larger issue or mood that added to the meaning of the whole story or suggested social commentary.
The writer used paragraphs purposefully, perhaps to show time and setting changes, new parts of the story, or to create suspense for readers. She created a logical, clear sequence of events.	The writer used a traditional—or slightly modified—story structure (rising action, conflict, falling action) to best bring out the meaning of his story and reach his audience.	The writer modified a traditional story structure, dealing with time in purposeful ways, to best suit her genre, bring out the meaning of her story, and reach her audience.	The writer used or adapted story structures and literary traditions (quest structure, coming of age story, cautionary tale, and so on) to fit the story, meaning, genre, and audience. The writer dealt with time purposefully (such as introducing multiple plot lines, flash-forwards, or flashbacks).

May be photocopied for classroom use. © 2014 by Lucy Calkins and Colleagues from the Teachers College Reading and Writing Project from *Units of Study in Argument, Information, and Narrative Writing* (firsthand: Portsmouth, NH).

	Grade 3	Grade 4	Grade 5
		DEVELOPMENT	
Elaboration	The writer worked to show what was happening to (and in) his characters.	The writer added more to the heart of her story, including not only actions and dialogue but also thoughts and feelings.	The writer developed characters, setting, and plot throughout this story, especially the heart of the story. To do this, she used a blend of description, action, dialogue, and thinking.
Craft	The writer not only told her story, but also wrote it in ways that got readers to picture what was happening and that brought her story to life.	The writer showed *why* characters did what they did by including their thinking. The writer made some parts of the story go quickly, some slowly. The writer included precise and sometimes sensory details and used figurative language (simile, metaphor, personification) to bring his story to life. The writer used a storytelling voice and conveyed the emotion or tone of his story through description, phrases, dialogue, and thoughts.	The writer showed why characters act and speak as they do by including their thinking and their responses to what happened. The writer slowed down the heart of the story. She made less important parts shorter and less detailed and blended storytelling and summary as needed. The writer included precise details and used figurative language so that readers could picture the setting, characters, and events. She used some objects or actions as symbols to bring forth her meaning. The writer varied her sentences to create the pace and tone of her narrative.
		CONVENTIONS	
Spelling	The writer used what he knew about spelling patterns to help him spell and edit before he wrote his final draft. The writer got help from others to check his spelling and punctuation before he wrote his final draft.	The writer used what she knew about word families and spelling rules to help her spell and edit. She used the word wall and dictionaries when needed.	The writer used what he knows about word families and spelling rules to help him spell and edit. He used the word wall and dictionaries when needed.
Punctuation and Sentence Structure	The writer punctuated dialogue correctly with commas and quotation marks. While writing, the writer put punctuation at the end of every sentence. The writer wrote in ways that helped readers read with expression, reading some parts quickly, some slowly, some parts in one sort of voice and others in another.	When writing long, complex sentences, the writer used commas to make them clear and correct.	The writer used commas to set off introductory parts of a sentence (*one day at the park.*). She also used commas to show when a character is talking directly to someone, such as "Are you mad, Mom?"

Grade 6	Grade 7	Grade 8	Grade 9
DEVELOPMENT			
The writer developed realistic characters, and developed the details, action, dialogue, and internal thinking that contribute to the deeper meaning of the story.	The writer developed the action, dialogue, details, and inner thinking to convey an issue, idea, or lesson. He showed what is specific about the central character. The writer developed the setting and the characters' relationship to the setting.	The writer developed complicated story elements: she may have contrasted the character's thinking with his or her actions or dialogue. The writer developed the central character's relationship to other characters. She showed character flaws as well as strengths to add complexity. The writer used details that related to and conveyed meaning or developed a lesson or theme.	The writer developed complicated story elements through key details—using them to add to tension or meaning. The writer showed character flaws, strengths, and aspects that make them unique or worthy of being written about. The writer used details to convey meaning or develop a lesson or theme.
The writer developed some relationship between characters to show *why* they act and speak as they do. He told the internal, as well as the external story. The writer wove together precise descriptions, figurative language, and some symbolism to help readers picture the setting, actions, and events and to bring forth meaning. The writer used language that fit his story's meaning and context (e.g., different characters use different kinds of language).	The writer developed contradictions and change in characters and situations. The writer used specific details and figurative language to help the reader understand the place and the mood (making an object or place symbolic, using the weather, using repetition). The writer varied her tone to match the variety of emotions experienced by the characters across the story.	The writer conveyed the pressures characters feel and the dreams they hold. He related those to their actions. The writer developed complicated characters who change and/or who change others. The writer created a mood as well as a physical setting, and showed how the place changed, or its relationships to the characters changed. The writer used symbolism to connect with a theme. The writer varied his tone to bring out different perspectives within the story, or to show a gap between the narrator's point of view and that of other characters.	The writer developed characters across scenes, offering insight into their troubles, hopes, relationships, and giving clues about how they change. The writer used setting to create mood and add to meaning. The writer used symbolism or metaphor for subtle as well as obvious connections to a theme. The writer varied the pace and tone to develop tension and/or develop different perspectives across the text.
CONVENTIONS			
The writer used resources to be sure the words in her writing are spelled correctly.	The writer used the Internet and other sources at hand to check spelling of literary and high-frequency words.	The writer used the Internet and other sources to check the spelling of literary, historical, and geographical words.	The writer checked spelling for accuracy, double-checking for misused homonyms or technologically created misspellings.
The writer used punctuation such as dashes, parentheses, colons, and semicolons to help him include extra detail and explanation in some of his sentences. The writer used commas and quotation marks or italics or some other way to make clear when characters are speaking.	The writer varied her sentence structure, sometimes using simple and sometimes using complex sentence structure. The writer punctuated dialogue sections accurately.	The writer used different sentence structures to achieve different purposes throughout his piece. The writer used verb tenses that shift when needed (as in when moving from a flashback back into the present tense of the story), deciding between active and passive voice where appropriate.	The writer was accurate and purposeful with conventions, using them to enhance the pace and tone of the text. If the write broke conventions, it was purposefully (for example, using fragments or dialect) when appropriate to the genre and purpose.

ON-DEMAND PERFORMANC

Narrative Writing

Say to students:

"I'm really eager to understand what you can do as writers of narratives, of stories, so today, will you please write the best personal narrative, the best true story, that you can write? Make this be the story of one time in your life. You might focus on just a scene or two. You'll have only forty-five minutes to write this true story, so you'll need to plan, draft, revise, and edit in one sitting. Write in a way that allows you to show off all you know about narrative writing.

"In your writing, make sure you:

- Write a beginning for your story;

- Use transition words to tell what happened in order.

- Elaborate to help readers picture your story.

- Show what your story is really about.

- Write an ending for your story."

Use the teaching rubrics to assess and score these pieces of on-demand writing.

Rubric for Narrative Writing—Sixth Grade

	Grade 4 (1 POINT)	1.5 PTS	Grade 5 (2 POINTS)	2.5 PTS	Grade 6 (3 POINTS)	3.5 PTS	Grade 7 (4 POINTS)	SCORE
STRUCTURE								
Overall	The writer wrote the important part of an event bit by bit and took out unimportant parts.	Mid-level	The writer wrote a story of an important moment. It reads like a story, even though it might be a true account.	Mid-level	The writer wrote a story that has tension, resolution, and realistic characters, and also conveys an idea, lesson, or theme.	Mid-level	The writer created a narrative that has realistic characters, tension, and change, and that not only conveys, but also develops an idea, lesson, or theme.	
Lead	The write wrote a beginning in which she showed what was happening and where, getting readers into the world of the story.	Mid-level	The writer wrote a beginning in which she not only showed what was happening and where, but also gave some clues to what would later become a problem for the main character.	Mid-level	The writer wrote a beginning that not only set the plot/story in motion, but also hinted at the larger meaning the story would convey. It introduced the problem, set the stage for the lesson that would be learned, or showed how the character relates to the setting in a way that matters in the story.	Mid-level	The writer wrote a beginning that not only sets the story in motion, it also grounds it in a place or situation. It includes details that will later be important to the story. These details might point to the central issue or conflict, show how story elements connect, or hint at key character traits.	
Transitions	The writer showed how much time went by with words and phrases that mark time such as *just then* and *suddenly* (to show when things happened quickly) or *after a while* and *a little later* (to show when a little time passed).	Mid-level	The writer used transitional phrases to show passage of time in complicated ways, perhaps by showing things happening at the same time (*meanwhile, at the same time*) or flashback and flash-forward (*early that morning, three hours later*).	Mid-level	The writer not only used transitional phrases and clauses to signal complicated changes in time, she also used them to alert her readers to changes in the setting, tone, mood, point of view, or time in the story (such as *suddenly, unlike before, if only she had known*).	Mid-level	The writer used transitional phrases and clauses to connect what happened to why it happened (*If he hadn't . . . he might not have, because of, although, little did she know that*).	

NARRATIVE: TEACHING RUBRIC—SIXTH GRADE (continued)

STRUCTURE (cont.)

	Grade 4 (1 POINT)	1.5 PTS	Grade 5 (2 POINTS)	2.5 PTS	Grade 6 (3 POINTS)	3.5 PTS	Grade 7 (4 POINTS)	SCORE
Ending	The writer wrote an ending that connected to the beginning or the middle of the story. The writer used action, dialogue, or feeling to bring her story to a close.	Mid-level	The writer wrote an ending that connected to the main part of the story. The character said, did, or realized something at the end that came from what happened previously in the story. The writer gave readers a sense of closure.	Mid-level	The writer wrote an ending that connected to what the story is really about. She gave the reader a sense of closure by showing a new realization or insight or a change in the character/narrator. The writer showed this through dialogue, action, inner thinking, or small actions the character takes.	Mid-level	The writer gave the reader a sense of closure by showing clearly how the character or place changed or the problem was resolved. If there was no resolution, he gave details to leave the reader thinking about a central idea or theme.	
Organization	The writer used paragraphs to separate the different parts or times of the story or to show when a new character was speaking.	Mid-level	The writer used paragraphs to separate different parts or times in the story and to show when a new character was speaking. Some parts of the story are longer and more developed than others.	Mid-level	The writer used paragraphs purposefully, perhaps to show time and setting changes, new parts of the story, or to create suspense for readers. She created a logical, clear sequence of events.	Mid-level	The writer used a traditional—or slightly modified—story structure (rising action, conflict, falling action) to best bring out the meaning of his story and reach his audience.	

DEVELOPMENT

	Grade 4	1.5 PTS	Grade 5	2.5 PTS	Grade 6	3.5 PTS	Grade 7	SCORE
Elaboration*	The writer added more to the heart of her story, including not only actions and dialogue but also thoughts and feelings.	Mid-level	The writer developed characters, setting, and plot throughout this story, especially the heart of the story. To do this, she used a blend of description, action, dialogue, and thinking.	Mid-level	The writer developed realistic characters, and developed the details, action, dialogue, and internal thinking that contribute to the deeper meaning of the story.	Mid-level	The writer developed the action, dialogue, details, and inner thinking to convey an issue, idea, or lesson. He showed what is specific about the central character. The writer developed the setting and the characters' relationship to the setting.	
							TOTAL:	

*Elaboration and Craft are double-weighted categories: Whatever score a student would get in these categories is worth double the amount of points. For example, if a student exceeds expectations in Elaboration, then that student would receive 8 points instead of 4 points. If a student meets standards in Elaboration, then that student would receive 6 points instead of 3 points.

NARRATIVE: TEACHING RUBRIC—SIXTH GRADE *(continued)*

DEVELOPMENT (cont.)

	Grade 4 (1 POINT)	1.5 PTS	Grade 5 (2 POINTS)	2.5 PTS	Grade 6 (3 POINTS)	3.5 PTS	Grade 7 (4 POINTS)	SCORE
Craft*	The writer showed why characters did what they did by including their thinking. The writer made some parts of the story go quickly, some slowly. The writer included precise and sometimes sensory details and used figurative language (simile, metaphor, personification) to bring his story to life. The writer used a storytelling voice and conveyed the emotion or tone of his story through description, phrases, dialogue, and thoughts.	Mid-level	The writer showed why characters act and speak as they do by including their thinking and their responses to what happened. The writer slowed down the heart of the story. She made less important parts shorter and less detailed and blended storytelling and summary as needed. The writer included precise details and used figurative language so that readers could picture the setting, characters, and events. She used some objects or actions as symbols to bring forth her meaning. The writer varied her sentences to create the pace and tone of her narrative.	Mid-level	The writer developed some relationship between characters to show why they act and speak as they do. He told the internal, as well as the external story. The writer wove together precise descriptions, figurative language, and some symbolism to help readers picture the setting, actions, and events and to bring forth meaning. The writer used language that fit his story's meaning and context (e.g., different characters use different kinds of language).	Mid-level	The writer developed contradictions and change in characters and situations. The writer used specific details and figurative language to help the reader understand the place and the mood (making an object or place symbolic, using the weather, using repetition). The writer varied her tone to match the variety of emotions experienced by the characters across the story.	

CONVENTIONS

	Grade 4 (1 POINT)	1.5 PTS	Grade 5 (2 POINTS)	2.5 PTS	Grade 6 (3 POINTS)	3.5 PTS	Grade 7 (4 POINTS)	SCORE
Spelling	The writer used what she knew about word families and spelling rules to help her spell and edit. She used the word wall and dictionaries when needed.	Mid-level	The writer used what he knows about word families and spelling rules to help him spell and edit. He used the word wall and dictionaries when needed.	Mid-level	The writer used resources to be sure the words in her writing are spelled correctly.	Mid-level	The writer used the Internet and other sources at hand to check spelling of literary and high-frequency words.	
							TOTAL:	

*Elaboration and Craft are double-weighted categories: Whatever score a student would get in these categories is worth double the amount of points. For example, if a student exceeds expectations in Elaboration, then that student would receive 8 points instead of 4 points. If a student meets standards in Elaboration, then that student would receive 6 points instead of 3 points.

NARRATIVE: TEACHING RUBRIC—SIXTH GRADE (*continued*)

	Grade 4 (1 POINT)		**Grade 5** (2 POINTS)		**Grade 6** (3 POINTS)		**Grade 7** (4 POINTS)		SCORE
		1.5 PTS		2.5 PTS		3.5 PTS			
			CONVENTIONS (cont.)						
Punctuation and Sentence Structure	When writing long, complex sentences, the writer used commas to make them clear and correct.	Mid-level	The writer used commas to set off introductory parts of sentences (*one day at the park,*). She also used commas to show when a character is talking directly to someone, *such as "Are you mad, Mom?"*	Mid-level	The writer used punctuation such as dashes, parentheses, colons, and semicolons to help him include extra detail and explanation in some of his sentences. The writer used commas and quotation marks or italics or some other way to make clear when characters are speaking.	Mid-level	The writer varied her sentence structure, sometimes using simple and sometimes using complex sentence structure. The writer punctuated dialogue sections accurately.		
							TOTAL:		

Teachers, we created these rubrics so you will have your own place to pull together scores of student work. You can use these assessments immediately after giving the on-demands and also for self-assessment and setting goals.

Scoring Guide

In each row, circle the descriptor in the column that matches the student work. Scores in the categories of Elaboration and Craft are worth double the point value (2, 3, 4, 5, 6, 7, or 8 instead of 1, 1.5, 2, 2.5, 3, 3.5, or 4).

Total the number of points and then track students' progress by seeing when the total points increase.

Total score: _____

If you want to translate this score into a grade, you can use the provided table to score each student on a scale of 0–4.

Number of Points	Scaled Score
1–11	1
11.5–16.5	1.5
17–22	2
22.5–27.5	2.5
28–33	3
33.5–38.5	3.5
39–44	4

Name: _____   Date: _____

Rubric for Narrative Writing—Seventh Grade

	Grade 5 (1 POINT)	1.5 PTS	Grade 6 (2 POINTS)	2.5 PTS	Grade 7 (3 POINTS)	3.5 PTS	Grade 8 (4 POINTS)	SCORE
					STRUCTURE			
Overall	The writer wrote a story of an important moment. It reads like a story, even though it might be a true account.	Mid-level	The writer wrote a story that has tension, resolution, and realistic characters, and also conveys an idea, lesson, or theme.	Mid-level	The writer created a narrative that has realistic characters, tension, and change, and that not only conveys, but also develops an idea, lesson, or theme.	Mid-level	The writer not only created a narrative with well-developed characters who change, he used the story to comment on a social issue, teach a lesson, and/or develop a point of view.	
Lead	The writer wrote a beginning in which she not only showed what was happening and where, but also gave some clues to what would later become a problem for the main character.	Mid-level	The writer wrote a beginning that not only set the plot/story in motion, but also hinted at the larger meaning the story would convey. It introduced the problem, set the stage for the lesson that would be learned, or showed how the character relates to the setting in a way that matters in the story.	Mid-level	The writer wrote a beginning that not only sets the story in motion, it also grounds it in a place or situation. It includes details that will later be important to the story. These details might point to the central issue or conflict, show how story elements connect, or hint at key character traits.	Mid-level	The writer wrote a beginning that establishes the situation and place, hinting at a bigger context for the story (revealing issues that have been brewing, showing how the setting affects the character, contextualizing a time in history, developing one out of many points of view).	
Transitions	The writer used transitional phrases to show passage of time in complicated ways, perhaps by showing things happening at the same time (*meanwhile, at the same time*) or flashback and flash-forward (*early that morning, three hours later*).	Mid-level	The writer not only used transitional phrases and clauses to signal complicated changes in time, she also used them to alert her readers to changes in the setting, tone, mood, point of view, or time in the story (such as *suddenly, unlike before, if only she had known*).	Mid-level	The writer used transitional phrases and clauses to connect what happened to why it happened (*If he hadn't . . . he might not have, because of, although, little did she know that*).	Mid-level	The writer used transitional phrases and clauses, grammatical structures (paragraphing, descriptive phrases, and clauses) and text structures (chapter divisions, extended italics) to alert his reader to changes in the setting, the mood, the point of view, or the time in the story.	

NARRATIVE: TEACHING RUBRIC—SEVENTH GRADE (continued)

	Grade 5 (1 POINT)	1.5 PTS	Grade 6 (2 POINTS)	2.5 PTS	Grade 7 (3 POINTS)	3.5 PTS	Grade 8 (4 POINTS)	SCORE
STRUCTURE (cont.)								
Ending	The writer wrote an ending that connected to the main part of the story. The character said, did, or realized something at the end that came from what happened previously in the story. The writer gave readers a sense of closure.	Mid-level	The writer wrote an ending that connected to what the story is really about. She gave the reader a sense of closure by showing a new realization or insight or a change in the character/narrator. The writer showed this through dialogue, action, inner thinking, or small actions the character takes.	Mid-level	The writer gave the reader a sense of closure by showing clearly how the character change(s) that followed from events in the story, or a resolution. If there was no resolution, he gave details to leave the reader thinking about a central idea or theme.	Mid-level	The writer gave the reader a sense of closure by revealing character change by showing clearly how the character change(s) that followed from events in the story, or a resolution. If there was no resolution, she wrote to convey how the events of the story affected the characters, and to circle back to a central idea, issue, or theme.	
Organization	The writer used paragraphs to separate different parts or times in the story and to show when a new character was speaking. Some parts of the story are longer and more developed than others.	Mid-level	The writer used paragraphs purposefully, perhaps to show time and setting changes, new parts of the story, or to create suspense. She created a logical, clear sequence of events.	Mid-level	The writer used a traditional—or slightly modified—story structure (rising action, conflict, falling action) to best bring out the meaning of his story and reach his audience.	Mid-level	The writer modified a traditional story structure, dealing with time in purposeful ways, to best suit her genre, bring out the meaning of her story, and reach her audience.	
DEVELOPMENT								TOTAL:
Elaboration*	The writer developed characters, setting, and plot throughout this story, especially the heart of the story. To do this, she used a blend of description, action, dialogue, and thinking.	Mid-level	The writer developed realistic characters, and developed the details, action, dialogue, and internal thinking that contribute to the deeper meaning of the story.	Mid-level	The writer developed the action, dialogue, details, and inner thinking to convey an issue, idea, or lesson. He showed what is specific about the central character. The writer developed the setting and the characters' relationship to the setting.	Mid-level	The writer developed complicated story elements: she may have contrasted the character's thinking with his or her actions or dialogue. The writer developed the central character's relationship to other characters. She showed character flaws as well as strengths to add complexity. The writer used details that related to and conveyed meaning or developed a lesson or theme.	

*Elaboration and Craft are double-weighted categories: Whatever score a student would get in these categories is worth double the amount of points. For example, if a student exceeds expectations in Elaboration, then that student would receive 8 points instead of 4 points. If a student meets standards in Elaboration, then that student would receive 6 points instead of 3 points.

NARRATIVE: TEACHING RUBRIC—SEVENTH GRADE (continued)

	Grade 5 (1 POINT)	1.5 PTS	Grade 6 (2 POINTS)	2.5 PTS	Grade 7 (3 POINTS)	3.5 PTS	Grade 8 (4 POINTS)	SCORE
DEVELOPMENT (cont.)								
Craft*	The writer showed why characters act and speak as they do by including their thinking and their responses to what happened. The writer slowed down the heart of the story. She made less important parts shorter and less detailed and blended storytelling and summary as needed. The writer included precise details and used figurative language so that readers could picture the setting, characters, and events. She used some objects or actions as symbols to bring forth her meaning. The writer varied her sentences to create the pace and tone of her narrative.	Mid-level	The writer developed some relationship between characters to show *why* they act and speak as they do. He told the internal, as well as the external story. The writer wove together precise descriptions, figurative language, and some symbolism to help readers picture the setting, actions, and events and to bring forth meaning. The writer used language that fit his story's meaning and context (e.g., different characters use different kinds of language).	Mid-level	The writer developed contradictions and change in characters and situations. The writer used specific details and figurative language to help the reader understand the place and the mood (making an object or place symbolic, using the weather, using repetition). The writer varied her tone to match the variety of emotions experienced by the characters across the story.	Mid-level	The writer conveyed the pressures characters feel and the dreams they hold. He related those to their actions. The writer developed complicated characters who change and/or who change others. The writer created a mood as well as a physical setting, and showed how the place changed, or its relationships to the characters changed. The writer used symbolism to connect with a theme. The writer varied his tone to bring out different perspectives within the story, or to show a gap between the narrator's point of view and that of other characters.	
CONVENTIONS								
Spelling	The writer used what he knows about word families and spelling rules to help him spell and edit. He used the word wall and dictionaries when needed.	Mid-level	The writer used resources to be sure the words in her writing are spelled correctly.	Mid-level	The writer used the Internet and other sources at hand to check spelling of literary and high-frequency words.	Mid-level	The writer used the Internet and other sources to check the spelling of literary, historical, and geographical words.	
								TOTAL:

*Elaboration and Craft are double-weighted categories: Whatever score a student would get in these categories is worth double the amount of points. For example, if a student exceeds expectations in Elaboration, then that student would receive 8 points instead of 4 points. If a student meets standards in Elaboration, then that student would receive 6 points instead of 3 points.

May be photocopied for classroom use. © 2014 by Lucy Calkins and Colleagues from the Teachers College Reading and Writing Project from *Units of Study in Argument, Information, and Narrative Writing (firsthand:* Portsmouth, NH).

	Grade 5 (1 POINT)	1.5 PTS	Grade 6 (2 POINTS)	2.5 PTS	Grade 7 (3 POINTS)	3.5 PTS	Grade 8 (4 POINTS)	SCORE
CONVENTIONS (cont.)								
Punctuation and Sentence Structure	The writer used commas to set off introductory parts of sentences (one day at the park,). She also used commas to show when a character is talking directly to someone, such as Are you mad, Mom?	Mid-level	The writer used punctuation such as dashes, parentheses, colons, and semicolons to help him include extra detail and explanation in some of his sentences. The writer used commas and quotation marks or italics or some other way to make clear when characters are speaking.	Mid-level	The writer varied her sentence structure, sometimes using simple and sometimes using complex sentence structure. The writer punctuated dialogue sections accurately.	Mid-level	The writer used different sentence structures to achieve different purposes throughout his piece. The writer used verb tenses that shift when needed (as in when moving from a flashback back into the present tense of the story), deciding between active and passive voice where appropriate.	TOTAL:

Teachers, we created these rubrics so you will have your own place to pull together scores of student work. You can use these assessments immediately after giving the on-demands and also for self-assessment and setting goals.

Scoring Guide

In each row, circle the descriptor in the column that matches the student work. Scores in the categories of Elaboration and Craft are worth double the point value (2, 3, 4, 5, 6, 7, or 8 instead of 1, 1.5, 2, 2.5, 3, 3.5, or 4).

Total the number of points and then track students' progress by seeing when the total points increase.

Total score: _____

If you want to translate this score into a grade, you can use the provided table to score each student on a scale of 0–4.

Number of Points	Scaled Score
1–11	1
11.5–16.5	1.5
17–22	2
22.5–27.5	2.5
28–33	3
33.5–38.5	3.5
39–44	4

Name: _____ Date: _____

Rubric for Narrative Writing—Eighth Grade

STRUCTURE

	Grade 6 (1 POINT)	1.5 PTS	Grade 7 (2 POINTS)	2.5 PTS	Grade 8 (3 POINTS)	3.5 PTS	Grade 9 (4 POINTS)	SCORE
Overall	The writer wrote a story that has tension, resolution, and realistic characters, and also conveys an idea, lesson, or theme.	Mid-level	The writer created a narrative that has realistic characters, tension, and change, and that not only conveys, but also develops an idea, lesson, or theme.	Mid-level	The writer not only created a narrative with well-developed characters who change, he used the story to comment on a social issue, teach a lesson, and/or develop a point of view.	Mid-level	The writer created a narrative with well-developed characters whose interactions build tension and change over time. The writer used that story to comment on a social issue, teach a lesson, and/or develop a particular point of view.	
Lead	The writer wrote a beginning that not only set the plot/story in motion, but also hinted at the larger meaning the story would convey. It introduced the problem, set the stage for the lesson that would be learned, or showed how the character relates to the setting in a way that matters in the story.	Mid-level	The writer wrote a beginning that not only sets the story in motion, it also grounds it in a place or situation. It includes details that will later be important to the story. These details might point to the central issue or conflict, show how story elements connect, or hint at key character traits.	Mid-level	The writer wrote a beginning that establishes the situation and place, hinting at a bigger context for the story (revealing issues that have been brewing, showing how the setting affects the character, contextualizing a time in history, developing one out of many points of view).	Mid-level	The writer wrote a beginning establishing a situation, place, and/or atmosphere; foreshadowing the problem(s); and hinting at questions, issues, ideas, or themes. The writer introduced a particular narrative voice and point of view.	
Transitions	The writer not only used transitional phrases and clauses to signal complicated changes in time, she also used them to alert her readers to changes in the setting, tone, mood, point of view, or time in the story (such as *suddenly, unlike before, if only she had known*).	Mid-level	The writer used transitional phrases and clauses to connect what happened to why it happened (*If he hadn't . . . he might not have, because of, although, little did she know that*).	Mid-level	The writer used transitional phrases and clauses, grammatical structures (paragraphing, descriptive phrases, and clauses) and text structures (chapter divisions, extended italics) to alert his reader to changes in the setting, the mood, the point of view, or the time in the story.	Mid-level	The writer used transitional phrases and clauses, grammatical structures to demonstrate the passage of time, to connect parts of the story, to imply cause and effect, to raise questions, and/or to make allusions (*long before, as when, just as, without realizing, ever afterward*).	

NARRATIVE: TEACHING RUBRIC—EIGHTH GRADE (continued)

	Grade 6 (1 POINT)	1.5 PTS	Grade 7 (2 POINTS)	2.5 PTS	Grade 8 (3 POINTS)	3.5 PTS	Grade 9 (4 POINTS)	SCORE
STRUCTURE (cont.)								
Ending	The writer wrote an ending that connected to what the story is really about. She gave the reader a sense of closure by showing a change in the character/narrator. The writer showed this through dialogue, action, inner thinking, or small actions the character takes.	Mid-level	The writer gave the reader a sense of closure by showing clearly how the character or place changed or the problem was resolved. If there was no resolution, he gave details to leave the reader thinking about a central idea or theme.	Mid-level	The writer gave the reader a sense of closure by revealing character change(s) that followed from events in the story, or a resolution. If there wasn't a change, or if there was no resolution, she wrote to convey how the events of the story affected the characters, and to circle back to a central idea, issue, or theme.	Mid-level	The writer gave the reader a sense of closure by returning to a theme, and/or revealing how characters change or make a change. If there wasn't a change or make a resolution, the writer made a connection to a larger issue or mood that added to the meaning of the whole story or suggested social commentary.	
Organization	The writer used paragraphs purposefully, perhaps to show time and setting changes, new parts of the story, or to create suspense for readers. She created a logical, clear sequence of events.	Mid-level	The writer used a traditional—or slightly modified—story structure (rising action, conflict, falling action) to best bring out the meaning of his story and reach his audience.	Mid-level	The writer modified a traditional story structure, dealing with time in purposeful ways, to best suit her genre, bring out the meaning of her story, and reach her audience.	Mid-level	The writer used or adapted story structures and literary traditions (quest structure, coming of age, cautionary tale, etc.) to fit the story, meaning, genre, audience. The writer dealt with time purposefully (eg, introducing multiple plot lines, flash-forwards, or flashbacks).	TOTAL:
DEVELOPMENT								
Elaboration*	The writer developed realistic characters, and developed the details, action, dialogue and internal thinking that contribute to the deeper meaning of the story.	Mid-level	The writer developed the action, dialogue, details, and inner thinking to convey an issue, idea, or lesson. He showed what is specific about the central character. The writer developed the central character's relationship to the setting.	Mid-level	The writer developed complicated story elements: she may have contrasted the character's thinking with his or her actions or dialogue. The writer developed the central character's relationship to other characters. She showed character flaws as well as strengths to add complexity.	Mid-level	The writer developed complicated story elements through key details—using them to add to tension or meaning. The writer showed character flaws, strengths, and aspects that make them unique or worthy of being written about.	

May be photocopied for classroom use. © 2014 by Lucy Calkins and Colleagues from the Teachers College Reading and Writing Project from *Units of Study in Argument, Information, and Narrative Writing* (firsthand: Portsmouth, NH).

*Elaboration and Craft are double-weighted categories: Whatever score a student would get in these categories is worth double the amount of points. For example, if a student exceeds expectations in Elaboration, then that student would receive 8 points instead of 4 points. If a student meets standards in Elaboration, then that student would receive 6 points instead of 3 points.

NARRATIVE: TEACHING RUBRIC—EIGHTH GRADE (continued)

DEVELOPMENT (cont.)

	Grade 6 (1 POINT)	1.5 PTS	Grade 7 (2 POINTS)	2.5 PTS	Grade 8 (3 POINTS)	3.5 PTS	Grade 9 (4 POINTS)	SCORE
Elaboration* (cont.)		Mid-level		Mid-level	The writer used details that related to and conveyed meaning or developed a lesson or theme.	Mid-level	The writer used details to convey meaning or develop a lesson or theme.	
Craft*	The writer developed some relationship between characters to show why they act and speak as they do. He told the internal, as well as the external story. The writer wove together precise descriptions, figurative language, and some symbolism to help readers picture the setting, actions, and events and to bring forth meaning. The writer used language that fit his story's meaning and context (e.g., different characters use different kinds of language).	Mid-level	The writer developed contradictions and change in characters and situations. The writer used specific details and figurative language to help the reader understand the place and the mood (making an object or place symbolic, using the weather, using repetition). The writer varied her tone to match the variety of emotions experienced by the characters across the story.	Mid-level	The writer conveyed the pressures characters feel and the dreams they hold. He related those to their actions. The writer developed complicated characters who change and/or who change others. The writer created a mood as well as a physical setting, and showed how the place changed, or its relationships to the characters changed. The writer used symbolism to connect with a theme. The writer varied his tone to bring out different perspectives within the story, or to show a gap between the narrator's point of view and that of other characters.	Mid-level	The writer developed characters across scenes, offering insight into their troubles, hopes, relationships, and giving clues about how they change. The writer used setting to create mood and add to meaning. The writer used symbolism or metaphor for subtle as well as obvious connections to a theme. The writer varied the pace and tone to develop tension and/or develop different perspectives across the text.	
							TOTAL:	

*Elaboration and Craft are double-weighted categories: Whatever score a student would get in these categories is worth double the amount of points. For example, if a student exceeds expectations in Elaboration, then that student would receive 8 points instead of 4 points. If a student meets standards in Elaboration, then that student would receive 6 points instead of 3 points.

PART II: THE ASSESSMENT TOOLS—NARRATIVE WRITING

NARRATIVE: TEACHING RUBRIC—EIGHTH GRADE (continued)

CONVENTIONS

	Grade 6 (1 POINT)	1.5 PTS	Grade 7 (2 POINTS)	2.5 PTS	Grade 8 (3 POINTS)	3.5 PTS	Grade 9 (4 POINTS)	SCORE
Spelling	The writer used resources to be sure the words in her writing are spelled correctly.	Mid-level	The writer used the Internet and other sources at hand to check spelling of literary and high-frequency words.	Mid-level	The writer used the Internet and other sources to check the spelling of literary, historical, and geographical words.	Mid-level	The writer checked spelling for accuracy, double-checking for misused homonyms and technologically created mishaps.	
Punctuation and Sentence Structure	The writer used punctuation such as dashes, parentheses, colons, and semicolons to help him include extra detail and explanation in some of his sentences. The writer used commas and quotation marks or italics or some other way to make clear when characters are speaking.	Mid-level	The writer varied her sentence structure, sometimes using simple and sometimes using complex sentence structure. The writer punctuated dialogue sections accurately.	Mid-level	The writer used different sentence structures to achieve different purposes throughout his piece. The writer used verb tenses that shift when needed (as in when moving from a flashback back into the present tense of the story), deciding between active and passive voice where appropriate.	Mid-level	The writer was accurate and purposeful with conventions, using them to enhance and pace the tone of the text. If the writer broke conventions, it was purposefully (for example, using fragments or dialect) when appropriate to the genre and purpose.	TOTAL:

Teachers, we created these rubrics so you will have your own place to pull together scores of student work. You can use these assessments immediately after giving the on-demands and also for self-assessment and setting goals.

Scoring Guide

In each row, circle the descriptor in the column that matches the student work. Scores in the categories of Elaboration and Craft are worth double the point value (2, 3, 4, 5, 6, 7, or 8 instead of 1, 1.5, 2, 2.5, 3, 3.5, or 4).

Total the number of points and then track students' progress by seeing when the total points increase.

Total score: _____

If you want to translate this score into a grade, you can use the provided table to score each student on a scale of 0–4.

Number of Points	Scaled Score
1-11	1
11.5-16.5	1.5
17-22	2
22.5-27.5	2.5
28-33	3
33.5-38.5	3.5
39-44	4

Name: _____ **Date:** _____

Narrative Writing Checklist

	Grade 6	NOT YET	STARTING TO	YES!
	Structure			
Overall	I wrote a story that has tension, resolution, realistic characters, and also conveys an idea, lesson, or theme.	☐	☐	☐
Lead	I wrote a beginning that not only set the plot/story in motion, but also hinted at the larger meaning the story would convey. It introduced the problem, set the stage for the lesson that would be learned, or showed how the character relates to the setting in a way that matters in the story.	☐	☐	☐
Transitions	I not only used transitional phrases and clauses to signal complicated changes in time, I also used them to alert my reader to changes in the setting, tone, mood, point of view, or the time in the story (such as *suddenly, unlike before, if only she had known*).	☐	☐	☐
Ending	I wrote an ending that connected to what the story is really about. I gave the reader a sense of closure by showing a new realization or insight, or a change in the character/narrator. I might have shown this through dialogue, action, inner thinking, or small actions the character takes.	☐	☐	☐
Organization	I used paragraphs purposefully, perhaps to show time and setting changes, new parts of the story, or to create suspense for readers. I created a logical, clear sequence of events.	☐	☐	☐
	Development			
Elaboration	I developed realistic characters, and developed the details, action, dialogue, and internal thinking that contribute to the deeper meaning of the story.	☐	☐	☐
Craft	I developed some relationship between characters to show *why* they act and speak as they do. I told the internal, as well as the external story.	☐	☐	☐
	I wove together precise descriptions, figurative language, and some symbolism to help readers picture the setting and actions, and to bring forth meaning.	☐	☐	☐
	I used language that fit my story's meaning and context (for example, different characters use different kinds of language).	☐	☐	☐
	Conventions			
Spelling	I used resources to be sure the words in my writing are spelled correctly.	☐	☐	☐
Punctuation and Sentence Structure	I used punctuation such as dashes, parentheses, colons, and semicolons to help me include extra detail and explanation in some of my sentences.	☐	☐	☐
	I used commas and quotation marks or italics or other ways to make clear when characters are speaking.	☐	☐	☐

NARRATIVE Student Checklists

NARRATIVE: STUDENT CHECKLISTS

Name: _____ **Date:** _____

Narrative Writing Checklist

	Grade 7	NOT YET	STARTING TO	YES!
Structure				
Overall	I created a narrative that has realistic characters, tension, and change, and that not only conveys, but also develops an idea, lesson, or theme.	☐	☐	☐
Lead	I wrote a beginning that not only sets the story in motion, it also grounds it in a place or situation. It included details that will later be important to the story. These details might point to the central issue or conflict, show how story elements connect, or hint at key character traits.	☐	☐	☐
Transitions	I used transitional phrases and clauses to connect what happened to why it happened (*If he hadn't . . . he might not have, because of, although, little did she know that*).	☐	☐	☐
Ending	I gave the reader a sense of closure by showing clearly how the character or place has changed or the problem has been resolved. If there wasn't resolution, I gave details to leave the reader thinking about a central idea or theme.	☐	☐	☐
Organization	I used a traditional—or slightly modified—story structure (rising action, conflict, falling action) to best bring out the meaning of my story and reach my audience.	☐	☐	☐
Development				
Elaboration	I developed the action, dialogue, details, and inner thinking to convey an issue, idea, or lesson. I showed what is specific about the central character. I developed the setting and the character's relationship to the setting.	☐	☐	☐
Craft	I developed contradictions and change in characters and situations.	☐	☐	☐
	I used specific details and figurative language to help the reader understand the place and the mood (such as making an object or place symbolic, using the weather, using repetition).	☐	☐	☐
	I varied my tone to match the variety of emotions experienced by the characters across the story.	☐	☐	☐
Conventions				
Spelling	I used the Internet and other sources at hand to check spelling of literary and high-frequency words.	☐	☐	☐
Punctuation and Sentence Structure	I varied my sentence structure, sometimes using simple and sometimes using complex sentence structure.	☐	☐	☐
	I punctuated dialogue sections accurately.	☐	☐	☐

Name: _____ Date: _____

Narrative Writing Checklist

	Grade 8	NOT YET	STARTING TO	YES!
	Structure			
Overall	I not only created a narrative with well-developed characters who change, I used the story to comment on a social issue, teach a lesson, and/or develop a point of view.	☐	☐	☐
Lead	In establishing the situation and place, I hinted at a bigger context for the story (revealing issues that have been brewing, showing how the setting affects the character, contextualizing a time in history, and/or developing one out of many points of view).	☐	☐	☐
Transitions	I used transitional phrases and clauses, grammatical structures (for example, paragraphing, descriptive phrases, and clauses) and text structures (such as chapter divisions and extended italics) to alert my reader to changes in the setting, the mood, the point of view, or the time in the story.	☐	☐	☐
Ending	I gave the reader a sense of closure by revealing character change(s) that followed from events in the story, or perhaps a resolution. If there wasn't resolution, I wrote to convey how the events of the story affected the characters, and to circle back to a central idea, issue, or theme.	☐	☐	☐
Organization	I modified a traditional story structure, dealing with time in purposeful ways, to best suit my genre, bring out the meaning of my story, and reach my audience.	☐	☐	☐
	Development			
Elaboration	I developed complicated story elements; I may have contrasted the character's thinking with his or her actions or dialogue.	☐	☐	☐
	I developed the central character's relationship to other characters. I showed character flaws as well as strengths to add complexity.	☐	☐	☐
	My details conveyed meaning and related to or developed a lesson or theme.	☐	☐	☐
Craft	I conveyed the pressures characters feel and the dreams they hold. I related those to their actions. I developed complicated characters who change and/or who change others.	☐	☐	☐
	I created a mood as well as a physical setting, and showed how the place changed, or its relationships to the characters changed. I used symbolism to connect with a theme.	☐	☐	☐
	I varied my tone to bring out different perspectives within the story, or to show a gap between the narrator's point of view and that of other characters.	☐	☐	☐
	Conventions			
Spelling	I used the Internet and other sources to check the spelling of literary, historical, and geographical words.	☐	☐	☐
Punctuation and Sentence Structure	I used different sentence structures to achieve different purposes throughout my piece.	☐	☐	☐
	I used verb tenses that shift when needed (such as when moving from a flashback back into the present tense of the story), deciding between active and passive voice where appropriate.	☐	☐	☐

NARRATIVE Student Checklists

Sample 1

Nubia
Section: 1   Personal Narrative

The curtains were closed but it felt like the audience's cheering was grabbing me. My heart fluttering, shifting from side to side thinking of running and hiding backstage. *Which* This is it. The time has come and the curtains were open. My heart felt to the pit of my stomach getting tied in a knot. I knew what the audience wanted, a great performance. The music blasted while the first pair of dancers stepped on stage. 1..2..3.. now me. I pasted a fake smile hoping the crowd won't notice and stepped in, the stage lights blinding me, noticing all the dancers... were they staring? But soon as I was dancing, I let the music get to me, let it flow. And that fake plastic smile, well let me tell you that in turned into a real one. In the crowd, somebody's momma yelled, "Work it girl!" I let the laughter bubble up inside me, like a cool bubbly soda on a hot summer day. this made me smile even more! I just knew that this feeling will just come back inside me for every piece, so for every dance move I let that big, tight, jumbled knot unravel bit by bit. Hip-Hop, Jazz, Modern, Ballet, Competition, West African, Tap, and all the other types of dance that I do, it's all my favorite and they all give me happiness. And, I know that the audience got what they wanted, a phenomenal show :)

Sample 2, page 1

By Emily

Look up and watch the show

I walked up the stairs of the subway. We were almost there! I had been waiting to see this for my whole life.

Five years before this I had been asking,
"Mom, can I go to the fireworks?"
My mom always replied, "No honey, maybe next year."
"Dad, can I go to the fireworks, all my friends have."
"You are too young and it is too late."
This went on for the next five years.

Finally I asked and they said "YES." I jumped up and down and kissed and hugged them eight times. They said I was now old enough. I couldn't wait to tell my friends.

And here we are an hour early staring eagerly at the star lit sky. I looked at the barges straight ahead of me. they were ready to fire! I imagined streams of color floating out of them in every direction. Like ten hoses with ten different colors of water.

For the next hour I asked my parents at least 100 times. "When is it starting?" My parents were giving me

2.

dirty looks. They were annoyed, but I really couldn't help myself.

Then BOOM crackle crackle BOOM red, orange, yellow, green, blue, purple, and white, all seemed to be falling on me screaming "Hi nice to meet you." They were saying to most of the other people, "I remember you from last year."

I glanced straight ahead of me and bats were flying away from all the commotion, and noise. It was eerie and exciting.

Amazing shapes, colors, and noises were bursting out of the four barges. Large booms from previous fireworks echoed from one building to another behind us.

Now the time I had been waiting for, to see the grand finale. Smiley faces and 100's of shooting stars shot high in the sky with large booms. Everyone was oohing and aahing But I knew I oohed and aahed the loudest. I was sure I was more excited than anyone else.

It was now over. Silence rang in my ears and a heavy smoke lingered in the sky. The smoke carried away with it all my dreams of (this) because now I had seen

and experienced my first ever upclose showing of the fireworks.

I hope my old dreams of seeing the fireworks for the first time is carried over to someone. And just like me they can have this great first-time experience and tell their friends all about it.

Now I have done it. I can tell myself I will never forget the first time I ever saw the fireworks. Now I understand what people mean when they say how magical the fireworks are.

May be photocopied for classroom use. © 2014 by Lucy Calkins and Colleagues from the Teachers College Reading and Writing Project from Units of Study in Argument, Information, and Narrative Writing (firsthand: Portsmouth, NH).

PART II: THE ASSESSMENT TOOLS—NARRATIVE WRITING

Gracie

Sample 1, page 1

On Demand Narrative Writing

"Hurry up Gracie!" Hazel yelled back at me as we rolled our bikes up the hill.

"Okay, Okay," I said rolling the tiny pink and white bike that I was borrowing up beside her. I watched as the light pink handlebars that I was holding onto swerved a little bit as I pushed the bike up the big hill.

"Hazel, I think that there is something wrong with the bike you gave me," I said showing her the handle bars.

"Don't worry, it always does that," she said and continued to march up the hill.

Soon we had made it to the top of the hill. My heart was beating fast because the bottom seemed so far down. I then realized something was missing.

"Shouldn't we wear helmets?" I asked Hazel starting to get even more worried.

"We don't have any helmets,"

Sample 1, page 2

Hazel replied stepping over her bike and getting ready to go down the hill. "I'll go first, and you come down after me, okay?" She asked putting her foot on the pedal.

In just a second she was halfway down the hill. She was going really fast, and this did not seem safe to me. I decided to trust Hazel and hope for the best. I sat down on the bike seat which also felt kind of wobbly, and put my hands on the handlebars. I pushed off and started down the hill, but something didn't feel right. The bike seat had turned itself all the way around and the handlebars would not stay in place. I tried to stop myself with my feet, but I was going too fast.

"Hazel!" I yelled, but she was already too far away. I then felt the bike flip over, and I was rolling down the hill. I could

Short Story:

I was driving my car by the old gas station. The car barley started this morning, my mom got me the one of the cheapest ones they had to offer at a dealorship And only know she wonders why.

Looking closer at the gas station, I noticed a car was parked there. Its sleek black chrome paint made the white chipping brick on the other stations barriers look like it belonged in a ghost town. All being noone had been in that station for years, it practically was its own little piece of an abandoned puzzle, that got mixed in with another.

"Hey ain't that Ty" someone from the back said. I couldn't tell who. I didn't really care, all I cared about was if Tyler really was there or not.

"Yeah that's him," rascal said next to me. "Been hangin' with those "new hope's" ever since he disrespected Willy."

"Don't even worry about it bro." Duke said. "Cause keep driving, I'm starving" His voice sounded weak. Like even though he said that, he didn't really think it was going to be true. And it probably wasn't.

Sample 2, page 1

---

feel the hard black gravel digging into my skin.

"Ha-azel!" I said as I tryed to stand up when I made it to the bottom of the hill. Everything around me was spinning, and I could barely keep myself on my feet. I couldn't see straight so I tried walking forward but soon a layer of dark red blood had covered my left eye. That was when I started to freak out.

"Mom!" I yelled hobbling over to the barn where all the parents were, or at least what I thought the barn was. I was instantly surrounded by parents.

"Please don't take me to the hospital, I don't want to get stiches," I stoed as my mom put a towel to my head.

"It will all be okay Gracie." my mom said sitting me down in the car, and before I knew it we were at the hospital.

Sample 1, page 3

Sample 2, page 2

"I will worry about it bro," I said raising my voice. "This ends today!" I slammed my foot on the breaks and did a U-turn. As I raced back to the gas station, hundreds of things raced through my head. But the only one I cared about was what to do when I got back to the gas station.

We pulled up. I turned the car so it was right by the back, where Ty sat smoking a cigarette. I got out first, before any of the New Hope members knew what happened.

I threw his cigarette down and then shoved Ty to the ground. By then my crew and New Hope grouped up. No one tried to stop us, for they knew we had to settle this once and for all.

A circle formed, half were the parked cars, and half were the people. They were so anxious about the fight to care about each other.

"What the hell man!?" Ty yelled at me, "what did you do that for?!" →

Sample 2, page 3

"You! You ruined me! You made everyone think it was me who attacked Bobby when it was really you!" I screamed. I had a fleeting thought of us fighting over a ball, not fighting like this. I wondered... was there another way to do this? I punched him hard in the gut. He coughed. He tried to talk, but couldn't get out the words. "He's my friend! Why would I want to hurt Bobo? You were the one who hated him! You were mad cause he was dating your ex!"

He looked at me, lying on the floor. I had hit him hard. I looked around at everyone(Pascal, Duke, everyone.

"And now your gonna pay,"

Hayley

On Demand Narrative Writing

Crunch! Crunch! Went the floor under my feet. It was a wet misty day, the air was fresh and had that sent of apples. It was chilly, and on my right hand I had a bag of apples that I picked.

Everyyear, my auncle takes my family apple picking. It's like a family tradition. It's a lot of fun because there is a little shop in the orched. With good stuff, like freshly made, warm apple pies, Jams, and my favorite... apple cider doughnuts. The trees were wet, but the best to climb to reach up and grab a Juicy, red apple.

"Hayley, remember the chickens we saw? I want to go there again. Please?" my little sister went. She was 4 years old and has been talking non-stop. But she loves apple picking because she is able to climb the trees like a monkey.

"Not now. We will go later," I said.

Hum?. She made a face, but I Just ignored it.

And there, up in the tree was the biggest apple I have seen. I had to get it, but it was to high for Amy to come up with me. So I called out to Tiffany my other sister.

"Tiffany! Please watch Amy while I climb this tree."

"OK," Tiffany responded

Tiffany came over the ground going Crunch! Crunch! under her feet, when she came over. I handed Amy's warm hand to her.

I climb and get the apple, and when I come down, I see Amy sitting on a rock, ok, she is fine I say to my self. We pick apples for like another hour and then its time to go.

"Hayley, go get Amy to put her in the car," my mom says.

"OK."

I go towards the wet rock were Amy was sitting on, but something wasn't right. Amy wasn't there.

She 's probably playing around with me, I think to my self. So I call out, "Amy! Come on were leaving."

But no response came

"Fine, I guess will leave you," which always worked on her.

But still, no response. Something was wrong. I ron back to my mom, my feet accidentally slipping in deep mud, but I don't care.

"Mom! Amy's missing! I can't find her," I yell frantically.

"Thats redicuious, Amy was over there a while ago." But when my mom looked, I saw that she knew I was telling the troth.

My mom ran to my dad telling him, and to my other relatives. We all frantically started looking and when my auncle looked at his watch, we knew there was more bad news. The orded was going to close in... 20 min! And still no sign of Amy.

③

Than a guy who works here came and said up had to start moving out.

"But we are missing my daughter" my mom tried to say as calmly as possible.

"Well, I'm sorry," he said in his rediculous looking hat.

"Maybe, someone found her and took her to the enterence of the orched," my sister suggest. She was just wearing a stripped T-shirt, Jeans and her worn out converse. I still thought it was crazy that she doesn't get cold easily, like me.

"Cool idea," my aunt said.

We drive to were the little shop is, for it was were the enterence was. We ask everybody if they have seen Amy, and we describe her, but they all said no. Dissapeinted and scared we start going back to the car.

I step short in my filthy shoes. I hear a little laughter, that sounds just like Amy's.

I spin around quickly on my feet, almost tripping and near to the shop is a little girl with a Jean-Jacket, Jeans, sneakers and curly ponytail.

The little girl was playing with the chickens.

I run without thinking, almost tripping, again, and when I reach the little girl, I see its Amy. I grab her and give her a tight hug, everyone else comes to, my parents were even crying of Joy.

"Why you all acting like that?" Amy asked confused.

⑤

We are to happy to be mad at her, we take her back to the car, and my dad buys fresh "apple" pie with two gallons of fresh cider. We eat and drink it happily, and we start going home. All of us thinking that it was a miracle that we found Amy 10 min. away from were we were picking apple, and two min. before the park closed.

I was just glad that we found my little sister, and i'll make sure it won't happen again, I won't take my eyes of her.

I just thought, I shuold of known that Amy would try to come to the chickens, that is what she has been talking about, but

The End

Xinyu

On-Demand Narrative Writing

I frantically searched the living room for a good place to hide. "Four, five, six..." I heard Lucy count in the other room. I looked at the table, countertops, the cupboards, and chairs. Nothing was appealing to me. Then it hit me the halls, I thought. Shall there be able to find me there. I tiptoed through the living room, careful not to bump into anything. Just as I was about to put my right foot down, my foot made contact with a sticky, gooey substance. I sighed, exasperated before directing my eyes to my foot. There, I stood in complete shock as the horror dawned upon me.

Earlier, when I arrived at Lucy's house, the first thing that attracted my attention was a yellow, glistening mouse trap that laided in the corner of the living room. "Watch your step," Lucy said as I dropped my bag on the side. It was those mouse traps where anything I made contact with it, the thing would get stuck. I bent down on my knees as I took a closer look and studied the two furry half-dead mice that unfortunately fell into the trap. "My mother's going to throw that out later, when she comes home from work," Lucy explained to me Lucy was 12, so she was allowed to stay home by herself. I and I, on the other hand was out only 8 at the time.

"Come on, get up," tartly she commanded I then reluctantly pushed off my toes and jumped onto my feet into an upright position.

Now, my right foot was glued to the mouse trap, and each worse, it was ontop on top of the two mice. I shortly shrieked in pure terror.

Sample 2, page 1

Xinyu

and prevent myself from

I tried to block my brain thinking of all the germs that were holden the in the mice's grey fur and how it has now in tested my foot by now. Lucy came running over when she heard my screams. She was about to ask me what's wrong but saw my predicament before she got her question out. She stared at me for a second before bursting out into hysterical laughter.

"I told you," she gasped for air, "to be careful."

I felt my hot, salty tears dripping onto my glasses and travelling down my flushed cheeks. I was so genuinely hurt and felt embarrassed that I was watch out she was laughing at me.

"Okay, okay," she said calmly after she calmed down from her uncontrollable fit of laughter of course She led me to her bathroom holding onto my hands as I hopped on my left foot. I sat down on the side of the bathtub as she grabbed a foot stool and sat in front of me.

"Ready?" Lucy asked I nodded shamefully. She grabbed the sides of the trap and pulled with all her might. Just as I feared, the trap would when wouldn't budge. She tried again but this time, more forcefully. The trap came off slowly the mice still intact while my right foot struggled to break contact with the mice. At last, I was free and when my foot and felt as if all the peace and tranquility were restored in my life once again.

"Pull harder!" I screeched,

Sample 2, page 2

Grade 6

> The writer's beginning not only sets the plot in motion, but it also hints at the larger meaning the story will convey.

> The writer developed realistic characters and developed the details, action, dialogue, and internal thinking that contribute to the deeper meaning of the story.

> The writer developed character traits and emotions through what characters say and do. She also developed some sense of relationship between characters to show *why* they act and speak as they do. In this way, she told the internal as well as the external story.

> The writer used punctuation to help set a mood, convey meaning, or build tension in the story.

> The writer wrote an ending that connects to what the story is really about. She gave the reader a sense of closure by showing a realization or insight or a change in the character/narrator.

My One Chance

It was the first day of school, and my sister Sara was going to her very first day of Kindergarten. She looked grown-up in her new clothes. I thought about when she was just a baby, and now she was in school.

"Come on down here and eat your breakfast!" yelled mom. We went downstairs and we got to pick out what we wanted to eat because it was the first day of school. I picked my favorite cereal with lots of sugar and Sara had eggs. My mom said to me that I had to be very careful and look before I crossed the streets, and hold Sara's hand the whole time. "OK," I said to my mom, but inside I felt annoyed. Then she kept talking about how she could trust me. I thought, "Why does she keep saying how she can trust me? It makes me think maybe she doesn't really trust me."

Then it was time to go, and we put on our new school shoes and got our bags. We hugged mom and said good-bye.

"Don't worry, Mom," I said. "I promise I'll take care of Sara."

Sara was already outside. She was skipping across the front yard. Mom was watching us from the kitchen window. I felt like she was watching because she didn't trust. I grabbed Sara's hand so Mom could see I was being responsible.

"Are you excited for your first day of school, Sara?" I asked, trying to make my voice sound like Mom's. Sara smiled and nodded her head yes. Her bow shook up and down. "Come on. I'll show you the way." I thought about my first day of school. Mom and Dad walked me and I was really nervous. I wondered if Sara felt nervous too.

We walked and saw trees that were bright green and flowers blooming. I felt happy and proud. I thought that I would finally prove I could be treated like a grown-up. But then suddenly I heard a growl.

We both saw it.

It was a large dog, with black hair and a big chain around its neck. It came closer and growled even louder. "GRRRR!!!" Sara jumped behind me.

I grabbed her hand again, hoping she wouldn't feel that my palm was sweating with fear. "I'm scared, Julie," she said.

"Everything will be okay," I said in my calmest voice. "I've got you."

"A plan. I need a plan," I thought to myself. "Be brave."

As the dog got closer I could see it was the size of a small pony, its fur standing up on its neck. "Maybe I'm not ready to be in charge," I thought.

I whispered to Sara. "When I say 'run,' run! Okay?"

I said, "Ready, set, RUN!"

We ran down the sidewalk. My feet hurt because I had new shoes. I yelled for Sara to go faster. "Run! Run!" Just then the bright red door of the schoolhouse came into view. Mrs. Crowley held it open as we ran in. We threw ourselves through the door and practically fell over trying to catch our breath.

"We did it," I said to Sara, giving her a high-five. "We made it."

I thought back to Mom's words earlier that morning. *I'm trusting you to get your sister to school safely.* "Maybe this whole grown-up thing is over-rated," I thought to myself.

Turning to Sara, I smiled. "Hey, Sara, I bet Mom will give us a *ride* to school tomorrow!"

> The writer wove together precise descriptions, figurative language, and perhaps even symbolism to help the reader picture the setting, actions, and events and to bring forth meaning.

> The writer used language that fits the story's meaning (e.g., in parts that have dialogue, different people use different kinds of language).

> The writer chose several key parts to stretch out and others to move through more quickly.

> The writer used paragraphs purposefully (perhaps to show time or setting changes, new parts of the story, or to create suspense for the reader). The sequence of events is clear.

> The writer used transitional phrases to connect what happened to why it happened.

Grade 7

Specific details not only set the story in motion but grounded it in a particular place and time.

The writer made some attempt to control time and pacing, by stepping outside of the central moment to give glimpses of the character's past, or other important moments.

The writer made comparisons effectively.

When comparisons were made, the writer repeated them to increase their significance and related them to the meaning of the story.

The central scene, where the problem and action were strongest, were slowed down and elaborated—the action wasn't over in two sentences, but was slowed down and released in parts. The writer attempted to bring out what was important in the story and reach the audience.

Sara woke up to the sound of her sister's voice. Sunlight streamed in, lighting up her posters of Taylor Swift performing at Madison Garden and Shaun White flying upside down on his snowboard at the X-Games. Someday Sara wanted to be just like them. She loved the way they were so strong, so fierce, and proud. Her life seemed so ordinary though—living on a quiet street in a quiet town. Would things ever change?

Julie was shaking her. "Wake up, Sara!!" Suddenly Sara remembered. It was her little sister Julie's first day of kindergarten, and Sara was going to walk her to school. This was Sara's small chance to prove herself. Her parents just didn't seem to realize she was grown up.

Sara lay in bed for a moment, dreaming of how dinner might go that night. Mom would lean in and ruffle her hair, saying, "I'm proud of you, Sara." With work, Mom didn't always seem to have a lot of time for Sara anymore.

When they got to the kitchen, Mom was pouring Cheerios in their bowls. "Eat up, kittens," she said. "And I'll drive you to school. We don't want anything to happen on Julie's first day of kindergarten."

Sara's jaw clenched. First, she was not a kitten. Maybe Julie was a kitten, but she was a lioness. Why wouldn't her mother notice that she was grown up? Second, they had already decided—she was taking Julie to school. It was her job to get her there safely.

"Mom, you said Julie could walk with me. I'll keep her safe." Sara tried to keep her voice calm. If she cried, her mom would think she was a baby, a kitten. She stood tall, trying to look as strong as confident as Taylor Swift was when she first performed onstage at twelve.

"I want to walk with Sara, Mommy." Julie said. "She'll keep me safe. She's brave like a lion." Julie put her hand in Sara's, and Sara felt bigger instantly. Sara glowed with pride. In her mind, she thought of how her mom would praise her that night.

Mom looked at the girls. Then she shrugged her shoulders. "Ok," she said. "But if anything happens, you're in big trouble, kittens."

As the girls left the house, the sun lit up the flowers in the yard. It was a quick walk to school—but there was one dangerous block. Sara's mind was filled with thoughts of how proud her mom would be, and she forgot to circle around the block where the big dog lived. Fang. You didn't want to go anywhere near Fang.

"GRRRR!" First, they heard it. "GROWLLL!" Then they felt its breath. Then they saw its red eyes. Fang was huge. Fang was fierce. Fang was ferocious. That's why Sara always skipped this block. Now here she was, alone with Fang and her five-year-old sister.

Sara didn't feel like a lioness anymore. She felt like a kitten. Fang crept closer. Inside, Sara thought about running. She was a much faster runner than Julie. She could get away.

The writer used compound sentences, and punctuated them accurately.

The specific language that characters use in dialogue revealed their character traits and/or emotions.

The writer included details that pointed to the central issue or conflict that would be developed later. Additionally, the writer set up complex relationships between characters.

Again, the writer stepped outside the central moment, controlling the story by introducing small scenes that linked the bigger scenes.

(continues)

7 NARRATIVE Annotated Writing
Developed through the Progression

Grade 7 (continued)

> The writer used dialogue to convey a sense of the character and her relationships.

> The writer used specific details to help the reader understand key aspects of the story.

Then Sara felt Julie's hand in hers. "Don't leave me," Julie whispered. She began to cry.

"GRRRRR!" Fang crouched low. His breath was hot. His fur bristled on his neck.

Sara stood there, her heart beating like a drum. She had to make a decision. Run, fast, alone? Or run slowly with Julie, and maybe get caught? She decided.

"GRRRRR!" Fang opened his jaws, full of razor sharp teeth. He looked ready to jump.

"Get back!" Sara shouted at Fang. Then: "Take my hand!" Sara shouted at Julie. With the sweetness and determination of Taylor Swift, she grabbed Julie's little hand. They ran and ran, together. Sara pulled Julie so they could both get away safely. Fang ran after but he couldn't catch them.

Afterward, they rested around the corner. "Hey Kitten, how are you?" Sara asked Julie, looking down at her tear-stained face. "I'm so sorry I didn't keep you safe."

Julie looked up at her. "You did keep me safe, Sara. Even when you were afraid, you stayed with me. I want to be just like you someday!" Julie said. Then she looked at the school building, which was across the street. "Kindergarten is going to be easy after this!" Julie laughed, and they ran towards school, together, loping like lionesses under the warm sun.

> The writer gave a sense of closure by showing how the problem had been resolved and the characters and their relationships changed.

May be photocopied for classroom use. © 2014 by Lucy Calkins and Colleagues from the Teachers College Reading and Writing Project from *Units of Study in Argument, Information, and Narrative Writing* (firsthand: Portsmouth, NH).

Grade 8

> The writer got to the trouble quickly—the story started with immediate tension or foreshadowing.

> The writer made allusions to other characters to compare character traits and suggest conflicts.

> The writer controlled, time effectively by stepping outside of the central moment to gave glimpses of the character's past, or other important moments.

> The dialogue the writers used revealed character traits and/or emotions.

> The writer made comparisons effectively. The writer's details related to and conveyed a larger lesson or theme.

Sara woke up to the sound of Julie's voice, and the feel of being shaken in her twin bed. Around the corner, Fang woke up to the smell of dog food, and the feel of his chain breaking.

"Wake up, Sara!" Julie shouted. It was Julie's first day of kindergarten, and Sara was taking her to school. Julie trusted Sara to keep her safe. Sara lay quietly, reviewing her plans. Above her bed, Shaun White flipped upside down on his snowboard, in a poster from the X-Games. Sara loved the way Shaun tried tricks that would terrify other kids. She loved the way he was fearless and lucky.

"I wish Mom and Dad wouldn't treat me like I was a little kid," Sara thought. There was no way in her small town to prove that she could be brave and strong. Until today. Sara couldn't start flying through the air on a snowboard. But she could seek out danger. In this town, danger looked like Fang. After she had protected Julie from Fang, everyone would see how brave Sara was, how strong and special.

Sara lay in bed for a moment, dreaming of how dinner might go that night. Mom would lean in, and ruffle her hair, and say, "I'm proud of you, Sara." With work, Mom didn't always seem to have a lot of time for her anymore. And Dad was busy trying to find work. Neither of them seemed to really *see* Sara anymore, unless it was to ask her to do a chore. Tonight they would notice her, though. Maybe they would toast her, they way they used to when they had parties, and people came over a lot.

When they got to the kitchen, Mom was pouring Cheerios in their bowls. "Eat up, kittens," she said. "And I'll drive you to school. We don't want anything to happen on Julie's first day of kindergarten."

Sara's jaw clenched. First, she was not a kitten. She was a lioness. Second, they had already decided—she was taking Julie to school. She kept her voice calm though. Otherwise, she thought, Mom would just send her to back to her room. "Julie's walking with me, Mom, remember? I'll keep her safe. What could happen?" Inside, Sara thought of Fang and her plans, and she cringed a little. Outside, she tried to look as confident as Shaun White before a competition.

Mom looked at the girls. Then she shrugged her shoulders. "Ok," she said. "But if anything happens, you're in big trouble, kittens."

> The writer hinted at what was to come—the action didn't just spring suddenly, but was developed.

> The writer showed more than one problem that the character faced, though not all problems were equally developed.

> The writer hinted about and developed the character's problems to build rising tension. Also, relationships were more than one way.

> Again, the writer hinted at rising tension by giving the reader clues about upcoming events and characters' inner thinking.

(continues)

Grade 8 (*continued*)

As the girls left the house, the sun slipped behind some clouds. It was a quick walk to school—just that one block you had to go around. Only this time, Sara didn't go around. Holding Julie's hand, she pointed up at the clouds. "Look at the shape of that one, Julie! It's like a snowman!" Pointing at clouds, laughing, she led Julie down the danger block before Julie noticed where they were.

> The dialogue the writer included furthered the plot or tension.

"GRRRR!" There he was. Black fur bristling on his neck. Red eyes. Razor sharp teeth. Drool. A metal collar with studs. FANG embossed in black.

> The writer used verb tense to indicate shifts in time and to bring out the meaning of the story.

Julie hid behind Sara. "Don't worry, kitten," Sara said. "I'll protect you." To Fang, she said in a firm voice, "Stay back!" Sara said this confidently, thinking about how yesterday she had come by and measured Fang's chain. She knew just how far he could reach. They were safe. Not that Julie had to know that.

"GRRRR!" Fang crept closer. And closer. He crouched, ready to spring. That's when Sara saw it. The chain dragging from his collar, the broken end loose.

> In the central scene, where the problem and action were strongest, the writer slowed the writing down and elaborated.

Sara didn't feel like a lioness anymore. She felt like a kitten. Fang crept closer. Inside, Sara thought about running. She was a much faster runner than Julie. She could get away. Then Sara felt Julie's hand in hers. "I'm not that fast, don't leave me," Julie whispered. Her small hand was sweaty. She began to cry.

> The writer made the problem clear, setting readers up for a lesson to be learned, making the meaning of the story clear.

"GRRRR!" Fang opened his jaws, full of razor sharp teeth. He looked ready to jump.

> The writer used dialogue to convey a sense of the character's language, emotions and tone of voice. Punctuation clarified meaning.

"Get back!" Sara shouted at Fang. She swung her backpack towards the dog, and he lept back, startled. Then: "Come on! " Sara shouted at Julie. With the speed and agility of an elite athlete, Sara swung her bag, grabbed her sister, and darted away.

"SNAP! GRRR! SNAP!" Fang was at their heels. Swoosh! Sara swung the backpack like a sword, trying to proetect Julie's small, running body. Fang stopped. Then . . . he sat.

Afterward, they rested around the corner. Julie looked up at her. "You were amazing, Sara! Wait until I tell Mom and Dad. I want to be just like you someday!"

> The writer's ending echoed its beginning, so that a clear lesson or change was conveyed.

Sara looked at her sister, who was panting and tear-stained. She thought about what had just happened and what had nearly happened. Maybe being kittens for awhile longer would be okay.

> In ending, the writer took the opportunity to reflect on the story, in this case, through the character's inner thinking.

Writing Process Learning Progression, Grades 5–8

	Grade 5	Grade 6	Grade 7	Grade 8
Generating Ideas for Writing	The student brings ideas and plans to her writing and can use a wide repertoire of strategies effectively to get more ideas, if necessary. The writer shows a willingness to grapple with one idea across multiple notebook entries. The writer is willing to write and rewrite entries about the ideas.	The student comes with ideas, a clear repertoire of strategies to draw on to get more ideas, and knows which pay off the most for him as a writer. He lets writing lead him to new work, perhaps working on an unfinished entry from other days, reflecting on writing to generate more.	The student independently and quickly tries out multiple ideas for writing, then sorts to decide which are worth following through on, based on the genre, purpose, and audience of the writing at hand. The writer sees a connection across her writing—she uses the notebook as a resource to bring prior thinking and writing to new projects, and makes clear through labeling or tabs which entries go together or are on hold for now.	The student can automatically generate some ideas for writing at this point. The student sorts through possible topics in his head, trying out only ones that he is confident are likely to pay off. The writer uses his own past writing, mentor texts, and understanding of the genre, purpose, and audience to create and connect entries that quickly move the writing toward a draft.
Planning and Drafting (Including Fluency, Stamina, and Volume)	The student plans before drafting, using supports from the unit or from the teacher to plan a clear structure within the genre of choice. The student can type three pages in a single sitting. The student can remain engaged in a writing project, which can include talking, planning, and drafting for an hour or more. The student at this level shows initiative on both independent and unit-based writing.	The student plans with some independence, using supports as a starting point, but trying more than one plan until he is confident. The student can write more than three pages in a sitting and can remain engaged for ninety minutes. The student at this level shows great initiative in writing work on both independent and unit-based projects for longer periods of time than required.	The student plans independently, using what she knows of the structure of the genre to guide her plans. The student can remain engaged in a writing project for over ninety minutes. At this level the student lets the project determine the time required, however far over the expectations.	The student plans efficiently and effectively, making use of her knowledge of the genre to create a workable outline that leads to a smooth drafting process. The student remains engaged in writing projects for however long is necessary or desired. His time is well spent and purpose-driven. At this point the quality of his work is just as or more important to him than the quantity.

WRITING PROCESS: LEARNING PROGRESSION, GRADES 5–8 (*continued*)

	Grade 5	Grade 6	Grade 7	Grade 8
Revising	The student revises not only drafts but also entries, ratcheting up her work using strategies, mentor texts, and partner talk. Rather than only revising key places, she will search for places where the writing feels weak, rewriting those parts. The student might also revise by experimenting with craft to bring out meaning or to appeal in specific ways to an audience. She considers the effect she wants her writing to have on readers and uses all she knows to achieve these effects.	Revision for the writer is not just about one piece growing stronger but about writing better in general. He can identify places where his writing is stronger and weaker in a single piece but also looks to find patterns. He might say, "The ending didn't feel right. I have to work on ending my pieces with more strength." He might talk with a partner or read a mentor text to help achieve these goals.	At this level a student revises based on the purpose and audience of a particular piece of writing, and her knowledge of herself as a writer. She seeks out critique from others, using it to grow stronger in her own ability to identify places where revision would help.	At this level, the student has a clear writing identity, which includes knowing how revision best fits into the process for him. He may revise as he goes or wait until he is finished, but he revises deeply and thoroughly, relying on strategies learned as well as an innate sense of when his writing feels weaker. He also might decide to read professional literature for writers, to support his development in particular areas, for example, saying, "I have trouble with maintaining conflict, so I'm reading *The Plot Thickens*."
Editing	The student at this level does not wait for the editing phase of the process to ensure that she is using correct spelling, punctuation, and grammar. At this level she is starting to see that editing is also about considering the tone and cadence of a piece, and she may start to vary sentence lengths to create a desired rhythm or meaning.	The student edits along the way and also at the end of a project, carefully rereading and using peer support to make sure the piece is publishable for the desired audience. The writer is starting to recognize the value of being precise and concise and eliminates wordiness and redundancy. The writer can explain why he has made certain language choices and the effect he believes he has created for his reader.	The student has developed an efficient and effective editing process, editing along the way to avoid lengthy end-of-project editing. The writer recognizes and eliminates wordiness and redundancy, and searches for the best language for her specific purpose and audience.	The student has developed an efficient and effective editing process, editing along the way to avoid lengthy end-of-project editing, consulting peers as well as other references to make sure the piece is correct and publishable for the desired audience. The writer makes decisions to suit his purpose as well as the conventions of the type of piece he is creating. He may choose to "break" grammar rules for effect and can explain his choices. He may emulate other authors' unconventional use of punctuation and grammar.

SAMPLE ON-DEMAND PERFORMANCE ASSESSMENT PROMPT FOR WRITING AND READING

READING INFORMATIONAL TEXTS AND WRITING ARGUMENT

(For complete access to a version of this assessment, and others like it, including links to texts and a scoring rubric, please visit the Teachers College Reading and Writing Project website: readingandwritingproject.com.)

Grade 7

STANDARDS ASSESSED

These are the primary standards to be assessed with this task.

Common Core State Standards

- Students will write in response to prompts to analyze explicit and implicit information from the text. They will also cite textual evidence from sources and analyze that evidence when supporting their position in an argument essay—work aligned with RI.7.1.

- Students will read a grade-level text and respond to prompts to demonstrate comprehension of that text—work aligned with RI.7.10.

- Students will write an argument essay on the topic of whether or not to ban bottled water in schools. They will base their argument on evidence from the provided texts and will consider the counterargument in their essay—work aligned with W.7.1.

Depth of Knowledge: Levels 2–4

GETTING READY

Duration of administration is two class periods across one or two days.

Preview Materials

- Video to stream: "CNN: Most Bottled Water Is Tap" (YouTube)
- Text: "Goodbye, Bottled Water?" (TCRWP website)
- Text: "International Bottled Water Association Statement"
- Student booklets (at end of this sample prompt)

Prepare Materials

- Make one-sided copies of student booklet (see student booklet template following this description).

- Make copies of the article(s) you've chosen to use.

- Make loose-leaf paper available for essay writing.

- Cue the video "CNN: Most Bottled Water Is Tap."

- Prepare a chart to hang in the classroom, outlining expectations for argument writing. On it, write the following:

Expectations for Argument Writing

- *Quickly plan how your argument will go: how your reasons and evidence will be grouped and organized and how you'll acknowledge the opposing position.*

- Introduce a position and acknowledge the opposing position.

- *Support the position using accurate, relevant sources.*

- *Use words, phrases, and clauses to provide clear transitions and connections between ideas and evidence.*

- Establish and maintain a formal style.

- *Provide a concluding statement or section that follows from and supports your argument.*

SETTING STUDENTS UP TO WORK

- Assemble all materials before the assessment day.

- Inform the students in advance of the date and time of the assessment.

- To help students remain aware of their pacing, the teacher might write "Time Started" and "Time Remaining" and change to indicate current time remaining after every ten minutes.

- Students who receive time-and-a-half or double time should receive the same modification for this assessment.

- Students who receive scribing or directions read aloud should receive the same modification for this assessment. To facilitate multiple students hearing the text read aloud, teachers may record the directions and the text and have students listen to the recording on individual devices (if available).

- During the assessment, teachers should take the opportunity to observe students' test-taking behaviors, recording observations that may lead to small-group instruction during test prep. (A sample observation sheet is available on the TCRWP website in the folder titled "assessment supports.")

You will need to alter the prompts that follow based on the language you've used to teach reading and writing nonfiction in your own classroom. It might sound something like:

"You're going to have a chance to show off what you know about doing quick, on-the-run, intensive research and composing an argument essay. Over the next couple of periods, you'll encounter a few texts that will provide you with information and claims about the pros and cons of bottled water. It will be up to you to really analyze the information and ideas, so that you can state your own claim and justify it, using researched evidence.

"For each text, you'll have a chance to respond to prompts that ask you to identify and explain key details in the text that support central ideas. Then you'll have some time to look over your research. Then, we'll imagine that our school is hosting a debate about whether or not schools should ban bottled water. You have to decide which side of the debate to argue. You can take the position that bottled water should be banned—in which case you want to gather convincing evidence from your research. Or you can make a claim to support bottled water in school—in which case you also want convincing evidence.

"One thing to tell you ahead of time—part of what makes a convincing argument is the ability to acknowledge the opposing claim and reasons, and refute those. So no matter which side you end up taking, be alert during your research for evidence that could be used for either side of the argument.

"This period is part one of this research project. You'll have a chance to watch a video and read two texts today, and to write to explain key details that help support the different points of view on this topic. At a later time, you'll write your position paper, or essay. You'll have a chance then to look over your notes and any of the texts again."

Task 1: Respond to Video "CNN: Most Bottled Water Is Tap"

"You're about to watch a news video about the relationship between bottled water and tap water. As you watch, think about the important ideas and information in the video. After I show the video a second time, write a central idea that this video teaches us, and fill in the outline with specific examples or evidence that the video gives to support that idea."

Task 2: Respond to Article "Goodbye, Bottled Water?"

"Now you'll have a chance to study an article about bottled water. After reading this, write two reasons that the article gives for why bottled water is a problem. For each reason, write a quote from the article that explains or supports that reason."

Task 3: Respond to "International Bottled Water Association Statement"

"Now you'll have a chance to read a response from the International Bottled Water Association regarding a state attorney general's decision to allow a town to ban bottled water. Read to find the strongest evidence that the Bottled Water Association gives in defense of bottled water. Write to explain why this evidence is convincing."

Task 4: Argument Essay Topic: "Should We Ban Bottled Water in Schools?"

"Researchers, you've done some good research now by studying this information and the ideas of these authors. Imagine that you are preparing for a debate, and that you have to take a stance on whether schools should or shouldn't ban bottled water, using evidence from the texts you've watched and read. Write an argument essay that you could read at the debate. First, you'll want to look over your reading responses and the texts and take a clear position on this issue.

"You'll want to clearly support one side of this argument, supporting that claim with convincing evidence you've gathered in your research. You'll want to include relevant information and details from the articles and video to support your claim, citing the source accurately. You'll also want to acknowledge the other side of the argument.

"Remember what's expected in argument writing." [*Read from chart.*] "Go ahead and start."

ASSESSING STUDENT WORK

Create teacher teams to assess student work. Ideally, set aside an hour for teams on a grade to come together to reach consensus about the scores for a few representative pieces of writing. A scoring rubric will help you. The complete rubrics can be found on our website, www.readingandwritingproject.com, under "Performance Assessments."

Seventh-Grade Informational Reading/Argument Writing Performawnce Assessment
Student Booklet

Name: _____ Date: _____

Task 1: Response to "CNN: Most Bottled Water Is Tap"

This video informs us about bottled water. What is a central idea in this video about bottled water?

```
_____
_____
_____
_____
```

What examples or specific evidence does the video give to explain or support this?

- Example or evidence: _____

_____

_____

_____

- Example or evidence: _____

_____

_____

_____

Name: _____ Date: _____

Task 2: Response to "Goodbye, Bottled Water?"

This article presents and explains many reasons why drinking bottled water is a problem. Complete the outline below with more than one reason that the article gives supporting this idea and at least one quote from the article to explain or support that reason.

According to the article, why is bottled water a problem?

One reason the article gives is . . . _____

_____

Write a quote from the article that explains or supports this reason.

- _____

- _____

- _____

- _____

According to the article, what is another reason why bottled water is a problem?

Another reason the article gives is . . . _____

_____

_____

_____

Write a quote from the article that explains or supports this reason.

- _____

- _____

- _____

- _____

Name: _____ Date: _____

Task 3: Response to "International Bottled Water Association Statement"

In this statement, the International Bottled Water Association attacks a town's decision to ban bottled water and defends bottled water as a necessary product. What is the **strongest** piece of evidence that the International Bottled Water Association gives in support of bottled water? Quote directly to capture the exact words that the author uses.

_____

_____

_____

_____

_____

What makes this evidence convincing? Write to analyze how this quote supports the International Bottled Water Association's position that bottled water should not be banned.

_____

_____

_____

_____

_____

_____

_____

_____

_____

_____

Name: _____ Date: _____

Task 4: Argument Essay

Your task is to take a position on whether or not bottled water should be banned in schools. Write an argument essay in which you clearly state your position either for or against bottled water in schools, and then support that claim with evidence from the texts you've read and watched. Be sure to:

- Quickly plan how your argument will go: how your reasons and evidence will be grouped and organized and how you'll acknowledge the opposing position.

- Introduce a clear position and acknowledge the opposing position.

- Support the position by referring to and accurately citing relevant sources.

- Use words, phrases, and clauses to provide clear transitions and connections between ideas and evidence.

- Establish and maintain a formal style.

- Provide a concluding statement or section that follows from and supports your argument.

Plan for argument essay:

May be photocopied for classroom use. © 2014 by Lucy Calkins and Colleagues from the Teachers College Reading and Writing Project from *Units of Study in Argument, Information, and Narrative Writing* (*first*hand: Portsmouth, NH).